Open Comput..., , ~ ~.~.~
To The Best Free UNIX Utilities

About the Enclosed Software

WARNING: MACINTOSH SYSTEM 7 USERS WILL NOT BE ABLE TO USE THE CD THAT COMES WITH THIS BOOK. EACH INDIVIDUAL PROGRAM MAY OR MAY NOT RUN ON A GIVEN PLATFORM. IF YOU DO NOT HAVE EXPERIENCE IN LOADING AND COMPILING UNIX SOFTWARE, WE SUGGEST THAT YOU ASK AN EXPERT TO HELP YOU WITH THE PROCESS.

Disc Contents

The CD-ROM that comes with this book has been created so that it could be useful to a maximum number of users; however, not all systems are supported. For instance, if you are a Macintosh System 7 user, you will not be able to use this disc. The CD complies with the ISO Standard 9660 using the Rock Ridge extensions and the files may be found in two formats. In one directory, you will find the files in **tar** format. Another directory is in the Rock Ridge format that includes each program in its original source code. Both formats require that the programs be compiled. Documentation is provided for each program for compilation on the CD. If you have not compiled code before, you may find compilation to be a time-consuming process.

There are 51 programs reviewed in this book. Almost all of the programs reside on the CD. These programs are arranged on the CD by chapter. The program reviews in the book start with Chapter 4. Therefore, if you go to the Table of Contents of the book, you can see what programs can be found in the directories on the CD. Osborne McGraw-Hill is providing the code on the CD as a convenience to the reader only. By using this CD you don't have to go to the trouble of downloading on the Internet. However, these programs are for your use only! This CD should not be distributed to others and the programs contained herein should definitely not be loaded back on the Internet. Many of the programs are updated frequently, so the disc is, in effect, a snapshot of the versions current when this book was put to press. Osborne McGraw-Hill has no rights to any of the programs on the CD nor can we offer support. The programs are provided on the CD as a convenience to the reader. Each description in the book has suggestions on where to look for support if it is needed.

Instructions for downloading the programs from the CD are included in the Introduction to this book and on the CD itself. Chapter 3 gives you step-by-step instructions on how to download from the Internet, as well as how to compile a typical program. Each program has a text file on the CD that explains how it should be compiled.

NOTE: IF, FOR ANY REASON THE CD-ROM IS NOT READABLE, CONTACT OSBORNE McGRAW-HILL AT (800) 227-0900.

System Requirements

The CD-ROM contains application software designed for the UNIX operating system. Most UNIX systems are supported. However, individual programs on the CD may not work on your specific system. Any ISO 9660-compatible CD should play the enclosed disc; however, it will not work with Macintosh System 7 computers.

Limited Warranty

Osborne/McGraw-Hill warrants the physical compact disc enclosed herein to be free of defects in materials and workmanship for a period of sixty days from the purchase date. If Osborne/McGraw-Hill receives written notification within the warranty period of defects in materials or workmanship, and such notification is determined by Osborne/McGraw-Hill to be correct, Osborne/McGraw-Hill will replace the defective compact disc.

The entire and exclusive liability and remedy for breach of this Limited Warranty shall be limited to replacement of defective compact disc and shall not include or extend to any claim for or right to cover any other damages, including but not limited to, loss of profit, data, or use of the software, or special, incidental, or consequential damages or other similar claims, even if Osborne/McGraw-Hill has been specifically advised of the possibility of such damages. In no event will Osborne/McGraw-Hill's liability for any damages to you or any other person ever exceed the lower of the suggested list price or actual price paid for the license to use the software, regardless of any form of the claim.

OSBORNE, A DIVISION OF McGRAW-HILL, INC., SPECIFICALLY DISCLAIMS ALL OTHER WARRANTIES, EXPRESS OR IMPLIED, INCLUDING BUT NOT LIMITED TO, ANY IMPLIED WARRANTY OF MERCHANTABILITY OR FITNESS FOR A PARTICULAR PURPOSE. Specifically, Osborne/McGraw-Hill makes no representation or warranty that the software is fit for any particular purpose, and any implied warranty of merchantability is limited to the sixty-day duration of the Limited Warranty covering the physical disc only (and not the software), and is otherwise expressly and specifically disclaimed.

This limited warranty gives you specific legal rights; you may have others which may vary from state to state. Some states do not allow the exclusion of incidental or consequential damages, or the limitation on how long an implied warranty lasts, so some of the above may not apply to you.

Open Computing's Guide to the Best Free UNIX Utilities

James Keogh
Remon Lapid

Osborne **McGraw-Hill**

Berkeley New York St. Louis San Francisco
Auckland Bogotá Hamburg London Madrid
Mexico City Milan Montreal New Delhi Panama City
Paris São Paulo Singapore Sydney Tokyo Toronto

Osborne **McGraw-Hill**
2600 Tenth Street
Berkeley, California 94710
U.S.A.

For information on translations or book distributors outside of the U.S.A., please write to Osborne **McGraw-Hill** at the above address.

Open Computing's Guide to the Best Free UNIX Utilities

 234567890 DOC 998765

ISBN 0-07-882046-4

We dedicate this book
to Anne, Joanne, Sandy, Lois, and Jessica

About the Authors

James Keogh is a software developer and an evening professor of computer science at Saint Peter's College in Jersey City, New Jersey. He has written more than 24 computer books.

Remon Lapid is a Wall Street UNIX consultant, and a developer of UNIX software for the financial services industry.

Contents At A Glance

Contents

Introduction

There's so much talk today about the electronic highway of the future that it's difficult to know what is hype and what is fact. This book isn't about to use a crystal ball and forecast traffic on this futuristic highway. Instead, we're going to give you a glimpse of today's electronic highway and uncover some of the treasures buried along the way.

The foundation of the electronic highway of the future is here today. It's hard to believe but, it's been around for years. The electronic highway that we're talking about is the Internet, a network of servers and computers that stretches around the world—literally circumnavigating the globe. This isn't science fiction! It's today's reality.

Just think of it. You can be sitting in your home or office holding a computer conversation with someone in Hong Kong. You enter your comments at the keyboard and your words travel along this unseen highway at nearly the speed of light to arrive on a computer screen in Hong Kong.

The cost? Not as much as you might think—just the expense of a telephone call to your local Internet host, which could be a local telephone number. The software? You'll need software to manage your long distance conversation. In this case, the software is free for the taking—just one of the treasures you'll find along the Internet roadside. Obviously, the Internet has been getting a lot of publicity lately. However, that same spirit of sharing is part of the UNIX culture. While much of the software comes from schools or government supported projects, programmers have dedicated hundreds of hours to developing rich products that will be supported on an array of UNIX platforms. This available software is often free on the Internet. This book is dedicated to making sure that you are aware of some of the best out there. However, we haven't begun to tap all the resources of the Internet. One of the goals of this book is to encourage you to "explore the net" yourself.

In this book, you'll learn about the software and hardware that you'll need to travel this world highway. You can probably use your current personal computer, modem, and communications software to connect to a local Internet host. A local host is your gateway to the Internet.

The term *Internet host* might seem confusing, but it will become clear to you in this book's second chapter, "Connecting To The Internet." There you'll learn all about an Internet host and how to find the one closest to you. We'll also show you how to make this connection at practically no cost to you.

The Internet is a strange highway but a rare find. It's a highway where every traveler has a sprit of community. This might sound a little hoaky but it's true. Let's say, for example, that you're having trouble using a particular software package. You can ask the Internet user community for help—and you can expect to receive more than a handful of responses to your call.

The underlying philosophy of the Internet is the belief that all information should be free. By information, we mean helpful tips as well as the software itself. No one on the Internet prohibits anyone from receiving this information. What's the catch? Strange as it may seem, there isn't any catch.

This book is really a treasure map to some of the more powerful and interesting software available on the Internet. Let's say that you need to create a typeset quality document. You could hunt around for commercially available software and pay a price for the privilege of using the software, or you could find a similar package on the Internet—available at no cost.

Well, practically no cost. You still have to pay for the phone call to your local host. You'll also have to spend time downloading the software to your system and building the binary files. Hold on! Where is this software located on the Internet and what's involved in building binary files?

Locating the software on the Internet can be tricky, especially since the software may be available on hosts located throughout the world. That's where this book comes in handy. Since we review the best software on the Internet, you can flip through the pages of this book and find the right software to do the job for you. In each review, we provide you with a location on the Internet where you'll find the software. We also provide the source on the enclosed CD-ROM so that you don't have to go hunting on the net.

In Chapter 3, "The Hacker's Guide," you'll find a sample session that walks you through the downloading process. Just type the commands that you see in this chapter and you'll have a successful file transfer each time. You'll be copying the source files for most of these utilities. This means that you must use your system's compiler to create the binary version of the utility.

Let's face it. Creating binaries can be a hassle. We realize this, so we made a special effort to provide you with a step-by-step guide to building binary files. Then we went the extra mile to provide you with tips and hints that you can follow if the binaries files don't run properly. Simply, if the software doesn't run, just follow our suggestions and you should be up and running in no time.

We provide you with everything that you need to know to use free software. You'll learn about the Internet itself and how to connect to this electronic highway of the future—today! You'll learn how to locate, download, and build some of the most powerful software packages that are available— available for the taking! And you'll have your own map that will lead you to these roadside treasures.

Mounting from the CD

The files on the CD are arranged in two directories. One of the directories contains all of the files compacted in **tar** format. The other directory contains the files in their source code form. Before you start, read the *README* on the CD for instructions. You can do this by typing

```
more /cdrom/readme.txt
```

Follow the instructions in the *README*. If you are in a big hurry, here are some quick instructions to allow you to mount the files.

NOTE
Different systems will require slight variations in the mounting instructions.

On a Sparcstation, the command line to mount the files would read

```
mount -r -t hsfs /dev/sr0/ cdrom
```

Here, the **hsfs** means the high sierra file system and **sr0** is the device. Again, depending on your system, these arguments may be different. If you are having trouble mounting, you should look at your system's manual under **mount** for instructions.

If you want to extract the sources from the *tar* files, you can use the next example as a model. We'll **move, configure,** and **make** one of the programs from Chapter 12.

To start, select a directory (in this case we'll use */usr/local/src*) using the following command:

```
cd /usr/local/src
```

Now we'll take the **tar** file and move it into this directory using these two commands:

```
tar xvf /cdrom/chapter12/gcc-2.5.8.tar
```

and

```
cd gcc-2.5.8
```

To configure, type

```
sh configure
```

NOTE
See the installation instructions for the package you're interested in. In some cases, you will have to edit the make file instead of running the configure script.

Finally, to make, type

```
make
```

Now you're all set.

To compile the programs correctly, you should read the documentation provided with each program on the CD. There will be hints in many of the reviews throughout the book. For an example of how the compilation process works, the second half of Chapter 3 provides a complete example of compiling one of the programs.

Support

Osborne McGraw-Hill cannot give you software support for the programs in the book. The nature of the UNIX environment makes support a ticklish issue because what may work well on one system may not on another. The best way to get support for your software is to ask questions over the Internet. Most of the programs in this book are in wide use. Therefore, it is likely that a user with a configuration similar to yours may be able to help you. Remember to read the documentation.

There are many companies that offer paid support for free UNIX utilities. For example, Cygnus Support of Mountain View, California is a developer of the GNU toolchain (so is the Free Software Foundation). They are the official maintainers of the GNU C++ Compiler, the GNU Debugger, and the GNU Assembler. Cygnus offers support and quarterly updates to the toolchains on a contracted basis.

For further ideas on support, look up each program in the book and refer to Chapter 2.

Free Software Foundation

This book idea came about as a result of the sharing attitude that has been born and fostered in the UNIX community and heightened by access through the Internet. There are several groups developing and maintaining free software on the Internet. Some of the contributors have been universities or government agencies, some like Cygnus (mentioned above) are for-profit companies, and some are non-profit organizations that make enough through selling CDs or support that they can support more free software development.

One of the leading proponents of free software is the Free Software Foundation. We include the following information from this foundation because we believe in the principles that it promotes. We feel it is a worthy cause and indeed supports what this book is all about. It should be noted that there are other organizations committed to the same goals. The following is an article provided by the Free Software Foundation for use in this book. Feel free to copy it if you wish, but no alteration is permitted.

Supporting Free Software

by the Free Software Foundation

The English word "free" has two meanings: one refers to price, and one refers to freedom. In "free software," the word refers to freedom, not price. Specifically, free software means you have the freedom to study, copy, distribute, change, and improve the software.

Distributing free software is an ethical opportunity to raise funds for writing more free software, and we shouldn't waste it. The price you pay for a copy of free software may be zero, or low, but that's not what "free software" is about. There's no need to aim for making distribution fees as low as possible, for the sake of impecunious users, precisely because they are welcome to get copies from their friends; they won't have to do without.

You don't have to pay the Free Software Foundation to get GNU software and use it. It is legitimate to get a copy of GNU software from an ftp site, from a BBS, from your friend, or from a commercial redistributor, without any contact with us. It's much better for you to do those things than not have the software.

But in the long run, how much you can do with free software is determined by how much new free software people develop. If you want to have more free software a few years from now, it makes sense to think about how you can contribute.

The GNU project is a cooperative one. GNU software is developed by the Free Software Foundation's paid staff and by volunteers. The most direct way to contribute to GNU is to volunteer—to write useful software and manuals, and donate them.

But if you can't donate your time and expertise, you can donate indirectly, by giving money to the Free Software Foundation. We will then use the funds to write more programs and manuals.

Donations to the Free Software Foundation are tax-deductible; however, many users find their office unwilling to make a "donation," but willing to support us by ordering our manuals, tapes and CD-ROMs.

Tapes and CD-ROMs support development better than manuals, because much of the price of a manual goes to cover printing and distribution. Nearly all of what you pay the Foundation for a CD-ROM goes toward development. We now distribute a CD-ROM containing the complete GNU source code, and another containing compilation software source plus executables for MS-DOS, Solaris 2, and HP/UX 9. We also offer tape and CD-ROM subscriptions. For details, contact *gnu@prep.ai.mit.edu*, or phone 617-876-3296 to ask for a GNU's Bulletin.

Your cooperation in 1993 has put the Free Software Foundation on a stable footing; but, like other charities, we will ask for your support year after year. If you have contributed, thank you; if you have not contributed recently, please do.

Another way you can help development is by encouraging for-a-fee distributors to contribute more—either by doing development themselves, or by donating to a development organization like the Free Software Foundation.

The way to convince distributors to do this is to demand it and expect it from them. So when you compare distributors, judge them partly by how much they give to free software development. Show distributors they must compete to be the one who gives the most.

To make this approach work, you must insist on numbers that you can compare, such as, "We will donate ten dollars to the Frobozz project for each disk sold." A vague commitment, such as "A portion of the profits are donated," doesn't give a basis for comparison. Even a precise fraction "of the profits from this disk" is not very meaningful, since creative accounting and unrelated business decisions can greatly alter what fraction of the sales price counts as profit.

Another thing to ask developers is what kind of development they support. Some kinds of development make much more long-term difference than others. For example, maintaining a separate version of a GNU program contributes very little;

maintaining a program on behalf of the GNU project contributes much. Easy new ports contribute little, since someone else would surely do them; difficult ports such as adding a new CPU to the GNU compiler contribute more; major new features or packages contribute the most.

By establishing the idea that supporting further development is "the proper thing to do" when distributing free software for a fee, we can assure a steady flow of resources into making more free software.

CHAPTER 1

An Inside Look At Free UNIX Software

You've just purchased one of the most valued books that you'll every need. No, we're not blowing our own horn. And we don't think this book is any competition for *Gone With The Wind*. But we do feel that the book is a road map to the best free UNIX utilities that you'll find anywhere. Underscore the word *free*!

You've heard about software being there for the taking on this worldwide electronic highway. This isn't news. But have you ever tried to find this free software? If you've made such an attempt, you soon discovered it's like trying to find a needle in a haystack. You know the software is out there—you might even know how to download to your system—but what are these software utilities and how do you find them?

We've spent years poking around the Internet and asking ourselves these questions. Now we'd like to share our findings with you. When we began this project, we sought to find the best free UNIX utilities that we could locate. There were only three qualifications to make our list. First, the utility had to be the best available within a category. Second, the source code, binaries, and documentation had to available on the Internet. And third, the utility must be available to anyone without any strings attached.

Admittedly, this is a tall order for any software to fill. Then, after several months of searching, we were surprised. We scratched the surface, then dug a little deeper in the Internet and there they were, a treasure of utilities that we feel you can't be without.

Before we begin to share our findings, we should establish a common understanding of the Internet and of the community of software developers who volunteered to build world-class utilities and make them available to you at no charge. That's right! You don't pay these developers anything, except maybe a compliment.

In Chapter 2, "Connecting to the Internet," you learn about the Internet itself. Sure, the Internet is the electronic highway of the future, but it's more than that. It's a world community where everyone is courteous and has a sincere desire to share information freely with each other.

You'll learn about how to connect to the Internet and about the unwritten rules, called "nettiquette," that make life easier for users of the Internet. Once you activate your connection, you too are expected to follow these rules.

Since we're talking about important utilities that you should have in your UNIX toolbox, we'd better show you how to download these files to your system. In this same chapter, you'll learn the techniques for transferring the utility's files from a remote host to your system. This is the first step in making the utility ready to run on your system.

Let's be honest. Taking free software from the Internet isn't the same as purchasing software at your local computer store. We'll provide you with the name of the utility and one of the locations on the Internet where the utility's files are stored. It's up to you to build these files into a working version of the utility on your system.

Say what? Sorry, but that's the way it is on the Internet. Don't be too disappointed—we realize that not every one of our readers is a computer hacker who can magically solve any incompatibility problem that might arise. We offer two support mechanisms to help you over those rough times when you're making your version of the utility.

Within each utility we review, you'll find the name of a netnews group where you can chat with other users of a particular utility. That is, if you run into a problem that you can't solve, connect to the netnews group that we recommend and post your question to the community of users. Shortly thereafter, you should receive a response.

If that fails, we've also provided you with an email address where you can send your bug reports. Sometimes this address is for a general service and other times it is the address of the author of the utility. In either case, we won't leave you in the dark.

But if this alone isn't enough help for you, we've sat down and remembered all of the problems that we've experienced building our first few Internet utilities. Actually, we did more than remember. We also noted the steps we took to avoid making the same mistakes twice. We share these experiences with you in Chapter 3, "The Hacker's Guide."

NOTE
The rest of this chapter is a quick overview of all of the programs reviewed in this book. If you wish, you can skip to Chapter 2 and leave the goodies for later.

General Utility Software

We begin the second part of this book (Chapters 4 through 12) with a review of the best general utility software that we could find. The first utility that we review is less. You'll find less an indispensable improvement over the standard more utility. Mark Nudelman, in creating less, has combined the best features of more and the pg utilities. This includes the capability to return to a previous page.

Next, we found a blend that is a hit; a UNIX shell that has the best of the Korn Shell, Bourne Shell, and the C Shell. We're talking about bash, which was developed by Brian Fox and Chet Ramey, and is the GNU Project's Bourne Again Shell. Bash uses Bourne Shell syntax to provide interactive command-line editing, job control (on architectures that support it), and the C Shell-like history feature. And this is just scratching the surface.

Every UNIX software developer must search for data. Searching for information using UNIX really isn't anything new. Your system already has some fine utilities that handle this chore very well. However, finding information is one thing, and managing data is another—that's where ingres comes into the picture.

Ingres is not another version of awk or grep. It is a relational database system that was developed by Bell Laboratories for Digital Equipment Corp. This program is not included on the CD. Ingres allows you to organize data properly by normalizing information into several tables. You can then join these tables as needed by drawing a relationship between a common field in both tables. Hold on! We don't what to give you the story here. You'll have to turn to Chapter 4 for the complete review.

We stumbled across another interesting utility that we just had to tell you about. Called screen, it allows you to hold multiple sessions on a dumb terminal. We can thank Oliver Laumann, Wayne Davison, Juergen Weigert, and Michael Schroeder, the authors of screen. You can learn where to find it, and how to install and use it, when you read its review in Chapter 4.

With the worldwide Internet network at your fingertips, wouldn't you like to be able to easily chat with someone, ask a few technical questions, or maybe talk politics? Some Internet users try to accomplish this by using netnews and posting questions and comments to a particular group. But then there's the problem of privacy—or the lack of it.

All that has changed. Edward Bennett found a way to allow two Internet users to hold a discussion without posting and without talking on the telephone. Bennett developed a utility called talk that is nearly as effective as talking on the phone. You'll learn the reasons why we selected talk in our review.

Now here's another problem solver that we found. Did you ever find a need to transmit a binary file via electronic mail? If you have, you already know some of the problems that you face. But you don't have to worry anymore thanks to Mark Horton, who with his associates developed uuencode. Now there's not much to uuencode, but what's there will save you a lot of aggravation.

Uuencode converts a binary file into an ASCII file that you'll have little problem transmitting. When the file reaches its destination, uudecode (uuencode's sister utility) is used to transform the ASCII file back to a binary file. The entire process is as simple as running both utilities.

Jerry Smith of Iris Computing Laboratories has developed a utility that we think you'll find to be a very handy addition to your UNIX toolbox. Xrolodex is a small, rolodex-like application that is designed for systems running X Windows. The xrolodex utility has a solid Motif—based user interface that will challenge any commercial software product that you can find on the market.

Text Processing Utilities

Our attention changes to another category of software: text processing in Chapter 5. We set out to find what we feel are the leaders in text processing. We didn't limit ourselves to editors; instead, we expanded this category to include any utility that will help you process text better than you do today. And we found some very worthwhile candidates.

Typical editors are no match for a true word processor. Sure, editors may not have all the formatting capabilities that you want, but that's not the purpose of an editor. If you're looking for an editor that can do word processing, look at TeX.

TeX was developed by Donald Knuth at Stanford University to take text file input from an editor and produce typeset output. In fact, a number of professional publishing firms use TeX for their publications. You'll find that TeX is a welcome addition to your collection of UNIX utilities.

Let's face it, most editors are not used to write a letter; they're used to create computer programs. You sit down in front of the editor and enter a few lines of code, then exit the editor to compile and execute your program. After you run your program, you discover a bug. Now it's time to call in the debugger utility to track down the problem, after which you return to the editor to correct the source code.

Does this sound all too familiar? If you've written programs for personal computers you know there is an easier way. Development tools from Microsoft and Borland International let you create and test your program without leaving the development environment. Don't you wish you had something like this for UNIX? You do! It's called emacs. Emacs has all of the facilities that you need to build your software without having to exit emacs. You'll learn all about emacs in our review.

Many of us have a problem with splling. Whoops! I mean spelling. Fortunately, Pace Willisson has come to our aid with ispell. Now we don't have any excuses for misspelled documents. In addition to pointing out possible spelling errors in a document, Willisson has incorporated a feature that you'll find indispensable. Ispell will actually make an attempt to provide you with the correct spelling. It's because of this that we've included ispell on our list.

Are you tired of printing those same dull reports time and again? You know, reports that look like they came from an old typewriter. Reports that are missing the pizzazz that immediately catches your eye and almost forces you to read the text. Well, those days are behind on you. Step back and take a breath of fresh air, then plow right in and learn how to use your latest tool in your UNIX utility toolbox.

We're talking about groff, which was created by James Clark. Clark has to be thanked for taking the time to develop a utility that so many of us can use every day. Groff is a front-end to the groff document formatting system and a post-processor for selected devices. These devices include ps for PostScript printers, .div for TeX, X75 for a 75-dpi X11 previewer, X100 for a 100-dpi X11 previewer, ASCII for typewriter-like devices, and latin1 for devices that use the ISO Latin-1 character set. Groff is a replacement for the standard UNIX nroff utility, and is discussed in Chapter 5.

Game Software

Not every program we looked at was for work. We also considered those times when you want a little enjoyment from your terminal. We didn't have to search too long before we found games that will challenge your reasoning skills. We also threw in an arcade game to keep you fingers nimble. You can read about all these games in Chapter 6.

The first game that made the list is chess. Don't expect Battle Chess! You won't see a knight lock swords with a pawn. But you will experience a challenging game when you run gnuchess. Stuart Cracraft and a whole host of other contributors have volunteered their time to create a game that provides a high-resolution display and executes numerous known strategies that will give most chess enthusiasts a good workout.

We then stumbled across two adventure games. Why include two adventure games on our list? We couldn't choose just one as the best—there was a tie. Let's begin our look at adventure games with moria.

It's dark and dreary and cold. You enter the dungeon with trepidation. Who's in there? No one. You're sure your wrong. There's someone in the dungeon just waiting for you—and it isn't with a warm greeting. But you're prepared. At least you think you have the proper equipment to handle anything. Only time will tell.

No this isn't a poorly written sci-fi novel. Instead it's an adventure game that's addictive. The game is called moria and has the same flavor as the famous Dungeons & Dragon games. If you've never played Dungeons & Dragons then you're in for a treat. Moria is an adventure game that requires you to think as if you were in the fathomless dungeon yourself searching for the hidden treasure and out to kill the Balrog. The Balrog resides 2,500 feet underground on the 50th level of the dungeon. That's 2,500 feet of deadly silence and terror stalking around every corner. Sound exciting? You bet it is—and plenty of intelligent fun.

The second adventure game is call nethack. Here you must prove your worthiness to the masters of your local adventurer's guild. The test is to enter the bowels of the dungeon to recover the Amulet of Yendor, an artifact that will bring you honor and full guild membership—and immortality, granted by the gods. It is a formidable challenge for anyone who thinks of himself as a master of adventure games. A word of warning! Don't start playing nethack an hour before you plan to go to bed. You'll find yourself staying up all night searching the Mazes of Menace.

Enough with adventure games. The next game that made our list is not a game at all. In fact, we classify it as a practical joke that you can play on anyone who is running X Windows. Remember when you walked into a dark basement in an old house? You got that creepy feeling that with each step you knew you weren't alone. You turned on the lights and there they were—hundreds of little creepy crawlers, scrambling for cover in all directions.

Well, these same bugs—or a computer representation—are in your system when you install the xroach utility. Now don't become excited. These aren't the bugs you find in your programs and they have no connection to viruses. They are computer roaches created by J.T. Anderson, the author of xroach, that scamper just like their relatives who visit dark, damp basements—except they do all their running on your screen. You really have to see it to believe it.

We conclude our list of the best games that we could find with an old favorite. Try it once and you'll find that you're addicted. You'll keep playing and playing in an attempt to beat the highest score. In fact, it has been known that the game pieces even enter your dreams. Sounds strange? Maybe, but let it be known that you've been warned.

The game that we're talking about is xtetris. Does the name have a familiar ring? It should, since xtetris is the public domain version of the very popular game tetris. Tetris requires quick reflexes and a sharp eye to fit falling blocks into the correct position on the game board. As the block moves down your screen, you use direction keys on the keyboard to rotate it into a snug fit among other blocks that have fallen to the bottom. Once you've completed a row of blocks, the row disappears, lowering the blocks above it one level. We think you'll find this game irresistible.

Communications Utilities

The heart of the Internet is data communications. So how could we assemble a list of the best utilities without including data communications utilities? In Chapter 7, you'll find utilities that handle data compression, file transfer, and even teleconferencing. Don't overlook this chapter.

Transferring large files is time-consuming and expensive, especially when the transfer occurs over telephone lines. But gzip can help. You'll still have to pay the cost of the connect time, but you can dramatically reduce the size of the file by using gzip. A smaller file means a shorter telephone call and reduced expense.

Now that we've compressed your data files, you still have to transfer the files. We found two file transfer programs that fit the bill. The first is kermit. Although you won't find Miss Piggy along side Kermit, you will be able to transfer files between all types of computers. Frank da Cruz and Christine Gianone are the authors of kermit.

The other file transfer utility that hit the top of our list is probably one of the most economical utilities that you'll ever find to transfer and receive files. It's called the zmodem utility. Zmodem uses the proper error correcting protocols to receive files over a dial-up serial port from a variety of programs. This allows you to receive files from programs running under DOS, CP/M, UNIX, and nearly any operating system that you can imagine.

Data communication was never this easy—and free! Well, the software is free. You'll still have to pay for the telephone call. The free software is pcomm, which converts your system and modem into a powerful tool that can reach around the world.

The pcomm utility is truly one of those great finds. It is designed to operate similarly to the Datastorm Technologies, Inc.'s DOS ProComm software. You'll find that pcomm walks you through the complete communications cycle, from dialing the telephone through transferring files. All you need to do is to respond to menus.

The next communication utility in our review is called sliplogin. The authors of this utility describe it as a serial-line link to a network interface. This sounds rather abstract, yet it is really a valuable utility for anyone who is looking to connect to the Internet. The concept is rather easy to understand. Let's say that you don't have an Internet connection. You search around for access through your local university but unless you're a student or a faculty member, they probably won't listen to you.

Next, you turn to a commercial firm that offers an Internet connection for a monthly fee. Although the firm supplies you with an IP address, you still must connect to the firm's host. This is where sliplogin comes into play. Sliplogin is a driver that handles the link between your system and your gateway into the Internet. It is a simple piece of software that you can't live without!

And to help you manage the file that you transfer to the host, we've included a review of special archival software. Let's face it. You're a professional and have all the necessary backups of the source in place—enough backup copies so you can easily recover from a mishap and retain your job.

However, when the MIS auditors get a hold of a project, those precautions that you've taken never seem enough to satisfy their need for a perfect audit. You won't have to face this problem again if you use the zoo utility. In fact, you'll invite the MIS auditors to examine your next project—to show off your new tool.

Zoo safely stores and retrieves your most valuable files. And it does so without interfering with your style of operation. There are many factors that make it a must have for serious developers, but ease of operation is number one.

We round out this communications chapter with a couple of truly unique utilities—a teleconferencing package and a hypertext browser. Let's say that you're ready to demonstrate the software package that you've worked months preparing. It works fine, but you must show your work to five end-user groups who are spread out over many locations in your firm. You could take your show on the road and visit each location, giving each group their own presentation. Or, you now have an alternative. You can teleconference all the end-user groups.

We're not talking about a video conference. We're talking about a networking conference that allows a single-user application to be shared among many end users. This means that you can start your application on your system and use the xtv utility to conference in each end user in the group.

Through a telephone line, you can take a participant through the steps that are necessary to use your software. Since all the groups are viewing the same instance of the application, they can hear your directions and watch the results on the screen. The xtv utility is a timesaver that can also let you dazzle your users with the latest in teleconferencing techniques.

And talk about dazzle, wait until you read our review about this next utility. We've seen the software that is breaking new ground by giving you the capability of using graphics, sounds, video, and text to make it easier to poke around the Internet. We're talking about mosaic, which we found to be a cut above all the other Internet browsers that you've used in the past. Mosaic can only be gotten free by downloading from **ftp**. It is not on the CD. We'll let you read the details about mosaic in Chapter 7.

Printing and Spreadsheet Utilities

Our list of the best free UNIX utilities wouldn't be complete unless we examined printing and spreadsheet utilities. We begin Chapter 8 by asking you a simple question. How would you like to print like the pros? Well, you can if you use the Ghostscript utility. Professional documents require the power of PostScript, a programming language that gives pizzazz to the traditional drab, single-font style that is used to print most text documents. However, if you can't have PostScript, you *can* have Ghostscript.

Ghostscript, created by L. Peter Deutsch, is a programming language similar to the Adobe Systems' PostScript (TM) language. Actually, Deutsch's Ghostscript is a set of programs that provide an interpreter for the PostScript language, as well as C programming language procedures that implement the PostScript graphics capabilities.

We continue discussing publishing utilities with a tool that will enhance your editor's capability. Making your publication look sharp using your favorite editor can be a nearly insurmountable task. Most editors are not designed to be a page-making tool. However, you won't have these problems anymore thanks to Angus Duggan, who built a series of publication tools that he calls the ps utilities.

The ps utilities are a group of programs that allow you to easily arrange pages into signatures, select pages and ranges of pages, rearrange pages, and print multiple pages on a single sheet of paper. Doesn't sound too impressive? Not unless you have to manually arrange pages for a publication.

We wind up this chapter with a brief look at the only spreadsheet utility that made it to our list. If you're looking for a simple yet powerful spreadsheet, then you're looking in the right place. We're talking about the sc utility, a powerful public domain spreadsheet that can handle nearly anything you can throw at it. Don't expect anything fancy. You won't find a macro language or graphic capabilities, but you will find built-in financial functions that are perfect for budgets and mortgages—and a lot more.

Software Development Utilities

The Internet has a wealth of tools for anyone who develops his/her own software. In fact, we were surprised by the vast amount of software development tools available for the taking. It took us awhile, but we were finally able to come up with a selection that we feel should be at the top of your list.

So, there you are. You've spent days working on a source code file. You've even worked on it at home. The boss should give you an award for your performance, but there is this little problem that you don't want anyone to know about. It goes like this. You copied the source code from your system at work to a floppy disk so you could work on it on your home system. Changes you made there were transferred back to the floppy and restored to your system at work. However, there were some days when you left the floppy at home—so you created another floppy disk.

Now you're confused. Which of the three source files is up-to-date? The one on your system at work or those on the two floppy disks? Choose the wrong one and you'll be days behind in your work. Sure, you know that you should have been more careful, but that's not going help you now. Relax, the diff utilities are here to come to your aid. These utilities will show you where each source code file differs with the others. With that information, you should be able to easily determine the version of the source code that you need to continue you work.

All of us know the difficulties that we experience when we try to stamp out bugs in our application. Here comes another debugger. So what! Well, don't be too quick to jump to conclusions. The gdb debugger is a timesaver that you should add to your arsenal of tools. It lets you see what is going on inside your program while your program is executing. And the gdb debugger will tell you what your program was doing at the moment your program crashed. You can read all about this powerful utility in Chapter 9.

Next, we turn our attention to a tool that will help you build a major portion of your next application. User interface can normally be tricky and time-consuming to create, but not any more if you use InterViews. InterViews is a C++ class library that speeds the development of user interfaces. The secret is that nearly all of the objects used to compose a typical application interface are available as part of the library. All you need to do is use these classes as part of your application.

Programmers, stand back for a blast that will give you a boost when creating your C language application. We're talking about a utility that will take all the hassles out of building a makefile. It's called makedepend, and it's yours for the taking.

Let's face it—all of us know that a makefile speeds the compiling and linking of application files during development. Once the makefile is created, you let the make utility worry about compiling just the source code that you changed. However, there's a price to pay for this assistance; it's up to you to write the makefile!

Admit it. You don't really write a makefile. If you're like many programmers, you "borrow" someone else's makefile and change it to suit your application. Not any more! You can thank Todd Brunhoff, the author of makedepend. He built a utility that reads your source code and identifies all the dependencies that are required for a makefile.

Finding the difference between two source code files is just half the problem of updating a version of your application. You still need to patch those differences into the file to create the next generation of your program. Larry Wall and his associates have come up with patch, which handles this chore for you.

The patch utility takes the output of the diff utility and uses the results to update a program file. This eliminates the need for you to go line by line to locate where the program file needs to be updated, then copy the appropriate lines of code into the program file. All the work is done for you, thanks to Wall's patch.

The next utility is a lifesaver. The rcs utility takes the pain and confusion out of managing your source code. As long as you faithfully use rcs, you'll never have to wonder which copy of the source code is the current version of your program. The rcs utility acts as a librarian by requiring you or other programmers on your team to check out the latest copy of the source code. Once the file is out, no one else can receive an editable copy of the file until the original file is checked in by rcs.

Anyone who has ever dealt with an end user soon realizes the main objectives of developing software. End users don't care what language you use, nor are they concerned about how efficient you write the code. All they care about are three things. Will it do the job? How easy is it to use? And can you deliver it tomorrow—before lunch? How can any programmer meet such a challenge?

One possible answer is to use Tcl, explained in Chapter 9, for your next development project. This utility is an embeddable scripting language that has many of the features you need to build a typical application. You can consider it your "little secret" weapon to combat typical—and sometimes unreasonable—requests made by the end user.

John Ousterhout developed the Tcl language at the University of California at Berkeley. The principle behind this language is that a single interpretive language (Tcl) controls all aspects of an interactive application. This includes the application interface and communication between applications. The Tcl utility will make programming X Windows simpler and reduce your development time 5 to 10 times from your present rate.

The last utility that we talk about in Chapter 9 is from James Peterson who has written a small but powerful utility that is perfect for keeping a watchful eye on a remote application. The xscope utility monitors the connection between an X11 server and a client program. Admittedly, this sounds a little like Big Brother looking over your shoulder, but sometimes this is required for fine tuning an application. It's a perfect tool for debugging your application in the field.

Graphics Utilities

In Chapter 10, we move into the world of graphics and explore the best utilities in this category. In today 's world of computing, very few users want to deal with raw data. In fact, many of them only want to see a dramatic picture of the information in the form of a graph. Let's face it—there are simple graphs that can be programmed in a few minutes. And then there are those graphs that can take hours to develop. Of course, users almost always prefer—and sometimes demand—complicated graphs.

Next time that this happens to you, don't duck. Instead, come out shooting because you'll be packing all the tools you'll need to produce the fanciest, most complicated graphics within minutes. You'll find your ammunition in gnuplot. What makes gnuplot so powerful is that all you need to create a publication quality graph is to describe the graph using simple commands. This utility could save you countless hours. All you need to do is to invest some of your time installing the utility on your system.

Here's a problem that anyone who works with graphics can appreciate. You spend days looking for the ideal bitmap for your graphics project. But when you find it, the bitmap is in a format that your graphics software doesn't recognize. You can't use the bitmap—until now!

Don't throw away a bitmap because your graphics software can't read the file. Instead, turn the problem over to the pbm utility to convert the bitmap into a file format that is acceptable to your graphics utility. Now, practically any bitmap that you can get your hands on can be incorporated into your graphics project.

Now, how about turning your terminal into an electronic canvas. It isn't a problem as long as you are using the xfig utility. Xfig can help you transform those graphic images in your mind to a bitmap. And when you combine xfig with the TransFig package, which comes with TeX, you can make hard copies of those images ready for your next presentation.

We close Chapter 10 with a look at a powerful graphics viewer. All of us know that computer images are really bitmaps of photos or art that were scanned into computer memory. Now you know that there are countless bitmaps available on Internet or from commercial sources.

But the bitmap are just half of the story. You still need software that will read the bitmap, display the image on the screen, and send the image to the printer. Where do you find such software? Right here! The xv utility can transform an image file into an attractive display on your computer screen.

But wait! It does a lot more than simply display an image. Execute the proper commands and you can have xv stretch or compress the image, rotate the image in 90 degree steps, flip the image around the horizontal or vertical axes, and even crop a rectangular portion of the image. Could you ever want more? Sure! And xv is not going to disappoint you. But you'll have to read our review of xv to find out.

Electronic Mail Utilities

Now for some interesting electronic mail utilities that we found along the Internet. The first one is elm. Elm is actually a user agent system that is designed to be used with sendmail, mail, or whatever email utility you have on your system. However, elm is also a full replacement for mail and mailx.

Inside elm, you'll find other software that can provide a list of your mail and that produces clean, paginated printouts of your email. Then there is a systemwide daemon that can automatically answer your email when you're unavailable. But probably the striking difference between elm and other email systems is how elm's features center around the screen. We won't give away all the details here.

Next we discovered a way for you to efficiently manage your netnews feed by using the cnews utility. Cnews allows your computer to have its own netnews node. It also includes three utilities that give you a rather primitive news reader. These are readnews, expire, and postnews.

And last but not least is a very powerful utility, NetFax, which allows you to send and receive a fax from your system. Put this review at the top of your list.

Programming Languages

If you own a personal computer, you're in for a treat. We found an X client server that's just what you're look for. It's called XFree86. XFree86 is a port of the X11R5 that supports several versions of Intel-based machines. See Chapter 12 for our review.

Also in Chapter 12 is a review of a utility that's just right for Fortran programmers. Here is a away to get a leg up on the C programming language, make you more productive, and save your employer money. The f2c utility reads your Fortran program and rewrites your program in C language. Too good to be true? Maybe, but you now can have your own copy of f2c to add to your UNIX toolbox.

We then move into the world of languages and libraries with a review of the gcc C and C++ compiler. Here's what you get: a compiler that will work with standard C and C++, one that contains new features that aren't found on a standard ANSI C compiler, and one that can convert your source code to standard ANSI C for portability.

And talk about portability, you're in for a treat if you develop applications that must run on various platforms. Gcc can compile your source code to run on a machine that is different from your own system. Hold on! We don't want to give away our review here. You'll have to read the rest for yourself.

Want to try your hand at some Artificial Intelligence applications? Nearly every programmer has taken a crack at trying to give a computer the ability to behave like humans. You've probably tried using the C programming language or some other general purpose programming tool.

Don't be surprised if you were disappointed with the outcome of your work. General purpose programming languages by themselves just don't have the power that is required for the symbol and list manipulation that is required for an artificial intelligence project. You've heard the old expression, "Use the right tool for the job." This holds true when you develop an AI application. Here are two of those tools: KCL, which is a LISP interpreter, and SB-Prolog, which is a Prolog interpreter. Both are perfect for AI and are reviewed in Chapter 12.

Another programming language that is worth mentioning is Perl. Granted, Perl won't be used for AI. Instead, Perl is an interpreted language that is specifically designed to efficiently read text files and extract information that will be printed in a report. Don't expect to write large, sophisticated applications with Perl. You can, however, expect to efficiently produce information for the more common system management tasks.

Larry Wall developed Perl by combining the best features of the C programming language and the sed and awk utilities, along with a few of the familiar conventions of Csh, Pascal, and BASIC-PLUS. This is one review that you can't miss.

We finish Chapter 12 with two worthwhile libraries. The first is the NIH Class library. Now you can directly benefit from your federal tax dollars and use classes that were built by the National Institutes of Health, an agency of the federal government. The National Institutes of Health designed their library to be used as a resource for software developers and to be portable to systems that use System V or 4.2/4.3 BSD.

The other library is readline, created by Richard Stallman. Readline enables you to incorporate the features of an editor in your application without the hassle of programming. And as a extra bonus, readline recognizes the same commands as emacs. This means your program conforms to a standard command set.

CHAPTER 2

Connecting To The Internet

In this book we review some of the most useful and powerful utilities that you should add to your UNIX toolbox. However, learning about these utilities isn't enough. You still must load them onto your system before you can use them. These software utilities aren't available in your local software store, but they are available on the Internet for a price you can't beat—free!

The Internet is the electronic highway of the future that you're hearing so much about these days on television and in the press. The federal government has focused efforts on developing this link to connect together every home, business, government agency, and educational institution in America.

Is this science fiction? Not really. Granted, there is a lot of public relations puff that is being thrown about, but when you look closely at the plan you'll find a solid base already in place. We're talking about the Internet. Right now, many government agencies, businesses, and educational institutions are connected together by this electronic highway.

It started back in the 1970s with a Defense Department-sponsored network called Arpanet. Arpanet wasn't really a network as we know it today, but instead was a collection of computer networks used to share defense-related information with selected businesses and educational institutions. These weren't for battle plans. They were studies and scientific discussions that played a role in the overall defense strategy of the United States.

Arpanet eventually evolved into the Internet. In the simplest terms, the Internet is an electronic link between your computer and systems all over the world. Yes, we really mean the world. You can sit in front of your computer at home and connect to your local Internet host via a modem and telephone lines (perhaps a toll free call), and send a message to your friend in Japan.

The Internet host is a server that is housed and maintained by an independent firm, your employer, or your local university. We'll talk more about how you connect with the Internet later in this chapter. However, once you log on to the host system, an entire universe of information is available to you by typing a few strokes at the keyboard.

So, what can this electronic highway do for you today? How about sending electronic mail to others on the Internet? For example, you could write a note on your word processor to the President, then send it electronically to *president@whitehouse.gov*. Within a fraction of a second from the time you press the ENTER key, your note is delivered to the electronic mail system at the White House.

While the delivery system bypasses the post office, no one is guaranteeing that you'll receive a reply any quicker than if you used your local mailbox. The address, *president@whitehouse.gov*, is the White House's Internet address. Once you are able to connect to the Internet, you too will have your own personal Internet address where you can receive electronic mail.

The Internet is more than a replacement for the Postal Service. It is a community of dedicated individuals who truly practice the concept of freedom of information. Unlike CompuServe and other commercial computer networks, the Internet is free of charge. And if you think that's rare in today's world, it gets better. Huge amounts of information on the Internet are also free!

Before you become too excited, there are expenses. First, you may have to pay a monthly fee to use a local host which will link your computer to the Internet. However, you might be able to connect through a local university or through your employer. In such cases, the university or the employer already has the computer and networking equipment to link to the Internet, so you probably won't be charged a fee for your connection.

Another expense is the cost of the telephone call to the host. You still have to pay for that. However, if you use a computer at your local college or are connected to the Internet through your firm's computer in the office, there probably won't be any charge.

The concept of free-flow information is key to the value of the Internet. In this book, we review the best UNIX utilities that we could find. These are utilities that cost you nothing to own because the authors of the utilities believe in the free flow of information. This includes free source code to these utilities.

What this means to you is that if you find a utility in this book that you think will be a valued addition to your UNIX toolbox, connect to the Internet and download the utility to your system. It's free for the taking. Think of it. You get the source code for the utility along with all the documentation that you'll need. Just copy the files and compile the source code so that the utility will work on your system.

You may be thinking that it sounded interesting until we said that you must compile the source code. Yes, compiling any source code successfully isn't necessarily an easy task. But don't become overly concerned. We did say that the Internet community believes in the free flow of information and that also includes help with software.

Although most of the utilities come with a ready-to-run makefile that is used to build the binary files of the utility, you'll also find step-by-step installation instructions included in the utility's documentation. And if you run into any problems, there are several ways to receive support for the software.

The first method is to read a netnews group that is interested in the utility you are installing. *Netnews* is a worldwide electronic bulletin board service on the Internet that facilitates the distribution of information. A *netnews group* is like a bulletin board that contains information about a particular subject such as information about your utility. We'll show you how to connect to a netnews group later in this chapter.

As you read information on the netnews group, you'll see comments that others have about the utility. You'll also see many handy tips for installing and using the utility. And there are always reports of known bugs that someone has found on a particular distribution of the utility. You might also find fixes or work-arounds for these problems posted on the netnews group.

But probably the most valuable aspect of the netnews group is that you can pose your own questions to the community of Internet users who are interested in the utility. This is called *posting* to a netnews group. Not long after you've posted your question, you'll find several suggestions to fix the problem. These suggestions are hints provided by other users of the utility who are interested enough to post a response to your question.

Nearly all the utilities that you'll find on the Internet have the electronic mail address of the utility's author or of the person who is maintaining the utility. Just write your problem in a note using your text processor, then electronically mail the note to the address that you find in the utility's documentation.

We should point out that all support that you receive on the Internet is volunteered. No one, including the author of a utility, is compensated for his or her efforts. All that you'll find on the Internet is provided in the spirit of free-flow information felt among the community of Internet users. Since others on the Internet are helping you as a courtesy, you must be careful not to overextend your welcome. You should also pay this kindness back by helping others as they helped you.

Therefore, you should abide by the rules of Internet courtesy. When asking for support, don't rush to send your problem to the author of the utility. This isn't polite. First, you should make sure that you haven't left out any steps during the installation process. Next, be sure that you reviewed all the netnews articles about the utility. And above all, post your question on netnews before contacting the author of the utility. We'll talk more about Internet courtesy in Chapter 3, "The Hacker's Guide."

We used the term *distribution*, which might be a little confusing. When a new utility is made available to the Internet community, the author copies all the necessary files to a host computer. All the files for that utility are called a *distribution*. You might think of a distribution as a version of the utility.

In fact, the utility can be found on many Internet host systems throughout the world. This is by design so that transmitting the utility to your system is efficient and economical. Let's say that you're on the West Coast of the United States and you want to acquire the ispell utility. This utility might be available on a host system at universities in Germany, San Francisco, Tokyo, and New York. Although there is nothing preventing you from copying ispell from the host system in Tokyo, it would be more economical to copy the utility from the university in San Francisco. This practice is also part of the Internet courtesy.

The Internet is a strange organization that truly blends the cultures of countries from around the world into one group that is willing to generously share information with its members. What is strange is that the Internet is not organized in the traditional sense. There are no leaders. No one owns the Internet. You don't need permission to join the Internet. And there are no rules for using the Internet, except for the unwritten rule of courtesy.

Connecting to the Internet

The Internet is an electronic network that joins together computers from all over the world. Each computer that is connected to the Internet is called an Internet *host*. An Internet host is typically a server that is on a local network such as the network that you find at universities or in businesses. It is common that personal computers and workstations are directly connected to the local network. Computers that are linked to an Internet host via a local network normally have access to the Internet. This assumes that all data security permissions from the local network administrator are in order.

If you can find your way onto such a network, you're in luck. You'll probably have access to the Internet free of charge. Just contact the local network administrator and ask to be provided with your own logon ID to the network. In many organizations, this process also results in the assignment of a personal Internet address for you.

Let's say that you're not associated with an organization that has their own Internet host. What do you do? Start looking for your local freenet. The concept of freenet started with the Cleveland Freenet, and has grown into a formal organization called the National Public Telecomputing Network (NPTN). NPTN and its' members provide free public access to the Internet. You can obtain a listing of freenet organizations in *The Internet Complete Reference* by Harley Hahn and Rick Stout and published by Osborne/McGraw-Hill.

A word of caution! Signing up for a freenet isn't without its drawbacks. Some freenets provide only limited access to the Internet and usually have their own rules you must obey. So before you connect to your local freenet, make sure you know if the freenet will give you complete access to Internet facilities.

Another way to connect to the Internet is to subscribe to a service that is provided by a commercial organization. Such a service will usually cost you a monthly charge and possibly a usage charge which is called *connect-time*. Keep in mind that you must still pay for the telephone call to the service. The Hahn and Stout book contains a list of some of these commercial organizations. Make sure that you select a firm that is a local call for your computer.

Inside Your Internet Address

Each Internet user is identified by a unique address. Here is a sample of an Internet address: *keogh_j@spcuna.spc.edu*. It may look a little strange, but there really is some logic behind the address. The address is divided into two major sections. These are the *user ID* and the *domain*.

The user ID is your personal login identifier that is used to sign you onto your system. In this example, *keogh_j* is the user ID. The domain section of the address begins following the at sign (@)—in this case, *spcuna.spc.edu* is the domain.

The domain is also divided into sections called subdomains. However, instead of reading the domain from left to right, we read it from right to left. The first subdomain in this example is *edu*, which means that the address is associated with an educational institution. Table 2-1 contains a listing of the major organizational domains.

The next subdomain in this example is *spc*, which is typically used to identify the institution. In this case the educational institution is Saint Peter's College in

DOMAIN	DESCRIPTION
com	Commercial organization
edu	Educational institution
gov	Government agency
int	International organization
mil	Military organization
net	Networking organization
org	Non-profit organization

TABLE 2-1.   *Top-Level Domain Codes by Organization*

Jersey City, New Jersey. Each institution creates their own subdomain letters. The final subdomain in this example is *spcuna*. This is the name of the computer where the user receives mail.

So, we can summarize the domain segment of the address as the educational institution Saint Peter's College's spcuna computer. Once the Internet locates the correct computer on the network, the user ID is used to identify the proper mailbox.

The example that we used is typical of an Internet address at a university. However, other Internet addresses might have a greater or lesser number of subdomains than is shown in this example. Some Internet addresses begin with a subdomain that indicates the country. Table 2-2 contains a sampling of geographical domains. Others just use two subdomains: the general subdomain such as *com* and the name of the computer. In all cases, the Internet address must have the user ID.

Finding Your Way on the Internet

There are thousands of Internet host systems on the network. Some of these hosts require special authorization for you to gain access to the system. For example, NASA, the National Aeronautics and Space Administration, has several hosts that are off limits to the general public.

However, there are many Internet host systems that are partially opened to everyone. This means you can connect to such a host and poke around without requiring any prior permission from the organization who owns the system. Keep in mind they have taken precautions to limit your access to the public areas of the system.

DOMAIN	DESCRIPTION
at	Austria
au	Australia
ca	Canada
ch	Switzerland
de	Germany
dk	Denmark
es	Spain
fr	France
gr	Greece
ie	Republic of Ireland
jp	Japan
nz	New Zealand
uk	United Kingdom

TABLE 2-2. *Top-Level Domain Codes by Geographical Location*

Let's say that you want to explore an Internet host other than your own host. The first thing that you need to do is know the Internet address of the remote host system. There are a variety of sources for these addresses. We recommend the Hahn and Stout book; it contains a wealth of addresses to Internet host systems.

Once you've located the address for the host system, you can then connect to the system. There are three Internet services that are used with a remote host. These are telnet, FTP, and client/server. All three services are available to nearly everyone who connects to the Internet. However, some freenets may not offer all the services. Firms that provide commercial access to the Internet may charge you extra for telnet and FTP.

Telnet is a service that allows you to start a session with a remote Internet host. Simply type **telnet** at the prompt, followed by the address of the remote system. The telnet service sends your request over the Internet and begins the logon process. If you logon successfully, you can use the remote system as though you had dialed in via modem.

FTP (File Transfer Protocol) is a service that is used to transfer files over the Internet. Here's how to copy files from a remote Internet host to your system. At your local UNIX prompt, type **ftp**, followed by the address of the remote host.

With an FTP connection, you can execute UNIX-like commands that are necessary for you to locate the file you want to transfer. Typically, you are allowed only to change directories and list the contents of a directory. After you've found the file that you need, enter the proper FTP commands to bring the file over to your system.

There are four basic FTP commands that will do most of the work for you. These are **bin**, **get**, **put**, and **close**. The **bin** command states that you want files transferred without any data conversion. This is necessary since you'll be transferring binary files and compressed files.

The **get** command is used to copy the file from the remote system onto your system. Type **get**, followed by the name of the file, and then press ENTER; the FTP service will transfer the file to the current directory on your system. Practically the same steps are used to send a file from your system to the remote host, except you substitute the **put** command in place of the **get** command. After you are finished transferring a file, you can execute the **close** command to break off the connection with the remote Internet host.

We can illustrate the difference between telnet and FTP services by trying to read the contents of a file on a remote host. If we created a telnet connection, we could use the UNIX cat utility to peek into the file. By contrast, if we connected using the FTP service, we'd have to copy the file over to our system before we could view the file. There is no command in the FTP service that allows you to read the file while the file remains on the remote host.

The client/server service is dramatically different from both telnet and FTP. While telnet and FTP are services that allow you to connect to a remote host, the Internet client/server service permits you to use the power of the remote host to help you find your way around the Internet. Probably one of the most frequently used client/server services is the gopher utility.

Gopher provides a menu interface to the Internet. When you type **gopher** at the prompt, the client portion of the utility contacts the gopher server for a copy of the initial menu. When this menu appears on screen, you can make your first selection. Each time you make a selection, gopher automatically connects to the necessary remote hosts on the Internet to meet your request. You'll find this to be a timesaver—like taking an electronic stroll through the Internet.

We've glossed over a very important aspect of using the Internet, that is, logging onto a remote host. Some remote hosts require that you make prior arrangements for a login ID with the organization that owns the host system. Just browse through the Internet addresses in the Hahn and Stout book (or other source), then give them a call to see what arrangement can be made to give you access to their system.

You'll find that there are many systems open to the public, and you can logon to them without making prior arrangements with the organization that owns the host. However, these systems do require you to login. What's you're login ID? It's anonymous. When you're prompted for your login ID, enter **anonymous**. Some systems will then ask that you use your email address as your password.

Finding Software on the Internet

The Internet is a large network of host systems all over the world. Somewhere on this network is the software that you need for your UNIX toolbox. But where is it? The first step in finding new software is to read our reviews in this book of the best free UNIX utilities that we've found on the Internet. Just thumb through each chapter and the index looking for software that meets your current needs.

Nearly all the software that we review in this book is available at more than one location on the Internet. In each review, we identify one of those locations. We tell you the directory and the Internet host that contains the utility.

We don't recommend that you connect to this location right away. Instead, use this location as your fail safe in case your exploration for the software on other Internet hosts turns out to be futile. Keep in mind that one of the rules of good etiquette of the Internet is that you locate software on the closest geographical host to your location. Therefore, the location we refer to may not be the ideal location for you.

A particular location contains the name of the remote host that has the utility. For example, we review many utilities that are distributed and maintained by the Free Software Foundation, Inc. These utilities are commonly referred to as GNU software. They are unique in that strict rules are enforced regarding the use of these utilities. No, they really don't restrict your use of the software. Instead, they prohibit anyone from preventing anyone else from using the software. You can read more about these restrictions when you read about the GNU utilities in this book.

The host that contains all of the GNU utilities is *prep.ai.mit.edu*. As you can imagine, this host is in very high demand. However, throughout the Internet there are hosts that mirror this system. This means that if the GNU host is not readily accessible, you can download the same utility from a host elsewhere on the Internet.

TIP
Keep on eye on the global clock. It is safe to presume that traffic on a host in your own time zone will have a heavy demand during normal working hours. However, this peak time may actually be the down time for a host outside of your time zone. You must weigh this factor against the geographical location of the host to determine which host is the most efficient to use to download your utility.

Although our software review contains one location for the utility, the question still remains, how do you find the other host locations on the Internet? At first you might think that you'd have to connect to each host and explore its directories. However, there is special software that does all the searching for you. This software is called the archie utility.

Here's how it works. A number of Internet hosts have archie software. If you can't find such as host, try this one: *archie.internic.net*. Log onto your computer, then type **telnet**, followed by the name of the remote host that contains the archie utility. Once the connection is made, you'll be asked to login. Login as **archie**. No password is required for this login.

Next, enter **prog**, followed by the name of the utility that you require. Archie will then tell you your position on the queue and the approximate length of time for the search. You'll then see a "working..." prompt on the screen. Archie will then return with the Internet address of the host, the last date the program was updated, the name of the directory that contains the program, and a profile of the file. (This includes the size of the file and the permissions for the file.)

After archie provides you with a list of locations, log off the remote host, then you can use the FTP service to connect to the new location. You'll notice that archie returns both the remote host Internet address and the parent directory that contains the software you are looking for. So, once you connect to the remote host using the FTP service, you can use the FTP directory commands to position yourself to the proper directory; then use the FTP commands to transfer the utility to your system.

When the software arrives on your system, you still must build the binary files. Almost all of the utilities that you download come with installation instructions and a makefile that is nearly ready to run. Nearly? That's right. You may have to tweak the makefile so that the settings conform to your system. We'll provide you with tips on installation in the next chapter, "The Hacker's Guide."

Some software comes bundled in a package that you may need to decode. Table 2-3 contains a list of suffixes, as well as information on how to decode the files.

Bugs and General Information About the Utility

You'll find that nearly all the software that you pick up from the Internet contains a wealth of information about how to install and use the utility. While these provide nearly all the information that you'll need to get started using the software, there is another place to find information about the utility.

The netnews service on the Internet consists of a wide variety of electronic bulletin boards, called *news groups,* where you can exchange information about topics that are of interest to you. You'll find many news groups devoted to utilities that are available on the Internet.

SUFFIX	HOW TO DECODE FILES
.tar	"Untar" the file with the UNIX tar command
.tz	Uncompress the file with the uncompress utility described in Chapter 7, then "untar" the file with the UNIX tar command
.tgz	Uncompress the file with the gunzip utility described in Chapter 7, then "untar" the file with the UNIX tar command
.zoo	Uncompress/unpack the file with the zoo utility described in Chapter 7
.shar	Follow the directions at the top of the file. The contents are readable

TABLE 2-3.   *Decoding Files from the Internet*

This means that you can connect to a particular netnews group and read through the listing of questions, answers, and comments that other users have about the utility. Where do you find these groups? In each review, we suggest a netnews group that you should use. Once you become familiar with netnews, you'll quickly find other groups that discuss similar utilities. Don't be afraid to explore.

One of the key reasons for connecting to netnews is so you can tap into the broad user community that is ready and willing to help you tackle those difficult questions about a particular utility. You can easily use your netnews reader, which you can get for free on the Internet, to post questions to a specific news group.

Although the technique for posting to a news group is unique for each netnews reader, we'll go through the steps that we use. These steps are similar to the way you use your netnews reader to post your questions or comments.

First, you select the netnews group. As you read through the postings, you usually have at least two choices available to you: to respond to a particular posting or to post your own message. There are menu options on your netnews reader to handle these functions. Just make your selection, then an editor appears on the screen. You can use the editor to enter your questions or comments. When you exit the editor, the netnews reader automatically sends your message to the netnews group. You'll be surprised at the response you'll receive.

While the netnews group is an excellent resource for assistance, we suggest that you try to find a posting that contains the most frequently asked questions. This is commonly referred to as the FAQ posting. Just by glancing through the FAQ file, you'll be able to learn all the basics that you'll need to know to use the software. A word of caution! Not all utilities contain a FAQ posting.

Keep in mind that you are using free software that is not guaranteed to work on your system. No one is trying to cheat you, but this is the reality of the Internet. With that said, we can assure you that most utilities do work on most systems. By sifting through our review, the utility's documentation, and reading the related netnews groups, you should be able to assess your chances of successfully running a particular utility on your system.

Some organizations assume that all free software is unsupported and therefore unreliable. They ignore the fact that if the software becomes popular it will be maintained by the Internet community. It is a different and arguably better level of support than can be achieved by any single private entity. The issue is to recognize which free software falls into this category, and that is one of the main purposes of this book.

Even if you are able to get the utility running, you still might uncover a bug or two. Yes, software on the Internet may have bugs. What do you do if you stumble across a bug? Don't panic. There's plenty of support to help you. The first step is to reread the documentation. We've found many utilities that list the known bugs in a section of the documentation. In fact, we try to provide you with information on some of these bugs in our review.

The next step is to refer to the netnews groups that we've been talking about. If you don't see your problem listed in the group, you can post your problem to the community of users. Chances are someone will confirm your finding and even provide you with a solution.

The last step is to send a bug report to an email address that is usually provided in the utility's documentation. We've also attempted to included these addresses in our reviews. Just send a description of your problem, including the steps that led up to it, as well as any input that you've given the utility to the email address.

Remember, this is all volunteer support. Don't expect anyone to drop what they're doing to fix the bug. Normally, serious bugs are addressed immediately and are incorporated into a new release of the utility. The announcements of these releases and their locations are usually broadcasted in the appropriate netnews groups.

Inside Our Software Reviews

Now that you have a good understanding about the Internet and how to capture some of the best free software that you'll ever find, let's take a look at what we have to offer you in this book. From the onset, we don't expect that this book will replace a good novel. Then again, a good novel won't help you work smarter using and developing software. Our book will help you do just that!

Somewhere out on the Internet, someone has developed a utility that you could add to your collection of UNIX tools and possibly include in the application that you're currently building. All you have to do is find this magic utility. All right, this is easier said than done. There are thousands of Internet host systems all over the world and you don't have time to electronically visit all of them.

With this book you don't have to! We've done this for you. We've spent months poking around the Internet to locate those special gems, and we decided to tell you about them in the form of a review. These reviews are a little more in-depth than the software reviews that you'll find in magazines.

Each review in this book is divided into about five segments. The first is a general introduction in which we give you a little bit of the history of the utility, along with a brief description of what it will do for you. In this section, we answer the question, "Why should I use this utility?" If the answer provided sounds interesting, you can read the next segment of the review.

We tried to place ourselves in the position of a potential user of the utility. The next question that we would expect you to ask is, "What do I have to do to install the utility?" All of us have heard raving reviews of software packages that later seemed burdensome and impractical to install.

Well, you can't be guaranteed a perfect installation the first time that you try to install any of the software that we review. However, the installation segment of the review provides you with some useful information about the installation process. Admittedly, you won't find all the information that you'll need to successfully install the utility if you just read our installation section. This section isn't designed to replace the utility's documentation.

However, you will find the Internet location of the utility and a few installation tips that we've found. We also provided you with direction for help if you are not successful in installing the utility on your system.

The next segment of the review talks about restrictions that are placed on the utility. You'll notice that many of the utilities have limited restrictions, the most common of which is that you can't prevent anyone else from receiving the utility free of charge. We've tried to summarize the restrictions that we found in the utility's documentation; of course, you must read the documentation for all the fine print.

We mentioned that the software available on the Internet can have bugs. That's a dreadful thought, considering that you might be adding the package to your toolbox. We try to help you survey the damage before you copy the utility's source files from the Internet host. In our review, you'll see a section that tells you about some of the bugs we found that were reported in the utility's documentation and in other sources. Granted, this isn't an extensive list of known problems, but it is at least a glimpse of what you can expect if you should decide to build a copy of the utility for your system.

The final segment of the review consists of a brief run-through of the utility. The contents of this section will vary with each review. However, in all the reviews we try to give you a flavor of what it is like to use the utility.

After reading a review, you will become an informed consumer. You'll have information that cuts through much of the hype about each utility. And above all, you'll know if the utility is worth investing your time to download to your system.

CHAPTER 3

The Hacker's Guide

Hey! Do you want to find some hot software? It's free! All you need to do is snoop around the Internet...no one will mind. We'll even show you how, right here, in this chapter. No, we can't provide you with a map, but we can show the correct way to find all those neat software utilities that we'll be reviewing in the next section of this book.

All right, finding the software is just one step. You know there might be pitfalls in downloading the software and building the binaries of the utility on your system. Sure, in other books you've read discussions of software utilities that sound exciting but you could never get to work on your system. We won't leave you hanging like that!

We refer to this chapter as a hacker's guide. In reality, we're just sharing with you years of experience of successfully downloading and installing software from the Internet to our own system. We'll make one general assumption; that is, that you've never downloaded and built software from the Internet before.

So, we begin the chapter with a step-by-step guide on how to get the software from the Internet to your system. We'll use the elm utility to illustrate this process. However, you can use the same procedure for any software that we review in this book.

Sometimes the installation and building of the software may not work smoothly. This is a fact of life and you shouldn't be alarmed. We said that we won't leave you hanging. After the tutorial, you'll find tips and hints that will show you how to overcome the more common problems that you may run into with software on the Internet.

Teaching you how to locate, transfer, install, and build software, it's all here! There is no excuse for not adding some of this hot software to your UNIX toolbox.

A Walk Through Finding Software on the Internet

It's easy to talk about how to locate, install, and run the software that we recommend in this book. The real test is for you to go through these procedures successfully. So, we thought the best way to ensure your success is to actually take you step-by-step through this process.

In this example, we'll hunt down the elm utility on the Internet and follow the process through installation and successful running of the utility. Each step is illustrated. If you simply execute each of these steps on your own system, you should see results similar to those presented here.

Let's establish a few ground rules that will help you better understand this process. First, we've boldfaced the words that you must enter at the keyboard. You'll also notice the word "bash$" in each illustration. This is our prompt. It's all right if you have a prompt on your screen other than bash$. The rest of the text shown in each figure is the text that was displayed on our screen as a response to our commands. You'll probably have similar text on your screen.

We should point out that at the end of some of the text, you'll see five periods (.....). This doesn't appear on the screen. We use the five periods to indicate that more text will be displayed than we show here. We simply don't have enough

Finding Software on the Internet
When Installation Doesn't Work

room to show you all the text that is displayed on your screen in response to a particular command.

Let's move on to locating, installing, and running the elm utility. Before beginning the process, create a directory on your system for elm. Type **mkdir elm**, then make elm the current directory by typing **cd elm**.

Where do you find elm? Good question. We'll use the archie utility to answer this question. Archie searches for all the remote hosts on the Internet that have elm (or for any software being sought). However, before we can use archie, we must find a remote host that offers the archie service. As illustrated in Figure 3-1, we use *archie.internic.net*. You can also use this host for your search.

You'll have to use the telnet service to open a connection to the archie host. Figure 3-1 shows you how this is done. Type **telnet**, followed by the name of the remote host that contains archie. The name of the remote host is one of two ways of expressing the Internet address of the system. The other way is by specifying the system's *octets*, a series of four numbers separated by dots. It may happen that the "text" version of the system name may not be known to your local computer. Use the octet version, which should always work. The telnet service also displays the real address on your screen (198.49.45.10).

Once the connection is made, a login message is usually sent to your screen from the remote host. (We provided a part of the message that we received.) The login message tells you a little about who owns the remote host and some of the ground rules for logging onto the remote host.

```
bash$ telnet archie.internic.net
Trying 198.49.45.10 ...
Connected to ds.internic.net.
Escape character is '^]'.
          InterNIC Directory and Database Services

Welcome to InterNIC Directory and Database Services provided by AT&T.
These services are partially supported through a cooperative agreement
with the National Science Foundation.

First time users may login as guest with no password to receive help.

Your comments and suggestions for improvement are welcome, and can be
mailed to admin@ds.internic.net.
.....
```

FIGURE 3-1.   *Locating the elm utility on the Internet*

The login for any archie host is "archie." As shown in Figure 3-2, type **archie** at the login prompt and press ENTER. Some archie hosts might prompt you to enter a password. In most systems, as is the case with the host that we connected to, no password is necessary. On those systems that ask you for a password, just enter your email address or follow the directions that are displayed in the login message.

Once you login as archie, the welcome message is displayed, which tells you about the local host and provides you with other general information. You're now connected to the remote host. What to do here? The remote host displays information that will help you interact with archie. In this example, you're told about the default terminal type, erase key, and the value of the search string type. Accept all the default settings.

Finally, you're ready to ask archie to do work for you. You'll notice that the screen will display the archie> prompt. In response to this prompt, type **prog**, followed by the name of the program that you need to find. In Figure 3-3, we typed **prog elm**.

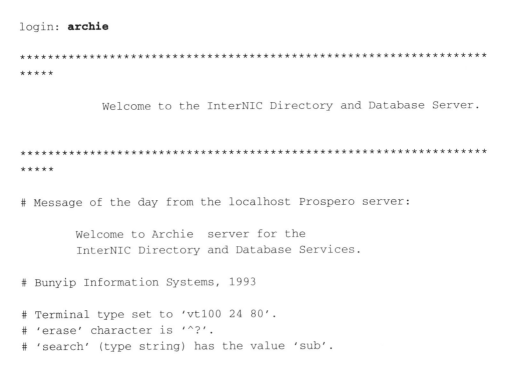

```
login: archie

* * * * * * * * * * * * * * * * * * * * * * * * * * * * * * * * * * * * * * * * * * * * * * * * * * * * * * * * * * * * * * * * * * * *
* * * * *

          Welcome to the InterNIC Directory and Database Server.


* * * * * * * * * * * * * * * * * * * * * * * * * * * * * * * * * * * * * * * * * * * * * * * * * * * * * * * * * * * * * * * * * * * *
* * * * *

# Message of the day from the localhost Prospero server:

      Welcome to Archie  server for the
      InterNIC Directory and Database Services.

# Bunyip Information Systems, 1993

# Terminal type set to 'vt100 24 80'.
# 'erase' character is '^?'.
# 'search' (type string) has the value 'sub'.
```

FIGURE 3-2. *Logging onto the remote host*

```
archie> prog elm
# Search type: sub.
# Your queue position: 1
# Estimated time for completion: 00:07
working...

Host ftp.cecm.sfu.ca    (134.87.46.67)
Last updated 10:02 27 Jan 1994

    Location: /pub/RMR/Accessories
       DIRECTORY      drwxr-xr-x      512 bytes  23:08  6 Aug 1993   Helmets


Hostsun.unicamp.br     (143.106.1.5)
Last updated 08:59 24 Feb 1994

    Location: /pub1/gopher-data/Frequently Asked Questions
       DIRECTORY      drwxr-xr-x      512 bytes  17:50 15 Dec 1993   elm
.....
Host gatekeeper.dec.com    (16.1.0.2)
Last updated 07:44 23 Feb 1994

    Location: /.0/BSD/386bsd/386bsd-0.1/unofficial/from-ref/public/elm
       FILE    -r—r—r—  785405 bytes  00:00 29 Nov 1992  elm2.4.tar.Z
```

FIGURE 3-3.   *Entering the search criteria for elm*

When you press ENTER, archie takes over. First, it places your request in a
queue. Sorry, but you're not the only one in need of help locating software on the
Internet. (Fortunately, in our case, we were the first in line.) Archie displays your
position number on the screen. If you find yourself waiting forever, you may want
to find another archie host.

On with our search! The next task for archie is to determine the length of time
that it will take to find all the locations of the software. (In this case, it only took 7
seconds for archie to report back with locations.) Archie will display an estimated
time on the screen, then indicate that it began the search.

Archie returns with a list of every location it could find that contains the
software we are looking for. In our example, there are many more locations than
we could fit into this book, so we've included only a few for illustrative purposes.

Archie displays pertinent information about each location. The first piece of data is the name of the remote host that contains the software we need. In this case, the first location archie found was on *ftp.cecm.sfu.ca* (the name of the remote host). You'll also see displayed the octet address for the host (*134.87.46.67*).

Next is a very key piece of information—the last update stamp. Although the rule of thumb is to download software from the nearest location, you also must be sure that the nearest location contains the latest version of the software. This is where the last update stamp will help you. You'll see the date and time of the last update of the software.

Another important piece of information is the location. Throughout this book, when we talk about locations we are referring to the name of the remote host, as well as the directory on the remote host that contains the software. By contrast, Archie refers to the directory as the location.

And the last piece of data displayed on the screen is the listing of a directory that contains the software. You'll see directory permissions and other typical UNIX file information. Notice that the time stamp of the directory might be different than the last update stamp. Don't confuse these dates. Rely on the last update stamp to decide which remote host you'll use to download the software.

Now we've found the elm utility. Next, we must leave archie and connect to the remote host location. As is shown in Figure 3-4, CTRL-D will log out of archie and close your telnet connection.

NOTE
Remember to make a note of the closest location before erasing your screen.

We'll use another UNIX service to copy the software to our system—the ftp service. At the prompt, type **ftp**, followed by the name of the remote host that contains the software. In this case, we're connecting to *gatekeeper.dec.com*. This is an unsupported service of DEC Corporate Research.

Once you're connected, you'll see a welcome message along with login instructions. We've included part of this message here. At the end of the message, you are asked to login. As an Internet standard, anonymous is used as the login ID. Just type **anonymous** and press ENTER. You'll be prompted for a password. Enter your email address or simply press ENTER. (Passwords are usually not required.)

If all goes well and you correctly spell anonymous, you'll be presented with an ftp> prompt on the screen. The ftp service uses some of the same commands as UNIX. So, the first command that you'll need to issue is **cd**, followed by the name of the directory that contains the software. In our example, the directory is

/.0/BSD/386bsd/386bsd-0.1/unofficial/from-ref/public/elm

```
archie> ^D
# Bye.
Connection closed by foreign host.

bash$ ftp gatekeeper.dec.com
Connected to gatekeeper.dec.com.
220- *** /etc/motd.ftp ***
     Original by:  Paul Vixie, 1992
     Last Revised: Paul Vixie, May 1993 ['locate']

     Gatekeeper.DEC.COM is an unsupported service of DEC Corporate
Research.
     Use entirely at your own risk - no warranty is expressed or implied.
     Complaints and questions should be sent to <gw-archives@pa.dec.com>.
.....

220 gatekeeper.dec.com FTP server (Version 5.84 Sun Apr 25 20:24:18 PDT
1993) ready.

Name (gatekeeper.dec.com:remon): anonymous
331 Guest login ok, send indent as password.

Password:
230 Guest login ok, access restrictions apply.


ftp> cd /.0/BSD/386bsd/386bsd-0.1/unofficial/from-ref/public/elm
250 CWD command successful.

ftp> bin
200 Type set to I.

ftp> get elm2.4.tar.Z
200 PORT command successful.
150 Opening BINARY mode data connection for elm2.4.tar.Z (785405 bytes).
226 Transfer complete.
local: elm2.4.tar.Z remote: elm2.4.tar.Z
785405 bytes received in 6.6e+02 seconds (1.2 Kbytes/s)

ftp> ^D
```

FIGURE 3-4.   *Ending the archie session and downloading the elm utility*

We found this name from archie.

Now we're in the correct place on the remote host. Our next step is to prepare the ftp service to transport our files to our system. Usually, all software files are in a compressed format, meaning they must be copied to your system without being modified during the transfer process. The ftp service uses a binary file mode to accomplish this task. However, this isn't the default setting; you must type **bin** before beginning the transfer process.

Let's get the transfer underway. The ftp **get** command will do the actual copying. Just type **get**, followed by the name of the program. All the software that you'll need for the utility is contained in a single file called a *tar* file. In our example, we typed **get elm2.4.tar.Z** to begin the transfer process.

The ftp displays information about the file as the file is being copied to your system. The file itself is placed in the current directory, which in this case is called elm. This is why it is important to position your system in the proper directory before beginning this process. When the transfer is completed, press CTRL-D to log out and close down the ftp connect with the remote host.

Hold on! You're not through yet. Let's make sure that the file arrived and that we can unpack it into all the smaller files that you'll need for the utility. In Figure 3-5, we use the UNIX command **ls** to list the directory. There should be only one entry in the directory if you're following along with our example.

Next, we must unpack the file. This is done by the zcat utility. Zcat reads in the compressed file that you specify on the command line and sends the uncompressed file to standard out. In this example, we actually use a UNIX pipe to send the uncompressed file to the tar utility. Tar is archival software that is used to, among other things, extract data from a tar file.

The tar utility command line is a little tricky, so we'll take a few moments to explain how we use it in this example. tar is passed four switches. The x switch tells tar to extract from a tar file. Next is the v switch, which instructs tar to display everything that it's doing. The f switch and the hyphen work hand in hand. The f switch specifies the name of the tar file, and the hyphen tells tar to read from standard in. When these switches are combined, tar is told that the name of the file is the string that comes from standard in, which in this case, is the output of zcat.

If this sounds too confusing, don't worry. Just enter the commands as they appear in Figure 3-5. When you press ENTER, zcat and tar will unpack the files and transform them into standard files. These are files that you can use to build your own version of the utility. You'll notice that as each file is unpacked, the name of the file is displayed on the screen. We just provide a sample of the list of file names here. The actual list is quite long.

We've come a long way. We located the software on the Internet, copied the software to our system, and unpacked the files. The only thing left to do is build the software. The place to begin is with the *README* file that is supplied with software.

```
bash$ ls
elm2.4.tar.Z
bash$ zcat elm2.4.tar.Z | tar -xvf -
x Changes, 3256 bytes, 7 tape blocks
x Configure, 111040 bytes, 217 tape blocks
x Instruct, 4359 bytes, 9 tape blocks
.....
```

FIGURE 3-5. *Checking that elm arrived*

In our example, shown in Figure 3-6, we used cat to display the contents of the *README* file for elm.

```
bash$ cat README
This is the 2.4 (USENET) version of the Elm Mail System

See the NOTICE and Instruct files for further details.

It is IMPERATIVE that all users rerun newalias after installing
elm 2.4 when upgrading from a previous version.  Elm's behavior
with aliases could be unpredictable if this step is not performed.

Where to find more info on Elm
   Much discussion on Elm including interim bug fixes, work arounds
and future plans occurs in the Usenet news group comp.mail.elm.  Also
a monthly status report on elm is posted there.  This status report
lists the archive sites that have the patches to Elm as well as
the latest version.

Patches to Elm are posted to comp.mail.elm and comp.sources.bugs as
soon as they are released.  They are posted to comp.sources.unix shortly
thereafter, to allow time for feedback of problems in the patches.
Patches should be available from the archive sites, or from the
archive server.  Mail archive-server@DSI.COM for details on how to
use the archive server program.  Ask it for help.
.....
```

FIGURE 3-6. *Finding the README file for elm*

NOTE
We suggest that you use your favorite editor instead of the cat utility since the *README* file can be very lengthy.

Although we have given you a sample of the elm utility's *README* file, you'll find important information about where to find installation instructions and other key procedures in the full file. It is critical that you read this file carefully; otherwise, you may find yourself skipping a step or two, which may cause the software to crash.

From the *README* file we learned that the elm utility comes with another file that contains all the steps you need to build the utility on your system. This is the *Instruction* file. We use cat again to display this file, as shown in Figure 3-7.

The process of creating your own version of elm or any utility that we review in this book, consists of installing and building. What's the difference? *Installing* is the process that creates all the necessary subdirectories from the elm directory, then places each file into its proper subdirectory for general use. On the other hand, the *building* process actually creates the utility's binary files.

The installation process can be time-consuming; however, elm as with most software on the Internet, comes with a Configure script that will do all the work for you. In Figure 3-8, we type **sh configure** to execute this script. The sh initiates the Bourne shell in batch mode, then executes all commands from a file called *Configure*. How do we know this? Because elm's *README* file told us.

We've only included a brief segment of the output of the Configure script. The actual output is too long to be printed here. However, you'll notice that several times during the execution of the Configure script, you'll be prompted to respond to questions posed by the script. For all the questions, we pressed ENTER and accepted the default settings.

We're almost at the finish line! All we must do now is build the binary files. Sound difficult? It isn't! The Configure script usually creates a makefile for you. The makefile contains all the information necessary for make to create the binary files. As is illustrated in Figure 3-9, just type **make** at the prompt and make will do the rest automatically.

You'll notice that make will display each file name as the file is compiled. This is a lengthy list, so we just provided you with a digest version here. Building the binaries will take a while, but when the process is completed, you'll be able to run the elm utility.

Well, there is one trick we should tell you about. You must find the executable *elm* file on your system. However, you don't need to pop in and out of directories; just let UNIX find it for you. We used the find utility to pinpoint the elm executable file. find requires several command-line arguments. The first is the starting

```
bash$ cat Instruct
                              Instructions
                              ------------


                        Last Update: $Date: 1992/11/15 01:07:19 $



        This file contains instructions on how to create and install
the entire ELM mail system.  It should be read BEFORE any attempts
are made at actually creating and/or installing any of the software
contained herein!

        There is actually really one step needed - unpack all the shar
files and then;
        $ cd <where-ever you're keeping the Elm sources>

        $ sh Configure

        Answer the questions of that program, then let it create the
localized Makefiles and system definition files for you.  When it's
done you can double check the configuration (or customize it further)
by reading the Configuration Guide and then rerunning Configure.
There are lots of neat features that are unique to this mailer - it's
worth a quick perusal at least!

        Once you're happy with the localized files, you then need to
create the documentation (so there's a bit of a catch-22 that you need
to format the Configuration guide before you are happy with the
localization but can't do that until you're happy with the
localization...oh well).
......
```

FIGURE 3-7. *Reading the instruction file*

directory. In this example, we used a period to represent the current directory. You do the same as long as the current directory is elm.

The next argument is actually a switch that works in conjunction with the third argument. The -*name* switch tells the find utility to locate the file that is named in the third argument which, in this case, is *elm*. The last argument, -*print*, is a switch that tells find to display the location of the *elm* file.

```
bash$ sh Configure

Beginning of configuration questions for elm2 kit.

First let's make sure your kit is complete.  Checking...
Looks good...
Making bin directory

Checking your sh to see if it knows about # comments...
Your sh handles # comments correctly.

Okay, let's see if #! works on this system...
It does.

Checking out how to guarantee sh startup...
Let's see if '#!/bin/sh' works...
Yup, it does.
Checking echo to see how to suppress newlines...
...using -n.
Type carriage return to continue.  Your cursor should be here—>

This installation shell script will examine your system and ask you
questions
to determine how the elm2 package should be installed.  If you get stuck
on a question, you may use a ! shell escape to start a subshell or execute
a command.  Many of the questions will have default answers in square
brackets--typing carriage return will give you the default.

On some of the questions which ask for file or directory names you are
allowed to use the ~name construct to specify the login directory belonging
to "name", even if you don't have a shell which knows about that. Questions
where this is allowed will be marked "(~name ok)".

 [Type carriage return to continue]
.....
```

FIGURE 3-8. *Installing elm*

So, after find has finished its work, the full path to the *elm* file is displayed on the screen. Just use the UNIX **cd** command, move to the proper subdirectory (*bin*), then enter the name of the executable file (**elm**) to run elm.

```
bash$ make
cd lib; /bin/make - all
/bin/chmod u+w ../hdrs/defs.h
/bin/touch ../hdrs/defs.h
/bin/chmod u+w ../hdrs/headers.h
/bin/touch ../hdrs/headers.h
cc  -g -I../hdrs    -target sun4 -c  add_site.c
cc  -g -I../hdrs    -target sun4 -c  addrmchusr.c
cc  -g -I../hdrs    -target sun4 -c  mk_aliases.c
cc  -g -I../hdrs    -target sun4 -c  mk_lockname.c
cc  -g -I../hdrs    -target sun4 -c  can_access.c
cc  -g -I../hdrs    -target sun4 -c  can_open.c
cc  -g -I../hdrs    -target sun4 -c  chloc.c
cc  -g -I../hdrs    -target sun4 -c  errno.c


. . . . .


bash$ find . -name elm -print
./bin/elm
bash$ cd bin
bash$ elm
```

FIGURE 3-9.   *Building elm*

You've located, installed, built, and run your first utility that we talk about in this book. The same procedures outlined here can be used to add any software that you find on the Internet to your UNIX toolbox.

And When the Installation Doesn't Work

As the example demonstrates, bringing up one of the packages from start to finish can be quite simple. Why then the hacker's guide? Because some of the software that you'll find on the Internet may not conform to the distribution style that we illustrated in the elm utility example.

Most of the software reviewed in this book comes with a configuration script that determines which flavor of UNIX you are working with and adjusts the *.h* files accordingly. Does that mean that every program will compile flawlessly on all UNIX systems? Of course not. In addition, we have noticed that support for System

V is weaker than for SunOs and appears not to be well tested in all cases. Basically the four types of problems you may find are that

- Sources fail to compile because UNIX ".*h* " files cannot be found

- Sources fail to compile because of syntactic errors

- Binaries fail to link because UNIX system calls cannot be found

- The program links, but doesn't run properly.

In this section, we'll talk about how to deal with these problems. The current way to solve many of these problems is to use the UNIX find utility. Therefore, we should take some time to give you some hints on how to use find.

- The UNIX find utility is powerful and flexible. Its purpose is to locate files with particular characteristics such as name, file type, or file content. You start the search for the file at a specified location in the UNIX file system. In theory, conducting a search from the root (/) directory will find the specified file if it exists. In practice, searching from the root has two problems: it can take a long time, and it can cause a large performance hit (slows your system down). If you are the only user on the system and the number of files on your computer is small, this will not be an issue. Otherwise, follow these recommendations before attempting the search.

- Although it helps to be familiar with find (and we do encourage you to learn it), you can follow our examples. We purposely use the subset of find, which in our opinion is most portable.

- Pay particular attention if your system supports symbolic links. find may not be able to cross symbolically linked directories. This means that even if the file is theoretically findable by following the link, find will not pick it up. Under System V.4, find has been enhanced to recognize the *-follow* switch, which will allow it to cross symbolic links. If you are reasonably sure that the file you are looking for exists and you suspect that a symbolic link is preventing you from finding it, there is a wonderful utility for finding out if there are any symbolic links. Its name? find. The following shows how to get find to tell you if any directory underneath the */usr/include* directory contains symbolic links.

```
find /usr/include -type l -print
```

Strategic Solutions

Let's take a few typical problems that you might run into and examine how you might solve them. The first problem is that the source file fails to compile because the *foo.h* file can't be found. The what file? If you're not familiar with UNIX, the term "foo" might seem strange to you. *Foo* is used as an alias for any file. This is the same way as John Doe and Mary Doe are used to represent any male or female name. Just substitute "foo" with the actual name in our examples.

What's your first step when the file fails to compile? Panic? Not yet. The listing below contains the first recourse you can take, which we'll call Strategy A. Strategy A assumes that the *foo.h* file exists but is not in the directories that are being looked at by the compiler. The first place to look is in the */usr/include* directory and all of its subdirectories. The following shows you the proper find command line to use to search for the *foo.h* file.

```
find /usr/include -name foo.h -print
```

So, you still can't locate the *foo.h* file. Is it time to panic now? No! Now implement Strategy B. You'll have to poke around your system to find other directories that might contain this file. Although we don't know how your system is organized, here are a few places that you might look: */usr/5bin/include, /usr/local, /usr/X11* and */usr/Motif.*

Come up empty-handed? What next? There's always Strategy C. There is a possibility that under your version of the operating system, the information that would otherwise have been in the *foo.h* file is really in another *.h* file.

For example, on some versions of UNIX, the string functions are declared in the *string.h* file, but on other versions they are found in the *strings.h* file. If you assume that this is the case, you may provide find with a *regular expression*. We suggest that you read your favorite UNIX book if you're not familiar the concept of a regular expression. However, we've provided you a sample command line for find.

```
find /usr/include -name "string*.h" -print
```

In this example, find will look for both the *string.h* and the *strings.h* files. In fact, it will find string anything *.h* since the asterisk is used as a wildcard.

Still no luck? Implement Strategy D. We call this the "shake the tree to see what falls out" strategy. First, edit the source with the reference to *foo.h* and comment out the *#include "foo.h"* line. Now attempt to recompile.

One of three things will happen: a symbol required for properly compiling your source will be missing and you will get an error message; no error message is produced and everything now compiles and runs properly; or no error message is produced and everything now compiles correctly, but doesn't run properly at all.

Let's look at the first situation where a symbol that is required for compiling your source is missing and you get an error message. Up until this point in your search, you've been looking for the *foo.h* file. However, to successfully build your program, you didn't need the file but you needed one or more symbols that are contained in this file. By commenting out the *foo.h* file, the compiler identifies the symbols that you need.

Now it's back to our find utility. Assume that the symbol the compiler complained about is called "boop". We can combine the power of find with that of grep to locate the file that contains the symbol "boop". This is done using the following line:

```
find /usr/include -name "*.h" -exec grep boop {} \; -print
```

Let's examine this command carefully. Find is told to start at the */usr/include* directory and look at any file in that directory and subdirectories for files that end in *.h*. (Remember, the asterisk matches any string of characters.) For each file that find locates, it will execute grep. This is accomplished by using the *-exec* switch.

Now grep goes into action. It will display any line in the file that contains the word boop. The line is followed by the path name of the file that contains the line. This is illustrated in this listing.

```
bash$ find /usr/include -name "*.h" -exec grep tm_mday {} \; -print
int tm_mday;
/usr/include/time.h
```

First, we enter the proper command line for find and grep. In this case, we're looking for any *.h* file that contains the symbol tm_mday. Notice that grep responds with the line itself (int tm_mday;) and on the next line grep displays the full path name and the name of the file that contains this line (*/usr/include/time.h*).

Now you've found the file that contains the symbol. What next? You must edit the source file that contains the #include line that you commented out. The first step is to uncomment the #include line. Next you have two choices. You can change the #include directive to use the new file that you found to contain the symbol. This might be the faster solution, but the source code will no longer be portable. The alternative is to use the #ifdef directive to conditionally include the proper file. This technique will continue to make the software portable.

The other typical problem that you might encounter is when the software compiles without a hitch—but the utility doesn't run. There are probably many reasons for this occurrence. We don't have a solution for you, but don't panic. It's time for you to share your problems with other users of the software. It's time to seek help from the Internet.

In each review in this book we have attempted to let you know which netnews group specializes in the utility that you are trying to get running. Post a message to that group. The message must describe the problem and be specific. Be sure to include which version of the operating system you are running and which version of the utility you are trying to build. If no one on the Internet can help you with a solution, email the author of the program, asking for help. The address of the author is usually contained in the utility's documentation. We've also included the same address in most of our reviews.

Another problem that you might have is that the source files fail to compile because of a syntax error. The most common reason for a source file to get such an error is that in your version of UNIX, additional *.h* files must be included in the source.

For example, if the typedef *ushort* is not known, you will have to find the proper include file that contains this symbol. Figure 3-10 shows you how to use find to locate the proper *.h*. In this example, we use both find and grep to locate the *ushort* typedef in the *types.h* file.

A word of caution! Older UNIX systems may have C compilers that are unfamiliar with constructs common to today's compilers. For example, you may have to hack together a replacement for **enums** with #defines. For example, the **enum** declaration,

```
enum LockType {ReadOnly, Update}
```

can be replaced by the code shown here:

```
#define ReadOnly 0
#define Update   1
```

```
bash$ find /usr/include -name "*.h" -exec grep ushort {} \; -print
typedef unsigned short    ushort_t;
typedef unsigned short    ushort;
/usr/include/sys/types.h
```

FIGURE 3-10.   *Using find to locate the .h file that contains the correct typdef*

NOTE
Be sure to turn on your compiler's flags to enable the modern C
language features before making this type of change. One such
compiler is on the Hewlett Packard 9000 series, which may require
the *-Aa* switch to recognize the more current dialect of C.

Here's another problem you might encounter—the binary files failing to link
properly because UNIX system calls cannot be found. This is the case of the
nomadic system call, one of the more common configuration problems that occurs
when building software from the Internet. To find a system call such as re_comp,
our best recommendation is to run the script illustrated in Figure 3-11 in the
bourne/ksh/bash syntax. Figure 3-12 shows the same script using the C Shell
syntax. The output will be a list of references to the routine you are looking for,
followed by the name of the file in which they were found. There are two types of
references: one to let you know that the routine is *used* in this *.a* file, and another
to tell you the routine is *defined* here. Obviously, we are looking for the latter.

The output of these scripts will depend upon how the **nm** command on your
operating system displays its output. Consult your operating system manual for
more information. Remember that the name of the library *precedes* the **nm** output.

Here are some more tips that might help you. First, the */usr/lib* directory may
not be the only directory to search. This directory may have subdirectories
containing libraries. Replace the first line of the *bourne/ksh/bash* script with:

```
for i in 'find /usr/lib -name "*.a" -print'
```

In the csh, the first line of the script should be

```
foreach i ('find /usr/lib -name "*.a" -print')
```

Be sure that you use back quotes (forward quotes will not work correctly).
Other places to search are */usr/ccs/lib, /usr/X/lib,* and */usr/local/lib.*

```
for i in /usr/lib/*.a
do
    echo Checking $i
    nm $i | grep re_comp
done
```

FIGURE 3-11. *Finding nomadic system calls using the bourne/ksh/bash syntax*

```
foreach i (/usr/lib/*.a)
   echo Checking $i
   nm $i | grep re_comp
end
```

FIGURE 3-12.   *Finding nomadic system calls using the C Shell syntax*

If your system supports shared libraries, you may want to also search the *.so* files. These scripts will work fine if you specify **.so** instead of (or in addition to) **.a*.

Many free utilities use a function called **alloca**. It is similar to **malloc**, but instead of allocating memory off the heap, it allocates memory off the stack. The advantage is that the memory is automatically freed upon exiting the function invoking **alloca**. This function has become so popular that many versions of UNIX incorporate it and often place it in a library called *libPW.a* or *libucb.a*. If your operating system does not have it, you can obtain the GNU version of it from many of the GNU utilities, such as bash.

The final problem that you might have to address is if the program links but doesn't run properly. Basically you have two choices. Since you have the source code you could theoretically run the utility in your favorite debugger until you found and repaired the problem. The alternative is to ask for help on netnews. Post your problem to the netnews group that we recommend in the review of the utility.

CHAPTER 4

General Utility Software

In this chapter you'll find information about a wide variety of general utility software that is sure to become a valued addition to your UNIX toolbox. We begin with the highly acclaimed replacement for the standard more utility. This is called—what else—the less utility. The improvements are well worth sending the more utility to the retirement home. This is truly well rounded and versatile paging software that will make any user of the more utility smile again.

Next we move to another utility that is looking to retire a current UNIX standard. This is the bash utility, which improves upon many of the features found in the Korn Shell. Do you really need another UNIX shell? Our knee jerk response was no. That was until we took a look at bash, and we think you should also do the same.

Continuing down our path of the best general utilities that we could find, we stumbled across an interactive database that caught our eye. This is ingres. Now, we're not saying that ingres should be the replacement for Sybase, but for an average database application, we feel ingres is a good fit.

Next, we uncovered a truly worthwhile package that can really come in handy. It's called the screen utility, which manages your dumb terminal's screen so you can have multiple sessions going on at the same time. Each session has its own logical window, which acts like a DEC VT100 terminal. We'll admit that screen isn't for everyone, but it rates high on our list as a session manager.

Another general UNIX utility that we found to be worth your consideration is talk. This is one of those software packages that isn't very exciting but can do a fantastic job for you. Did you ever want to converse with another Internet user? (We mean a conversation using your keyboard.) You both can type at the same time and messages are received ungarbled.

We conclude the list of the best general utility software on the Internet with two small but handy utilities. We're talking about uuencode and xrolodex. They're both worlds apart from each other but are very handy to have in your UNIX toolbox. Uuencode has a special knack for converting binary files to ASCII files. Granted, this isn't something most of us do every day, but a utility like this can help you out in a pinch.

Xrolodex is, as the name implies, a handy little telephone directory that can keep names, addresses, and telephone numbers, along with comments about the person. One reason that this utility made the list is that there isn't a limit to the number or size of entries. Another factor that makes xrolodex stand out is that the database is free-form, allowing you to use the data with other utilities.

The less Utility: Paging Software
The bash Utility: A Replacement for the Korn Shell
The ingres Utility: An Interactive Database
The screen Utility: Multiple Screen Software
The talk Utility: Terminal Communication Software
The uuencode Utility: A Binary to ASCII File Converter
The xrolodex Utility: Telephone Directory Software

The less Utility: Paging Software

You'll find the less UNIX utility an indispensable improvement over the standard more utility. Mark Nudelman, in creating less, has combined the best features of more and the pg utilities. If you have ever been frustrated when more exited after scrolling to the end of the file, or if you paged too far and wished you could return to a previous page, then you're in for a treat when you use the less utility.

The less utility is a paginator that allows you to move both forward and backward in a file (such as when you read complex man pages). In addition, less enables you to mark particular selections of the file for quick reference. Best of all, you already know the commands used to control less. They are based on the same commands that are used for more and the vi editor.

The less utility starts up faster than most text editors. The reason is in its design—most text editors read the complete file into a buffer, then edit the buffer copy of the file—less reads only a portion of the file at a time.

Another interesting aspect of less is that it uses termcap or terminfo depending on your system. This allows less to run on a variety of terminals. There is even limited support for hardcopy terminals.

Restrictions

Nudelman imposes very few restrictions on the use of less. This means that you can freely use and modify it. All you need is to provide the necessary copyright notice and the restriction notice on the copy of less that you distribute. The info file that you'll find with less contains the restriction notice. You can also sell the less utility; however, before doing so you'll need Nudelman's written consent.

You can contact Nudelman by using Internet's electronic mail. Send your email to one of the following addresses:

sun!pyramid!ctnews!UNIX386!mark
decwrl!pyramid!ctnews!UNIX386!mark
hplabs!pyramid!ctnews!UNIX386!mark

Another advantage of using less is that you can make your own modifications to it by using lesskey that Nudelman also authored. See the discussion about lesskey later in this chapter.

A Fast Installation

You'll be able to find less in */pub/packages/utils* on *nigel.msen.com*. Once you locate it, create a new directory for your copy of less, then copy the utility's source code into the new directory. Unfortunately, the less utility is not ready to run.

You'll have to do a little work before you can run your copy. Enter the **sh** command to unpack the distribution files, then type **sh linstall** to begin the automatic installation process.

NOTE
Unpacking instructions might be different depending on the distribution of the less utility that you download. Be sure to follow the instructions that came with your copy of less.

The numerous hardware and operating system combinations makes binary distribution of less impractical.

The installation program will prompt you for information about your UNIX environment. Based upon your responses, the installation program will set the necessary internal switches that will make your copy of less compatible with your equipment and version of UNIX. The installation program will also create a makefile and a *defines.h* file. You may want to review both these files to be sure that various settings (such as the path) are correct for your environment. Keep in mind that any free software on Internet is not the same as purchasing off-the-shelf software. The level of support for the program exceeds anything you can get commercially at any price. Since tens of thousands of technicians use free Internet software and have access to the source code, bugs are fixed quickly.

After you review the makefile, use make to build the binary files for less. Type **make** at the command line. The make utility will generate the binary copy of less in the *less* directory that you created. You can install less in a public directory also by using make. Execute make using the install parameter (**make install**).

A Quick Start

With less successfully installed, enter the **less** command at the prompt, followed by the name of the target file (**less** *filename*). You can include several filenames on the command line, then use the less utility's file management commands to switch among files.

Although some of the important features of less are discussed in this chapter, more information is available by using the on-line help command, **H**. This command displays a summary of the less utility commands. You can also use the man utility with the corresponding man files that are provided with less. Table 4-1 also provides a quick reference of the commands.

CAUTION

Some commands may not operate properly depending on your particular installation of less. These are the **v**, the **!**, and the **!!** commands. The **v** command invokes an editor from within less. The editor must be specified in the EDITOR environment variable; otherwise, the vi editor is executed by default. The **!** command invokes a shell to run a shell command that you specify. If you don't supply a shell command, less will invoke the shell specified in the SHELL environment variable. By default the sh shell is invoked. The **!!** command repeats the last shell command.

You can exit less by issuing the **q**, **:q**, or **ZZ** commands.

Scrolling Is a Breeze

Two key features of the less utility are its ability to move forward and backward within the file, and to position the cursor at a particular line in the file. Moving within the file is controlled by a host of movement commands, most of which will be familiar to you if you know vi. All of these commands accept a number parameter, which enables you to specify the number of lines that will be skipped.

Pressing the ENTER key moves the cursor to the next line, which is expected. However, Nudelman has provided several commands to move forward one or more lines. These are **e**, CTRL-E, **j**, and CTRL-N. They are synonymous. Each may be preceded by an integer that tells less how many lines to scroll. This book uses the pound sign (#) in conjunction with commands to denote a numeric argument. You should use the command that most closely resembles the scrolling command of you favorite text editor.

Replace the pound sign (#) with the number of lines that you want to move forward in the file. If you don't specify the number of lines, less will default to a single line. You can also use the #**D** and the #CTRL-D commands to scroll forward. These are slightly different than the **e**, **E**, **j**, and **J** commands. The **d** and **D** commands use half a screen instead of a single line as the default value. In addition, the number of lines that you specify becomes the new default value for subsequent **d** and **D** commands.

There are many commands that allow you to scroll backward in the file. These are the #**y**, #CTRL-Y, #**k,** and the #CTRL-K commands. Each one moves the cursor backward a specified number of lines with a single line as the default value. The #**u** and the #CTRL-U are used for the same purpose; however, the default value is a half screen and the line number that you supply becomes the new default value for these commands. Finally, there are the #**b**, #CTRL-B, and the #ESC-V commands. These also move the cursor backward, and have a default value of one window.

You can move to a specific line in the file by using the #**g**, #**<**, and the #ESC-< commands. If you don't specify a number, less will move the cursor to the beginning of the file. Nudelman also makes use of the #**G** or #**>**, and the #ESC-> commands for the same purpose, except the default value is the end of the file if you leave off the line number.

CAUTION
The less utility could run slowly on a large file, or if the line number isn't specified and the standard input rather than a file is being read.

If you are unsure of the line number, you can display a percentage of the file by using the #**p** and the #**%** commands. In this case, the pound sign (#) represents the percentage of the file that you want displayed on the screen. The percentage must be between 0 and 100.

Mark Text for Reference
Another key advantage that Nudelman has built into less is the ability to mark positions in the text. This allows you to quickly move to sections of the file without having to remember specific line numbers.

You can use the **m** command followed by any lowercase letter to place a mark at the current position of the cursor. Return to that position from anywhere in the file by typing a single quote ('), followed by the letter used as the mark. The CTRL-X, CTRL-X (press CTRL-X twice) command can be used in place of the single quote.

CAUTION
All placement marks are lost when you examine another file.

Here is an example of how to mark text in a file:

```
Jones, Bob, 555-1234
Smith, Mary, 555-2345
Adams, Roger, 555-3456
```

Suppose these lines are at the top of your screen. Setting a mark by typing **m**, **a** allows you to return to this exact screen later. Here's how it's done. Enter a single quote ('), or use the CTRL-X, CTRL-X command, then type **a**. Press ENTER and less redisplays the screen as it was when you typed **m**, **a**.

Searching for Text

The less utility enables you to search forward or backward through a file for a pattern that you specify. You can also search for lines that do not contain the pattern. The pattern is any regular expression that is recognized by the ed utility.

A forward search of the file is conducted by executing the **#/pattern** command. (Substitute a line number for the #.) For example, typing **2/pattern** tells less to find the second line that contains the match to the pattern. If no line number is specified, then the default value of 1 is used for the search. The search begins at the second line of the file, although you can use the -a option to change this default setting. (See the discussion about options later in this chapter for more information about how to use the -a option.) The **#?pattern** command is very similar to the **#/pattern** command, except a backward search is conducted. The search starts at the line immediately before the top line of the display.

You can search for lines that don't match the pattern by using the **#/!pattern** and **#?!pattern** commands. The **#/!pattern** command conducts a forward search of the file while the **#?!pattern** searches backward through the file. After less has located a line that fulfills your search requirement, you can use the **n** command to continue the search through the file.

Working with Files

When you run less you can specify the name of one or more files on the command line. The first file on that list is displayed on the screen. Within less, you can use several file management commands to select files to examine. For example, the **E** [*filename*] command displays the file that you specify in the command. If you don't specify a file name, the current file will be displayed.

The **#N** and the **:#n** commands are also used to examine files on the list. (Substitute the pound sign [#] with number of the file on the list.) If you leave out a number, the less utility will examine the next file on the list. The **#P** and **:#p** commands function similarly to the **#N** and **:#n** commands, except you specify a previous file to be examined. Another way to call up a previous file is to use the pound sign (#) command. This command recalls to the screen the last file that you examined.

Less also provides a way to display information about the current file by using the = and the CTRL-G commands. When either of the commands is executed, less displays the name of the current file, the number of the line that contains the cursor, and the offset of the bottom line being displayed. If there is room on the screen, less also displays the length of the file and the percentage of the file that has been displayed.

KEY	DESCRIPTION
H	Displays help
q	Exits
#f, #SPACE	Moves forward # lines, default one screen
#b	Moves backward # lines, default one screen
#e, #j, #CR	Moves forward # lines, default 1 line
#y, #k	Moves backward # lines, default 1 line
#d	Moves forward # lines, default half screen or last # to d/u
#u	Moves backward # lines, default half screen or last # to d/u
r	Repaints screen
R	Repaints screen, discarding buffered input
/#pattern	Searches forward for # line containing the pattern
?#pattern	Searches backward for # line containing the pattern
n	Repeats previous search
#g	Goes to line #, default 1
#G	Like g, but default is last line in file
#p, #%	Positions to # percent into the file
m<letter>	Marks the current position with <letter>
'<letter>	Returns to a previously marked position
''	Returns to previous position
E [file]	Examines a new file
N	Examines the next file (from the command line)
P	Examines the previous file (from the command line)
=	Prints current file name
V	Prints version number of the less utility
-<flag>	Toggles a command-line flag
_<flag>	Displays the setting of a command-line flag
+cmd	Executes the less cmd each time a new file is examined
! command	Passes the command to the system to be executed (by $SHELL)
v	Edits the current file (with $EDITOR)

TABLE 4-1.   *Command Quick Reference*

The Options Play

You can change the way less functions by using the appropriate option. There are three ways to execute the option. These are:

■ entering at the command line

■ using an environment variable

■ changing the option while the less utility is running

When you execute less, you can specify a list of options by preceding the option with a hyphen (-). (For example, less -c *filename*.) The -c option causes less to scroll down the screen. (The default setting scrolls from the bottom to the top of the screen.)

You could also create a LESS environmental variable, then assign options to the variable. (For example, setenv LESS -c.) Each time less is executed, the contents of the LESS variable is read to set the options for the session. The LESS variable is parsed before the command line is read. This allows you to override the options assigned to the LESS variable by specifying new option settings on the command line.

For example, you can negate the effect of the -c option that is stored in the LESS variable by executing less with the -C option (less -C *filename*). The -C option causes less to clear the screen before executing the top-down scrolling of the display.

Most options can be changed while less is running by using the - command. The same general option format is followed. For example, the -c option has the same effect as assigning the option to the LESS variable or passing it on the command line.

Before you change any options, display the current setting for that option. You do this by executing the _ command, followed by the letter of the option that you want to examine. For example, _c will display a message describing the current setting of that option. You can reset the option to the default by issuing the + command, followed by the letter of the option that you want to reset.

The Search Options

Normally, less conducts the forward search just after the top line of the display. This is actually the second line on the screen. However, you can use the -a option to have the search begin just after the bottom line of the display. This means that the text currently on screen isn't searched.

By default, all searches by less are case sensitive. This can limit the scope of the search, especially if there is inconsistency in the way text is entered into the file. You can tell less to ignore the case during the search by using the -i option. This option also tells less to ignore text that is underlined or overstruck.

The Display Options

You can control how information is displayed on screen by using the less utility's display options. For example, you can change how less represents lines that are past the end of the file by using the -w option. (By default, the tilde (~) character is used to represent these lines.) The -w option causes blank lines to be used instead of the tilde character.

Another useful display option is the -s option. This option causes consecutive blank lines to be squeezed into a single blank line. You'll find this feature useful when viewing nroff output. Besides reducing the number of blank lines that are displayed on the screen, you might find it advantageous to suppress the line numbers on the screen. By default, less automatically counts the lines so it can use them with the = and **v** commands, which may cause it to run slowly if a very large input file is being used. The -n option allows you to suppress line numbers.

You can tailor the prompt used by less by using the -P option. The less utility actually has three prompts called the short, medium, and long prompt. The -P option changes the short prompt, while the -Pm option changes the medium prompt, and the -PM option changes the long prompt. Each of these options must be followed by a string that will be substituted as the prompt. A *string* consists of a sequence of letters and special escape sequences.

Rather than entering a prompt option at the command line, you should place it in your LESS environment variable. The prompt option must be either the last option in the LESS variable, or terminated by a dollar sign ($).

If you don't want to customize the less utility prompt but don't want to use the default colon (:) prompt, you can use the -m option to change the prompt. The -m option causes less to use the percent sign (%) and the file name as the prompt just like the more utility.

The File Options

You can control how less handles file management by using one of two file options: -l and -L. The -l option causes less to copy the input to the file as the file is being viewed. You must specify the name of the file as part of this option. (For example, -l *filename*.) If the file already exists, less will ask for confirmation before overwriting the file. The -L option has a similar function; however, an existing file is overwritten without asking for confirmation.

Create Your Own Commands

Nudelman has opened the door allowing you to substitute your own commands for the less utility actions. You can read the details of these procedures in the man pages, which are supplied with less. However, here are the procedures in a nut shell.

Place your set of command keys and the action that is associated with each key into a text file called *.less*. The *.less* file must be in your home directory. Each line in the *.less* file must take on a special form: string *white space* action *newline*. The string is the command key that invokes the action. You can use up to a sequence of 15 command keys in the string, and each command key can be a literal key or a prefix such as a caret to indicate a control key. White space is any sequence of one or more spaces and/or tabs. The action is the name of a less utility action as described in Table 4-2.

Once you have prepared the *.less* file, you can run the lesskey utility: lesskey [-o output] [input]. The output file is the file that is used by the less utility. If you don't specify an output file, the lesskey utility will use *$HOME/less*. The input file is the text file that contains your command keys and actions. Lesskey will use the *$HOME/.less* file by default if you don't specify an input file.

DEFAULT KEY	ACTION
k	back-line
y	back-line
^K	back-line
^Y	back-line
^P	back-line
b	back-screen
^B	back-screen
33v	back-screen
u	back-scroll
^U	back-scroll
?	back-search
E	examine
^X^V	examine
+	first-cmd
e	forw-line
j	forw-line
^E	forw-line
^J	forw-line
^M	forw-line
^N	forw-line

TABLE 4-2.   *The less Utility Actions*

DEFAULT KEY	ACTION
f	forw-screen
^F	forw-screen
40	forw-screen
^V	forw-screen
d	forw-scroll
^D	forw-scroll
/	forw-search
G	goto-end
>	goto-end
33>	goto-end
g	goto-line
<	goto-line
33<	goto-line
'	goto-mark
^X^X	goto-mark
H	help
N	next-file
%	percent
p	percent
P	prev-file
q	quit
ZZ	quit
^L	repaint
^R	repaint
r	repaint
R	flush-repaint
n	repeat-search
m	set-mark
!	shell
=	status
^G	status
-	toggle-option
_	display-option
V	version
v	visual

TABLE 4-2. *The less Utility Actions* (continued)

The bash Utility: A Replacement
for the Korn Shell

If you're looking for a UNIX shell that has the best of the Korn Shell, Bourne Shell, and the C Shell, step back and make way for bash. The bash utility is the GNU Project's Bourne Again Shell that uses Bourne Shell syntax to provide interactive command-line editing, job control (on architectures that support it), and the C Shell-like history feature. And this is just scratching the surface.

Brain Fox (*bfox@ai.mit.edu*) and Chet Ramey (*chet@ins.cwru.edu*), the authors of bash, realized that there was a need to blend the worlds of Korn Shell, Bourne Shell, and C Shell. So they set out to satisfy the needs of many UNIX programmers who prefer the semantics of the Bourne Shell over those of the C Shell but still wanted to use some of the features found in the C Shell.

You'll find that bash uses the standard C Shell editing commands such as **!!** to repeat the last command. But bash doesn't stop there. Bash also recognizes the emacs-style editing commands, which include incremental searching as well as Korn Shell-style vi editing. For example, the following contains the output of the history feature of bash.

```
50 make -f Make.sun CFLAGS=-g
51 gdb xyzzy
52 emacs foo.c
53 history
bash$
```

Suppose you want to run make again. Just press CTRL-R, then enter the string of characters that are in the command you want to run. CTRL-R is the reverse incremental search command. In this example, we want to search for make in the history list.

Let's leave out the 'm' in make to illustrate the power of bash. If we press CTRL-R, **a**, bash steps backward through the history list and finds emacs *foo.c*. This is the first occurrence of the letter 'a' in the history list. However, by next pressing **k**, bash immediately locates make *-f Make.sun CFLAGS=-g*. You actually watch the search as you type. This allows you to stop typing immediately when a match occurs.

Installing the bash Utility Is Easy

You'll find bash in */pub/Z* on *cs.oswego.edu*. Just create a directory for bash on your disk, then copy all the files into that directory. The bash utility comes with a makefile all ready to run. All you need to do is type **make** and the binary version of bash will be created for you.

If you have problems making and running bash, you can contact the Free Software Foundation directly through email. The first step is to review the bash utility's discussion list that is available on request at *bug-bash@ai.mit.edu.* This list contains information about new ports of the bash utility, new features, and modifications that users of bash would like to see implemented in future releases.

Another place to look for information about bugs is in the gnu.bash.bug news group. And finally, if you still can't find the solution to your problem in running bash, you can post your problem to the *gnu.bash.bug* newsgroup. Chances are very high, given the number of people using bash, that someone who has run into the same problem and solved it, is reading the group and will post a reply or email you directly. In many cases you will receive multiple responses. This is the power of the Internet. If all else fails, you can contact the developers who maintain bash at *bash-maintainers@ai.mit.edu.* Keep in mind that no one promises to fix all the bugs.

Ready To Run
Bash is easy to run. Just type **bash** and press the ENTER key. Once the utility has settled down, you'll see the bash$ prompt on the screen. Now bash waits for your commands. You can also modify how the utility operates by specifying command-line options.

There are several useful options that can be set when you run bash. Actually, you'll find two types of options when you read the man pages that are supplied with bash. These are the single character and multi-character shell options. For example, you can determine how bash reads commands by using the single character shell options.

Here's a time saver. Start bash by using the -c option; the bash utility then reads commands directly from a string. (For example, bash -c "ls -l"). This behaves the same as in the Bourne Shell. An alternate way to start up bash is by using the -s option, which causes the commands to be read from standard input.

The -s switch prevents interpretation of the positional parameters as a shell script with parameters. For example, from within the shell, you can later ask to see the positional parameters. Let's say that "bash a b c" means run script a and pass it arguments b and c. Launching the bash utility using bash -s a b c will cause bash to run interactively. Later in bash, you can type **echo $1 $2 $3**, which will return a b c.

You'll also find a few of the multi-character options handy.

CAUTION

Multi-character options must appear on the command line before the single character options. For example, by default bash reads the personal initialization file and the profile file when the utility starts to run. The personal initialization file (~/.bashrc) is read if the utility is in the interactive mode. Likewise, the profile file (~/.bash_profile) is read when bash is invoked as the login shell.

These files are initialization files that you can use to set environment variables such as your search path. For example, the lpr command (print a file) will print on the default printer unless you specify -P *printername*. However, if you have an environment variable called PRINTER, the **lpr** command will automatically print to the printer whose name is the value of the PRINTER environment variable. This saves you the need to remember and enter the name of the printer that is closest to your desk.

There are a whole host of other options that you'll fine useful to use such as -quiet, which hides the shell version and other information that is normally displayed at start up. You'll find a complete description of these options in the man pages.

Plenty of Shell Variables to Use

The bash utility is loaded with many useful shell variables that you an easily incorporate into your scripts and programs. Many of them may be familiar to you already since they are used in the Korn Shell, Bourne Shell, and C Shell. For example, you can probe the PPID shell variable to find the process ID of the shell's parent and UID or EUID variable to find out information about the current user.

The PWD variable is also familiar. You'll use this to determine the current working directory that is set by the **cd** command. You can also use the OLDPWD variable to retrieve the previous working directory.

However, bash also comes with additional shell variables that can provide valuable information at your fingertips. Consider the BASH variable, which returns the full path name used to invoke the current instance of the bash utility, and the BASH_VERSION, which displays the version number of bash. And you can always use the PATH variable to set the search path. All you'll need to do is separate directories with a colon when you specify the search path Bourne shell style.

The bash utility even has a few variables that you might find handy for those special programs. The RANDOM variable returns a randomly generated integer each time that you refer to the RANDOM variable. The SECONDS variable returns the number of seconds since bash was started. And we've only scratched the surface. You'll find more in the man pages.

Special Treatment for Email

You'll find that bash will keep you informed about your electronic mail through the use of four shell variables. These are MAIL, MAILCHECK, MAILPATH, and MAIL_WARNING. The MAIL variable contains the name of the file that receives electronic mail. Bash will check for mail every 60 seconds. You can change the period between checking the mail by assigning the time in seconds to the MAILCHECK variable.

The MAILPATH variable allows you to specify the path names that are to be checked for mail. And you can also write your own response message. The following shows how it works.

```
MAILPATH='/usr/spool/mail/mbox?"You have mail $_ has mail!"'
```

The MAILPATH variables is assigned the path to the mail file called *mbox*. The question mark (?) prints the quoted text when new mail is found in the file. The $_ stands for the name of the current mail file, which is *mbox*.

The MAIL_WARNING variable also displays a message on the screen. However, this message informs you that the mail file has been read.

Customizing the bash Prompt

You call the shots, if you wish, when it comes to the prompt that is used by bash. When bash is running in the interactive mode, there are two types of prompts, contained in the PS1 and PS2 shell variables, that can be displayed. The PS1 prompt is used when bash is ready to read a command. The PS2 prompt, called the secondary prompt, is used when more input is needed to complete a command.

Best of all, you can customize these prompts. Table 4-3 contains prompt commands that allow you to easily use known shell information as part of the prompt. An example of this is shown here:

```
PS1="Enter your command here -> ".
```

If you don't customize the prompt, the default prompts will be used. The PS1 default value is bash$ and the PS2 default value is the greater than sign (>).

COMMAND	DESCRIPTION
\t	The time
\d	The date
\s	The name of the shell
\w	The current working directory
\W	The basename of the current working directory
\u	The username of the current user
\h	The hostname
\#	The command number of this command
\!	The history number of this command

TABLE 4-3. *Commands Used to Customize the Prompt*

The Timesaving History List

You'll find the history feature of bash one of the most economical highlights of this program. It allows you to re-enter commands without having to type the command. This becomes extremely useful when complex expressions are entered on the command line. Want to see the history list? Just type **history** at the bash prompt and press the ENTER key. The bash utility will display the history list for you.

You'll notice that each line in the history list contains a number. You refer to this number whenever you want to have the bash utility re-enter the command on the command line. For example, type **!5** and press the ENTER key. The bash utility will automatically run the fifth command on the history list. Press ENTER and you've just executed the fifth command by pressing three keys. It's even easier if you want to re-execute the last command. All you need is to type **!!** at the bash prompt, then press ENTER. Bash does the rest. Read the man pages for more history commands.

You can include your own customized controls to this feature by using the three history shell variables. These are HISTSIZE, HISTFILE, and HISTFILEZE. You can specify the maximum number of commands that can be stored on the history list by using the HISTSIZE variable. For example, HISTSIZE=40 causes the history list to contain a maximum of 40 commands.

The history list is saved after you exit the session in the *.bash_history* file in your home directory, You may change this file name by specifying the file name as the value of the HISTFILE variable—for example, (HISTFILE=hislist).

CAUTION
The history file can grow in size. It's best to have bash automatically control the size of the file by specifying the maximum number of lines that the file should contain. This value is assigned to the HISTFILESIZE variable. For example, HISTFILESIZE=40 will truncate the history file at 40 lines.

Create Your Own Commands Using Aliases

You'll find the alias feature of bash a fast way to create your own commands. An alias can be assigned a command and arguments by using the bash utility's built-in alias command. Once an alias is set, the alias can be used in place of the assigned command. Bash automatically replaces the alias that you typed on the command line with the command that you assigned to the alias.

Let's see how that's done. We'll create the command **dir** using the **alias** command. The **ls** command will be assigned to the dir alias (bash$ alias dir=ls). When you press the ENTER key, bash automatically adds the dir alias to the list of current aliases. We can type **alias** at the command line, then press ENTER to see the list of all the current aliases—including dir. Typically, you put all your aliases in the *.bashrc* file so they are available to you as soon as the bash prompt is displayed.

The next time that we want to list the contents of the current directory, all we need to do is to type **dir** and press ENTER. Bash will substitute and execute the **ls** command for the dir alias. Don't worry if you make a mistake. Any alias can be cancelled by using the **unalias** command (**unalias dir**). There's a lot more you can do with the bash utility's alias feature, so examine the man pages.

Controling Jobs Is No Problem

Probably one of the more sophisticated features of bash is its ability to control jobs. Job control refers to the ability to selectively stop the execution of a process, then resume execution at a later time. This assumes that the operating system supports job control.

Here's how it's done. The bash utility associates each job with a pipeline and maintains a table of each job that is currently executing. You can view this table by using the **job** command. The listing below shows a sample display that is generated by the **job** command. The "one" in square brackets [1] indicates the job number, and "25650" is the job's process ID.

```
[1]  25650
```

You can suspend the current job by pressing CTRL-Z. Bash will immediately stop the job and return you to the bash prompt. Rather than stopping the process right away, you can issue the CTRL-Y command, which causes the job to stop the next time it attempts to read input form the terminal. At that time, control is returned to bash. These are just some of the ways that you can utilize the job control feature. Read the man pages for more techniques on using job control.

You Control the Flow

In addition to a host of commands that you expect from a powerful utility such as bash, there is a series of control features that allow you to create sophisticated scripts. You'll find that bash has the for loop, the while loop, and the until loop. These loops function just like their Bourne Shell counterparts. The **break** command is also available as an exit from within any of the loops, and you can use the **continue** command to resume the next iteration of the loop.

The bash utility also has conditional controls that redirect the execution of the script. These are **case..esac** and the **if..fi**, and they function in the same way as their counterparts in other shells. Another very useful addition to bash is the ability to define functions. The **function** command enables you to execute a list of commands whenever the script calls the function.

Commands, Commands, and More Commands

You'll find that bash responds to most of the Bourne Shell and C Shell commands that you are familiar with. Table 4-4 contains a brief listing of commands. Most of these are simple commands that may take an optional argument. You can read the man pages for a more complete treatment of each command and its options.

COMMAND	DESCRIPTION
alias	Alias with no arguments prints the list of aliases on standard output. When arguments are supplied, an alias is defined for each name whose value is given
bg	Executes a suspended program in the background
cd	Changes the current directory to a specified directory
declare	Declares variables and/or gives them attributes. If no names are given, it displays the values of variables instead

TABLE 4-4. *Useful Built-in Commands*

exit [n]	Causes the bash utility to exit with a status of n
fg	Executes a suspended program in the foreground and makes it the current job
help	Displays helpful information about built-in bash utility commands
history	Displays (with no options) the command history list with line numbers
jobs	Lists the active jobs
logout	Exits a login shell
pwd	Prints the pathname of the current working directory
read	Reads from the standard input. The first word is assigned to the first parameter, the second word to the second parameter, and so on
test expr	Tests a specified expression and returns a 0 (true) or 1 (false), depending on the evaluation of the conditional expression
unalias	Removes names from the list of defined aliases

TABLE 4-4.   *Useful Built-in Commands* (continued)

Restrictions on Using the bash Utility

The bash utility is free software, which means you can copy and modify the utility. The only restriction is that you can't place any restrictions on the use of bash, even if you distribute your modified version of the program. The Free Software Foundation holds the copyright for the bash utility. Typically copyrights are used to limit your use of the software; however, the Free Software Foundation's objective is to assure that no one limits anyone's use of the software. Therefore, you'll have to include the Free Software Foundation's copyright and restriction notices with your modified or copied version of bash. You can read more about the restrictions in the documentation that is supplied with the software.

The ingres Utility: An Interactive Database

Searching for information using UNIX really isn't anything new. Your system already has some fine utilities that handle this chore very well. However, finding information is one thing. Managing data is another and that's where ingres comes into the picture.

The ingres utility is not another version of awk or grep. It is a relational database system that allows you to organize data properly by storing information in tables. You can then join these tables as needed by drawing a relationship between fields in both tables.

Now, there's nothing magic about ingres—except that it's free! If you have the technical skills and the time, you can write a version of ingres yourself. In fact, ingres is written in the C programming language and the source code is provided for you. You can poke around the code to see how it's assembled or simply install ingres on your system and create your own information management system.

Not just a stand-alone database system, ingres can be conveniently shared with other users, and is ready and willing to become the heart of a multi-user system that provides multi-access to the same database concurrently. You'll find that ingres has built-in data integrity features that guarantee that the concurrent access of data won't corrupt the database.

Is ingres industrial strength? Good question to ask and the answer is yes. It has been used as the database of choice for accounting systems, managing student records, managing a telephone company's wiring diagrams, and for a host of other typical applications.

Now, there are some improvements underway. One is a higher-level user language that allows recursion and user-defined functions and features designed to make a database administrator's life a lot easier. Don't be too concerned about these shortcomings. They will be removed in future releases.

Installation

Installing ingres on your systems can be a little tricky. The ingres documentation covers these steps in detail. We'll just provide you with a few hints to get you on your way. Before you copy any ingres files to your system, create a user name called ingres, then login to your system as **ingres**. (The utility won't work if you fail to do this.) Next, create a parent directory called *ingres*.

You'll find ingres in the */pub/database* directory on *qiclab.scn.rain.com.* Now you're ready to copy the files. Be sure you're in the ingres home directory before beginning this process. Table 4-5 contains a listing of the minimal subdirectories that are required to run ingres. The ingres documentation contains a further listing of these.

The documentation for ingres provides more detail about these installation procedures. However, an important point to keep in mind is that you must set the proper permission for the directories and programs that are used by ingres. Table 4-6 contains a sampling of the proper **chmod** commands to use to set the permissions for the ingres directories. Table 4-7 shows the permissions for several key files.

If you have any problems installing ingres, log onto the Internet and read *comp.databases* for help. According to Joe Kalash, who tackles some of the bug

DIRECTORY	CONTENTS
/bin	Binary programs
/files	Files used by various parts of ingres
/data/base/	User-created databases
/demo	Used by the "demodb" command
/doc	Documentation
/lib	Object libraries
/source	Source code

TABLE 4-5. *Subdirectories for the ingres Parent Directory*

reports, over two-thirds of the bugs could have been fixed if the user had referred to the ingres documentation. So, read the documentation carefully before alerting everyone that a bug exists in ingres.

NOTE
The ingres utility originated at the University of California and is made available free to educational institutions as described above. However, there is a commercial Ingres database product published by the ASK Group in Alameda, California. This product is greatly enhanced and you may choose to use it. For reasons associated with the dual nature of this product, the Ingres database can not be found on the CD accompanying this book.

DIRECTORY	SETTING	DIRECTORY	SETTING
/bin	755	/files	7555
/data	700	/lib	755
/data/base	777	/source	755
/demo	755	/any database	777
/doc	755		

TABLE 4-6. *A Sampling of chmod Commands for Setting Permissions for ingres Directories*

FILE	SETTING	FILE	SETTING
copydb	-rwx--x--x	ingres	-rws--x--x
creatdb	-rws--x--x	printr	-rws--x--x
demodb	-rwxr-xr-x	purge	-rws--x--x
destroydb	-rws--x--x	monitor	-rwxr-x--x
equel	-rwx--x--x	vaxingres	-rwsr-----
helpr	-rws--x--x		

TABLE 4-7. *Permission Settings for Key Files*

Known Problems

The ingres utility received a bad rep when earlier versions of the database executed slower than many users expected. Don't worry! All is well—in the current version the problem has been fixed. Another concern is with Quel, which is the SQL-like language that is used to query an ingres database. Quel, however, doesn't support recursion. This means that you'd have to write recursion routines in the C programming language using the precompiler. Sorry, no fix yet, but it's planned for a future upgrade.

The wish list doesn't end with recursion. Here are a few more potholes that should be filled. The Quel language needs to be expanded to include user-defined functions, multiple target lists for a single qualification statement, and an if-then-else flow control structure. In addition, there is a need for a better report generator. Currently, only the PRINT command is available for reports.

And the last item that might give you some concern is the COPY command. This routine hasn't been very dependable. It'll work fine for most situations, but not all bulk copying is performed successfully. You can read more about these and other known problems in the ingres documentation.

Up and Running

It isn't difficult at all to launch ingres. Before you begin, make sure that your login is in the ingres users file. This is the file that contains information such as status and permissions for each person who has permission to use ingres. The documentation contains all that you need to know to enter yourself in this file.

There are two ways of starting ingres: by providing the name of the database on the command line, or by executing a program that is written using the Equel precompiler.

If you just want to have ingres use a specific database, type **ingres** *<database>* on the command line, where *<database>* is the name of the database that you want to use for the session. Now ingres enters the terminal monitor mode where it accepts commands from the keyboard. Table 4-8 contains a sampling of these commands. You'll find a complete listing of terminal monitor mode commands in the ingres documentation.

As you enter commands at the prompt, ingres reads them and carries out your instructions. If ingres runs into any problems, an appropriate error message is displayed on the screen. This is an ideal way to make fast, one-time queries about information in the database, but for more permanent queries, you should consider creating a Quel program.

A Quel program is a series of database query language commands (an alternative to SQL) that are entered into a file, which is then read by ingres. This is basically the same process you use to create a shell script, except Quel commands replace UNIX shell commands in the script. Another technique that you can use is to use Equel instead of Quel.

Equel is the embedded version of the Quel language. This means that you enter Equel statements inside your otherwise ordinary C program. Next, you must run this program through a preprocessor that translates the Equel statements into pure C code, which is then ready for your C language compiler.

You'll notice that Quel has its roots in the data languages ALPHA, SQUARE, and SEQUEL. If you are familiar with any one of these languages, you shouldn't have any difficulty assimilating Quel.

The following example gives you a glimpse into the Quel language.

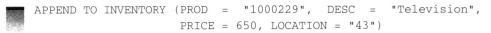

```
APPEND TO INVENTORY (PROD   =   "1000229",   DESC   =   "Television",
                     PRICE = 650, LOCATION = "43")
```

COMMAND	DESCRIPTION
#	Erases the previous character
@	Erases the current line
\r	Erases the entire interaction and resets the workspace
\p	Prints the current workspace
\e	Enters the UNIX text editor and begins accepting editor commands
\g	Processes the current query (go)
\q	Exits from ingres

TABLE 4-8. *A Sampling of ingres Terminal Monitor Mode Commands*

Here, a new product is being entered into the inventory database. In this case, we're adding information about a television set. As you can see, the Quel language isn't complicated at all; in fact, you can even ask ingres to perform simple math for you. As illustrated in the example below, ingres is told to increase just the price of a specific television by 20%.

```
REPLACE   (PRICE BY 1.2 * PRICE)
    WHERE PROD = "1000229"
```

Anyone who has ever developed a complex database application knows that there are times when more than one database table must be used. Traditionally, query languages require you to preface the field of the database with the name of the database. For example, to refer to the PRICE field in our INVENTORY database, we might be required to use INVENTORY.PRICE.

Fortunately, the authors of ingres realized that this method of referring to a field could be time-consuming and cumbersome. Having to enter the name of the database each time you use a field is something no programmer looks forward to doing.

With ingres, you can abbreviate the name of the database by using the RANGE OF command. Let's say we want to use the INVENTORY database. The RANGE OF command allows us to refer to the database as the letter I. At the beginning of the query we would write the following command:

```
RANGE OF I IS INVENTORY.
```

All we need to do is place the I before the name of the field to refer to the field in the query. For example, I.PRICE has the same affect as INVENTORY.PRICE.

Is this all there is? Not quite! You've just seen the tip of the iceberg when it comes to Quel commands. Our intent is to whet your appetite for more, not to provide you with a tutorial. Table 4-9 contains a sampling of other Quel commands. Want more? Sure you do! Now it's time to load ingres onto your system and crack open the documentation. You'll find that the ingres documentation is filled with clear, concise examples of the Quel language. These are examples that you can copy into your own Quel program, then modify as needed—a great time saver!

The screen Utility: Multiple Screen Software

Who wouldn't like to have several sessions running at the same time with each session in its own window, even though all you may have is a "dumb" terminal? Now you can, thanks to the work of Oliver Laumann, Wayne Davison, Juergen

COMMAND	DESCRIPTION
RETRIEVE INTO	Determines where to place matched data
WHERE	Sets selection criteria
AND	Joins two selection criteria
DELETE	Deletes records that match selection criteria
REPLACE	Replaces a value in a field
COUNT	Counts the number of records
MAX	Returns the maximum value in a field
MIN	Returns the minimum value in a field
AVG	Returns the average value of a field
CREATEDB	Creates a specific database
DESTROYDB	Removes a specific database
COPY	Bulk copies records
PRINT	Prints records
MODIFY	Changes the storage structure access method
INDEX ON	Creates a secondary index on a database
HELP	Provides information about the database

TABLE 4-9. *A Sampling of Quel Commands*

Weigert, and Michael Schroeder. They are the authors of screen, which manages multiple sessions on your screen. Each session occupies the entire screen; despite that, these sessions are referred to as *windows*. And if you ever called in to work on a "dumb" terminal and miss having another X Window to work in, then screen will be a lifesaver!

Each logical window contains its own interactive shell and acts like a DEC VT100 terminal. Want more? You've got more! You'll find a scrollback history buffer for each window and a swift copy-and-paste feature that allows you to move the contents of any window to another window. You'll find this feature very handy for a quick copy and paste of code between programs.

The screen utility's roots began with Laumann's custom windows utility. Davison and his associates then enhanced Laumann's work to what we know of today as the screen utility. Actually, screen's real name is the iscreen utility to distinguish it from the original screen utility. However, you'll find that all of the documentation that is supplied with screen still refers to it as screen rather than iscreen. We'll do the same in this chapter.

Enough about history. Let's talk more about this powerful utility that has just become part of your UNIX toolbox of utilities. There is a hidden benefit of using the screen utility; it fixes bugs that are found in VT100 terminals. We'll let you read the documentation for more details about this. And for the emacs utility users, screen also allows you to enter the CTRL-S and CTRL-Q commands on all terminals. All you need to do is create the following alias: alias emacs "screen emacs". The screen utility then acts as a buffer between emacs and your real terminal.

Straightforward Installation
You'll probably have little trouble installing screen if you follow the installation documentation that is supplied with the utility. One of the places you can find screen is in */archive/gnu* on *tamu.edu*. First, create an empty directory on your system, then copy the screen utility's files to your machine. The authors of the utility supply two key files that will save you time during the installation. These are the configure shell script and the install files.

The configure shell script creates the necessary makefiles based upon variables that the script finds on your system. The script also creates the *config.status* file that contains the current configuration. You can use this file to recreate the current configuration, if necessary.

Once the configure shell script has finished running, type **make install** to create the binary files of the screen utility and install them. If either the shell script or the install files has problems running, there is a good chance that your system requires special settings in either file. The installation files that come with screen provide some helpful tips on how to modify the configure or install files.

If you still experience problems with the installation or just want to pass along your comments, send an email to *jnweiger@immd4.informatik.uni-erlangen.de* (Juergen Weigert) or to *bug-gnu-utils@prep.ai.mit.edu*.

Known Problems
There are some known difficulties with screen. For example, the utility will not run on a system that does not include pseudo-ttys, the select system call, and UNIX domain sockets.

Besides these limitations, you can't change the $TERMCAP environment variable when you are reattaching under a different type of terminal. This is due to the fact that support for termcap is very limited. You'll also notice that the screen utility does not recognize hardware tabs.

These are just a few of screen's existing shortcomings. Be sure to read the complete listing along with the latest bugs in the utility's documentation.

A Fast Start

Now that you've installed screen and are aware of a few known bugs, you're ready to enter that magic command that creates a logical multi-window display out of your single terminal. Stop waiting and begin typing. Type **screen** and press ENTER. The screen utility will create a single window on the terminal. The shell prompt is displayed, ready for your next command.

Although you can't see it, screen is still running quietly in the background. Enter the proper screen utility command and you can create a new window, kill an existing window, or switch among windows. There's more! You can copy and paste text, view the history of commands, and even display a list of the current windows.

The windows aren't just window dressing! You can have separate programs running in each window. The screen utility reads each command that you enter at the keyboard and passes it directly to the program in the current window. That is, except for screen's own commands.

All screen commands begin with the CTRL key. Could these commands interfere with the commands of your favorite program? Sure! If screen recognizes a command as its own, the command will not be passed along to the program. However, don't be too concerned. The authors of screen allow you to customize the screen's commands in the *.screenrc file*. The documentation shows you how to do this.

Table 4-10 contains a sampling of the commands that you'll use with screen. The utility's documentation contains a complete listing of commands, but if you don't like to read documentation, type CTRL-A, **?**. The utility will display a list of commands on your terminal.

TIP
If the screen utility isn't displaying text properly on the screen, check that you have the proper termcap setting. And while you're looking at the termcap setting, make sure that you deactivate the termcap's automatic margins feature. Screen will then be able to accurately update the display quickly.

In addition to specifying commands at the prompt, you can control screen by using command-line arguments. Table 4-11 contains a sampling of these arguments. A full discussion about how to use these arguments can be found in the screen utility's documentation.

Restrictions

The screen utility is covered by the Free Software Foundation's GNU General Public License. This means that the only restriction is that you can't restrict the use

COMMAND	DESCRIPTION
CTRL-a, X	Switches to the window where X is the number of the window
CTRL-a, CTRL-a	Switches to the window displayed previously
CTRL-a, c	Creates a new window with a shell and switches to that window
CTRL-a, C	Clears the screen
CTRL-a, h	Prints the contents of the current window to the hardcopy.n file
CTRL-a, k	Kills the current window and switches to the previously displayed window
CTRL-a, l	Redisplays the current window
CTRL-a, SPACEBAR	Switches to the next window
CTRL-a, p	Switches to the previous window
CTRL-a, W	Toggles the window width between 80 and 132 columns
CTRL-a, ?	Displays a help screen
CTRL-a, CTRL-\	Kills all windows and terminates screen

TABLE 4-10. *A Sampling of screen's Commands*

COMMAND	DESCRIPTION
-a	Includes all capabilities
-A	Adapts the sizes of all windows to the size of the display
-c file	Overrides the default configuration file
-f	Turns flow-control on, off, or to automatic switching mode
-h	Specifies the history scrollback buffer to be num lines high
-l	Turns login mode on or off
-R	Attempts to resume the first detached screen session it finds

TABLE 4-11. *A Sampling of Command-line Arguments*

of this utility, even if you modify the utility and incorporate it into your own application. Otherwise, you are free to use screen any way you wish.

However, before taking our word for this, we suggest that you read the complete text of the GNU General Public License that is contained in the screen utility's documentation.

The talk Utility: Terminal Communication Software

If you are running System V and long for the ability to converse with other people on your local-area network, you need the same program that BSD users have had for years. It is called talk, but has not been available under System V.

At least not until now. Edward Bennett found a way to allow two users to conveniently hold a discussion without talking on the telephone. Bennett developed a part of the BSD utility called talk that is nearly as effective as talking on the phone.

The talk utility is technically an inter-terminal screen-oriented communication. It allows both parties to converse by typing at the same time using their terminals without having garbage displayed on the screen. If you try this without a communications manager such as talk, you'll notice that the display of the outgoing message interferes with the incoming message and scrambles characters on your screen. But this doesn't happen if you use talk.

Installation

Create a directory on your system for talk, then copy the talk utility files from the Internet. You can use the archie utility to locate the closest host that contains a copy of talk. One place you can find talk is the */usenet* directory on *ftp.uu.net*, in the file *talk.sysv.verb.Z.*

You'll find that most of the work in building the talk utility binaries is done for you. The utility comes with a makefile. However, you'd better review the settings in this file to be sure that they correspond to your system's requirements. We suggest that you also review the definitions in the *talk.h* file for compatibility with your system.

When you are satisfied with these settings, type **make install** at the prompt. This will create and install three binary files: *talk, talkdemon,* and *stoptalk.* The *talk* binary is the interface that you'll use to chat with another system on the Internet. The *talkdemon* binary sits in the background and supervises the conversation. The *stoptalk* binary removes the talk message queue.

It is important that talk is able to exchange signals independently. Therefore, the utility must be able to run setuid. We also suggest that you restrict the 'other' permissions for the *talkdemon* and *stoptalk* binary files. This will prevent others from tampering with these files. You can set the owner and group permissions in any way.

Next, we suggest that you set up your system so that the talkdemon process automatically begins and ends. You can do this by inserting these two lines,

```
echo talkdemon started
/etc/talkdemon
```

in your startup script, and these two lines,

```
echo Talk msgqueue being removed
/etc/stoptalk
```

in your shutdown script. The utility's documentation talks about this in greater detail.

The above code is needed because when your system is shut down in the single user mode, the talk utility's message queues are not removed. When your system comes down, the talkdemon process is killed with a -9 signal, which prevents the process from removing the message queue.

The last step in the installation process is to make sure that your TERM environment variable is set. This is required because talk uses the curses(3X) screen management library. This library uses the TERM variable as the handle to your display.

Restrictions
Bennett holds the copyright to talk. He's given you permission to use the utility any way that you see fit. The only catch is that you must include the copyright notice and preserve the author's name in the header of your distribution.

Known Problems
We'll warn you that you might find a few bugs with the talk utility. However, none of these will give you a reason for not loading this utility onto your system. For example, one of the known problems is a conflict between the talk utility and the System V curses package. The conflict causes text to be lost from one of the screens if a party to the conversation presses the BACKSPACE key.

Another problem with curses is that on some systems the cursor will jump from the beginning of the line and back to the current cursor position when a character is entered on the screen. A talk utility user reports that this problem doesn't cause any harm but is annoying.

Also on some systems, you'll notice that talk has a high CPU usage. The problem stems from a low-precision sleep call on some System V distributions. This causes the main loop of talk to run as fast as the system itself.

These are just a few of the bugs. You can find a complete discussion about these and other known problems with the utility in the utility's documentation. You can also read the *comp.sources.unix* group on netnews to see what other talk users have to say about their experiences.

Keep in mind that you may also stumble across a few new bugs of your own. If so, you may want to report the bug to Bennett. Drop him an email at:

ihnp4!cbosgd!ukma!ukecc!edward.

Up and Running

The talk utility is probably one of the easiest programs that you'll ever use. At the prompt, just type **talk**, followed by the login ID of the person you want to talk to. Keep in mind that the talkdemon must be running on both systems. You may run into a little difficulty establishing the conversation if the other person is logged in more than once. In such a case, you must specify the tty to which you want to connect as the second argument to talk.

After you initiate the talk process, talk connects to the other person's system and informs them that you want to begin a conversation. The talk utility will wait for a response and resend its message every 30 seconds. If the other person fails to respond, you must interrupt talk to exit.

Once the other person agrees to converse with you, both of you can begin typing your conversations at the keyboard. First, you'll see your message displayed on the screen, then the other person's response. Although you'll find that talk is very good at managing the communication, there might be times when your screen becomes garbled. This is rare but it does happen. Don't be too concerned; press CTRL-L and talk will refresh your screen.

The uuencode Utility: A Binary to ASCII File Converter

Did you ever find a need to transmit a binary file via electronic mail? If you have, then you already know some of the problems that you face. But you don't have to worry any more, thanks to Mark Horton. He and his associates developed the uuencode utility. Now, there's not much to uuencode, but what's there is enough to save you a lot of aggravation.

The uuencode utility converts a binary file into an ASCII file, which you'll have little problem transmitting. When the file reaches its destination, uudecode, uuencode's sister utility, is used to transform the ASCII file back to a binary file. The entire process is as simple as running both utilities.

Well, there is a slight problem if the ASCII file is larger than 64K. Some UNIX mailers will refuse to work with messages longer than 64K. You'll have to shrink the ASCII files down to size using the UNIX split utility. The split utility automatically breaks the file into chunks that are about 64K in size. The file must be reassembled using a standard editor before the uudecode utility can be used to convert the file back to a binary file.

TIP
Here's another trick using uuencode. When you need to transmit a very large ASCII file, you should shrink the size of the file by using compress. Here's how it's done. First, compress the ASCII file using the compress utility discussed in Chapter 7. This will produce a binary file. Use uuencode to convert the compressed binary file back to ASCII. This will result in a smaller ASCII file than the file you started with, and will reduce the amount of time that is necessary to transmit the file. On the receiving end, you'll have to recreate the binary file using uudecode, then use the compress utility to decompress the file back to its ASCII form.

Up and Running Quickly

Create a directory for uuencode in your home directory, then copy the source code for uuencode and uudecode. One source of the code is in */pub/lispusers/medley* on *nervous.cis.ohio-state.edu*. You can use the UNIX C compiler and linker to create the binary versions of this program. No makefile is provided. Once you have both utilities compiled, you're ready to convert your first binary file.

Type **uuencode** at the prompt, followed by the name of the binary that will be converted (uuencode *input file output file*). You'll also need to enter a name for the file to be created by uudecode. In most cases, the conversion process takes less than a minute. If the file is less than 64K in size, you can use the UNIX mail utility to transmit the file; otherwise, you'll have to use the split utility to divide the file into smaller files. You can then transmit each of the smaller files.

The uudecode utility is run in the same manner as uuencode. At the prompt, type **uudecode** *filename*. The file will then be reconverted to a binary file using the second parameter to uuencode. However, you'll have to reassemble files that were created by the spilt utility before running uudecode if the original file was too large.

The most efficient use of uuencode is to pipe the converted file directly into the mail utility (uuencode *filename* output file | mail user@machine). For most UNIX mail readers, you can take a piece of mail and send it through a pipe. At the mailer prompt, the recipient could type "| **uudecode**". This works for the older mailers such as mail and mailx. However, if you are using the newer X Windows mail readers and the pipe facility is not available, you can always save the mail to a temporary file and run uudecode on the temporary file. See the uuencode man pages for more information about this process.

Watch Out for...

The size of the converted binary file is automatically increased by about 35% since uuencode adds a byte for every three bytes in the file. In addition, uuencode also adds control information to the file. Although these are stripped away by uudecode, you will have to transmit this additional data, which could extend transmission time.

Another point to consider is that the user who is reconverting the file using the uudecode utility must have write permission on the directory before running uudecode.

If you run into any problems with uuencode or uudecode, you can contact the authors of these utilities directly. Although we don't have an address for Horton, his associates can be reached at these addresses:

Alan J Rosenthalt (*flaps@utcsri.UUCP*)
Fred Fish (*well!fnf*)
and
Bryce Nesbitt (*ucbvax!cogsci!bryce*)

The xrolodex Utility:
Telephone Directory Software

Where is that darn telephone number? If you're like most of us, you can answer this question within seconds by pressing a few keys on your pocket rolodex. Enter the first few letters and up pops the name, address, and telephone number. That is, unless you left your pocket rolodex at home!

Let's face it. We've all gone through this more than a few times during the year. And if you frequently use the telephone during the day you know how much of an inconvenience this is for you. But Jerry Smith of Iris Computing Laboratories has developed a utility that we think you'll find to be a very handy addition to your UNIX toolbox.

The xrolodex utility is a small, rolodex-like application that is designed for systems running in the X Windows environment. Now, we're not talking about a rolodex that you can slap together using a few basic shell script commands. We're not even talking about a character-based utility.

The xrolodex utility has a solid Motif-based user interface that will challenge any commercial software product that you can find on the market. All you have to do is press a few buttons on the screen and select items from classy-looking menus; xrolodex does the rest for you.

Once you've loaded xrolodex onto your system, you'll find yourself reaching for your keyboard rather than your pocket the next time you need a telephone number. Your pocket rolodex will become your traveling companion as the xrolodex utility becomes your deskmate.

Installation

One place where you can find the xrolodex utility files is in */archives/mirror3/linux/X11/motif* on *cs.columbia.edu* on the Internet. You can use the archie utility to find a host that is closer to your location. Copy the utility's files to your system. You'll find that xrolodex comes with a ready-to-run makefile called *xrolo.make.*

   You should take a few minutes and review the settings in this file before attempting to make the xrolodex utility binary files. You may have to modify some of these settings to conform to the environment on your system. You'll find complete installation instructions as part of the utility's documentation. Refer to the documentation if you have questions about the *xrolo.make* file.

   Once you're sure the settings are proper, type **make -f xrolo.make**. The make utility will crunch away for a few minutes and when it stops you'll have a working copy of xrolodex ready to run on your system.

Restrictions

Iris Computing Laboratories holds the copyright to xrolodex, but this shouldn't stop you from using the utility pretty much as you please. As you'll read in the utility's documentation, Iris Computing Laboratories gives you permission to use, copy, modify, and distribute the source for any purpose and without any fee.

   The only limitation is that you're expected to include the formal copyright notice (that you find in the utility's documentation) when you distribute the software. In addition, you can't use the Iris Computing Laboratories name as part of the advertising or publicity that pertains to the redistribution of the utility.

   You can read all the fine print about these restrictions in the documentation. You'll also learn that there are no warranties associated with the utility. Iris Computer Laboratories specifically disclaims any implied warranties of merchantability and fitness for the software. In non-legalese this means you're on your own when using the software.

Known Problems

The documentation claims that there are no known errors or problems with xrolodex. We found nothing to dispute this claim. The utility has been extensively tested on the Sun SPARCstation in the MIT X environment with Motif 1.1.x, using Code Center/Saber-C.

CAUTION

Don't rename the xrolodex utility to xrolo. This is an easy mistake to make; however, there is a different utility that carries this name. Eliminate the confusion before the problem arises.

While there aren't any problems with the utility noted in the documentation, we suggest that you keep a watch out anyway. You can do this by reading the *comp.sources.x* group on netnews. If you think that you discovered a problem with xrolodex, drop Jerry Smith a note and a bug report at *jsmith@spectro.com*.

Up and Running

Type **xrolodex** at the prompt; your screen will be filled with a utility that will maintain a set of virtual business cards for you. The display is divided into four major areas; the menu bar, the name of the current rolodex file, a control panel, and the edit window for editing and viewing a rolodex entry.

The xrolodex utility allows you to specify the name of the rolodex file that you want to use for the session. This is done by specifying the file name as an argument on the command line. For example, type **xrolodex business** and the business rolodex file will be used with xrolodex. You can also create a new rolodex file from within xrolodex by selecting the Open menu item, then specifying the name of the rolodex file.

Working within the utility is intuitive since xrolodex uses all of the normal Motif editing commands and standard widget sets. For example, within the edit window, you can copy, cut, and paste text for the current entry by using standard menu items.

There are two ways to move among the rolodex entries. You can use the pull-down menus from the main menu bar or the convent push buttons that are located on the control panel. These buttons allow you to move the first, last, next, or previous entries in the current rolodex file.

All editing is limited to the current rolodex entry. You can't view or edit the complete rolodex file directly from within xrolodex. The scroll bar will not move across entries in the rolodex file. You can always use the copy and paste menu items to move text among various entries in the file.

Smith designed the xrolodex utility's rolodex file as a free-form database. You won't find any limitations on the number of entries that the rolodex file can hold. And there are no limitations on the size of each entry. This means you can include notes along with names, addresses, and telephone numbers. Instead of creating a fixed record length for each entry, Smith decided to delimit each entry with "#" characters.

The free-form design of xrolodex's database is ideal for experienced UNIX programmers because you have full access to the database without having to use the utility. You can manipulate any rolodex database file by using any of the many text processing tools that are available in the UNIX environment. This means that you might be able to download and upload files to/from your pocket rolodex system if it has a communications port.

The xrolodex utility functions very much like a standard Motif editor. The current rolodex file is loaded into memory when you start the utility. Additions, deletions, and modifications that you make to entries occur in memory. The file on the disk is updated only when you select xrolodex's Save menu item.

Now, here is probably the best feature of xrolodex. Locating an entry isn't limited to a few database key fields. When you select the Find Entry menu item, you are prompted for a search string. This string can be anywhere in any entry. The xrolodex utility will examine all the information that you entered in each entry in the rolodex file and try to match the search string. Searches can be conducted case sensitive or insensitive depending on the setting of a radio box on the screen.

We've found xrolodex to be just the right tool for maintaining a personal list of friends and business contacts. However, we won't recommend xrolodex as the software of choice for the on-line corporate telephone directory. But this utility goes to the top of the list when it comes to your personal telephone directory.

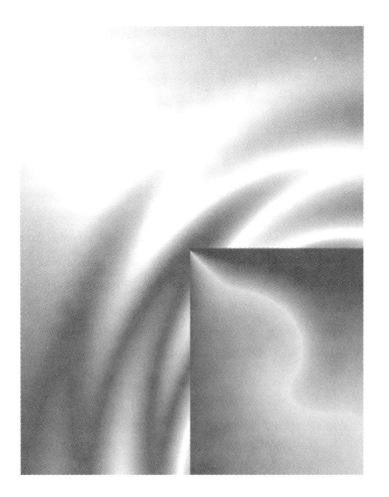

CHAPTER 5

Text Processing
Utilities

Y ou're on the verge of adding some powerful text processing utilities to your UNIX toolbox. No, we're not talking about another editor for creating text files. You probably have enough of those utilities on your system already. We're talking about *text processing utilities* that make a real impact on your work.

In this chapter, we'll take a look at the TeX utility, which enables you to produce typeset-quality documents for your basic correspondence and reports. And just think what it can do for those special documents that you use for presentations. TeX is even used by some serious publishing houses as a typesetting tool.

After the TeX utility, you'll explore the world of emacs—an editor, and then some. Emacs can be used to simply enter text into a file or be used as a development environment where you can compile and link your application without leaving emacs. This is truly a convenient way to build your application.

Anyone who has ever written a document knows the pain when it's returned with misspellings underlined in red. Embarrassed? Sure, but there's no need to have it happen again, thanks to the ispell utility, a spelling checker that you can use on any text. You can even use it from within the emacs. Just as you would expect, the ispell utility compares words in your document with words in its dictionary. You'll be alerted to any mismatches and receive a list of suggested correct spellings for the word.

We'll round off this chapter with a look at another useful utility called groff. The groff utility is a replacement for the nroff utility that is standard on most UNIX distributions. You'll find that groff handles the latest devices and allows you to print man pages on a PostScript printer.

And the best thing about the TeX, emacs, ispell, and groff utilities is that they're all for the taking, free of charge.

The TeX Utility: Typesetting Software
Emacs: More Than Just an Editor
The ispell Utility: A Spelling Checker
The groff Utility: Text Formatting Software

The TeX Utility: Typesetting Software

So you've looked at the editors that we've included in this book and discovered that something is lacking. They're just no match for a true word processor. Sure, editors may not have all the formatting capabilities that you want. But that's not the purpose of an editor. What you're looking for is the TeX utility.

TeX was developed by Donald Knuth at Stanford University to take text file input from an editor and produce typeset output. In fact, a number of professional publishing firms use TeX for their publications.

You'll find the TeX utility a welcome but complicated addition to your collection of UNIX utilities. (Underline the word *complicated*.) However, with a little patience and practice, you'll be producing publishing quality documents in a very short time.

The TeX utility is keyword driven; that is, if you want text to be displayed in bold type, you enter the bold keyword immediately before the text. Likewise, if you want to define settings for the complete document, you specify a group of global commands at the beginning of the TeX file. It's that easy.

Installation

We can't give you any quick installation instruction because installing the TeX utility on your system is just too complicated to explain here. But don't be too concerned. You'll find all the information that you'll need for a successful installation in the TeX utility's documentation. Just take your time, read it carefully, and you'll have TeX up and running shortly.

You'll find the TeX utility at various locations on the Internet; one of them is */pub/unix/software/tex* on *knot.queensu.ca*. You can also read information about TeX on the *comp.text.tex* netnews group.

Once you've successfully installed TeX, you may find it beneficial to join the TeX Users Group, called TUG. This is a nonprofit organization that supplies up-to-date information and publications about TeX. Drop them a line at this address:

TeX Users Group
P.O. Box 9506
Providence, RI 02940

Restrictions

The TeX utility is coverd by the Free Software Foundation's GNU General Public License. You can read the details in the documentation. However, feel free to use TeX without charge—as long as you don't charge anyone for it. You can modify and incorporate the utility in your application without prior permission from the Free Software Foundation.

Keep in mind that no warranties or guarantees come with the TeX utility, so use it at your own risk. You should also let this fact be known to anyone who uses an application that includes TeX.

Up and Running

The TeX utility comes with an on-line tutorial that helps you get up to speed in no time. In addition, the user's group can supply you with a list of publications that show you how to use TeX. Probably one of the more popular books is *The TeX Book,* published by Addison Wesley, Reading, MA. In this section, we'll just highlight some of the more important features and let you read the TeX documentation for a complete discussion of the various features of TeX.

You can use the TeX utility in the interactive mode or in the batch mode. We recommend the batch mode, which will give you better control over text formatting.

Before beginning TeX, create a file using your favorite editor. A word of caution! If you create the file using a word processor, make sure that you save the file as an ASCII file and not in the word processor's format. TeX can't deal with control characters that are found in a word processor formatted file.

Once the file is created, type **tex** *filename.* Many who use the TeX utility use a set of TeX macros called LaTeX, which is invoked as "latex". (The LaTeX macros are described in *LaTeX: A Document Preparation System* by Leslie Lamport, Addison Wesley, Reading, MA, 1986.) TeX takes your file and converts it into a DVI (device independent) file. The DVI file is then read by a device-specific program that produces typeset output. The DVI file and the device driver allow your document to be used by various devices such as a laser printer, an X Windows display, and even a phototypesetter. Once your text file is converted to the DVI format, your document can be read by any device, without your having to reprocess the file through TeX.

TIP
Before developing a complex document, write a few lines and pass it through the TeX utility; then display or print the file using the device driver. If the text output is the same as the text in your original file, then TeX is operating properly and you can proceed to create more complicated documents.

So where's the fancy formatting? For this, you must return to your original text file and embed special TeX utility keywords. Table 5-1 contains a sampling of these commands. Notice that each command is preceded by a backslash (\).

NOTE
Beautiful typesetting is both an art and a science. In that spirit, TeX provides commands that allow you to specify what you want rather than how to do it. You can, however, tighten parameters, which will allow TeX more or less leeway in its formatting. For example, you can control how much space to use in separating words, which will determine where lines wrap and if hyphenation will be attempted.

A Brief Look Inside

We don't intend to teach you how to use TeX. The utility's documentation does an excellent job of this. However, we can't leave you without showing you what a TeX-formatted document looks like. Figure 5-1 contains a typical timesheet. You'll

KEYWORD	DESCRIPTION
\beginuser	Begins the batch block
\enduser	Ends the batch block
\noindent	No indentation
\displaytext	Prints or displays text
\section	Creates a new section of the document
\subsection	Creates a new subsection of the document
\item	First item in a list
\maketable	Creates a table in the document
\halign	Aligns text horizontally
\bf	Makes text bold
\noalign	Doesn't align text
\hrule	Creates a horizontal rule
\smallskip	Skips a small amount of space
\vbox	Creates a box
\bdots	Creates a bullet
\bigskip	Skips a large amount of space
\center	Centers text
\nopagenumbers	Doesn't include page numbers
\eject	Begins new page
\vfill	Places leftover vertical space at the bottom of the page
\hsize	Sets the horizontal width of the text on the page
\vsize	Sets the height of the main text
\hoffset	Moves text to the right
\voffset	Moves the text up
\footnote	Creates a footnote

TABLE 5-1. *A Sampling of TeX Keywords*

notice that the page style information is at the beginning of the file. This is followed by the title of the worksheet.

```
\documentstyle{letter} \vspace*{1 in}
\begin{document}
\large
\pagestyle{empty}
\begin{center} {\bf Work Performed By John Jones for Random Walk Investors, Inc.}
\end{center}
\vspace{.5 in}
\begin{tabular}{|||r|||} \hline
 Date & Hours  & Description  \\ \hline
11/05/93 & 8 & Researching bogus investments \\
11/08/93 & 8 & Investing in bogus securities \\
11/09/93 & 8 & Collecting profits from bogus securities \\
11/10/93 & 8 & Filing for bankruptcy \\
11/11/93 & 8 & Avoiding Federal agents \\
11/12/93 & 8 & Attempting to bribe Federal agents \\
11/15/93 & 8 & Calling attorneys \\
 \hline Total: & 56 & \\ \hline
\end{tabular}
 \\
 \\
{\bf Total clams due:\$4,872.00}
\end{document}
```

FIGURE 5-1. *A sample timesheet in LaTex format*

The {tabular} command is given to instruct TeX to create a table of dates, hours, and activities. The ampersand (&) is used to delimit columns, and double backslashes (\\) are used to delimit each row. Lines are added to the table using two different techniques. The \hline command is used to draw a horizontal line. When the timesheet is printed using a PostScript printer, it looks like Figure 5-2.

emacs:
More Than Just an Editor

So you think you've just acquired another editor. Just what you need. But hold on a minute! Don't be too quick to jump to conclusions. Is emacs an editor? Sure, but it's more. And that's what makes it a worthwhile addition to your system.

Let's face it, most editors are used for more than just writing a letter. They are used for creating computer programs. Here's a scenario you may have experienced: you sit down in front of the editor and enter a few lines of code, then

Work Performed By John Jones for Random Walk Investors,
Inc.

Date	Hours	Description
11/05/93	8	Reasearching bogus investments
11/08/93	8	Investing in bogus securities
11/09/93	8	Collecting profits from bogus securities
11/10/93	8	Filing for bankruptcy
11/11/93	8	Avoiding Federal agents
11/12/93	8	Attempting to bribe Federal agents
11/15/93	8	Calling attorneys
Total:	56	

Total clams due: $4,872.00

FIGURE 5-2.   *The PostScript printed version of the sample timesheet*

exit the editor to compile and execute your program. After you run your program, you discover a bug. It's time to call in the debugger utility to track down the problem. Finally, you return to the editor to correct the source code.

Does this sound all too familiar? If you've written programs for personal computers you know there is a easier way. Development tools from Microsoft and Borland International let you create and test your program without leaving the development environment. Don't you wish you had something like that for UNIX? You do! It's called emacs.

Emacs has all of the facilities you need to build your software without having to exit emacs. Now, we'll admit that emacs doesn't look like the development tools that are available for personal computers. Then again, looks aren't everything; it's functionality that counts. Emacs lets you float in and out of your favorite compiler, linker, and debugger without having to lose sight of your source code. But there is just too much to emacs to describe here. We'll point you in the right direction and let you explore emacs for yourself.

Unpacking and Installation

Before you attempt to install emacs, make sure that your system has sufficient swap space. The emacs program takes up 400K and has a data area that can extend beyond 600K. How much space is enough? Well, the minimum requirement is 400K for the program and 150K for the data. However, emacs will give you an error message if the utility requires more space than is available. Here is one place to locate emacs: */pub/gnu/emacs* at *sunsite.unc.edu*. You can learn about emacs by reading one of the following netnews groups: *comp.emacs, gnu.emacs.announce, gnu.emacs.bug, gnu.emacs.help,* and *gnu.emacs.sources.*

As you'll read in the installation instructions that are provided with the emacs documentation, you'll need to create at least two directories: one directory for the installed emacs files and the other for the build files. Assign these directory names to the EMACS and BUILD environment variables.

Follow the directions contained in the installation procedural files and copy the appropriate files into the proper directories. Emacs comes with two files that help you with the installation: the build-install and install.sh scripts. The build-install script helps you setup the file, and you can use the make utility with the install file (make install) to create emacs' binary files.

Restrictions

Emacs is covered under the permission rules set down by the Free Software Foundation. Generally, you can freely use, modify, and distribute emacs as long as you don't prohibit anyone else from doing the same. The emacs documentation contains a complete description of these restrictions.

You'll also find somewhat different restrictions placed on the emacs tutorial and other documentation provided with the utility. Be sure to read all the permission requirements before you modify and distribute emacs documentation.

Up and Running

Once you've built emacs, you're ready to learn how to master a very powerful software development tool. Type **emacs** at the prompt to begin the utility. If you specify a file name, the file is displayed on the screen.

Most of the commands that you'll use to control emacs are single letter commands that are prefaced with the CTRL key or the META key. For example, to end the session, you type CTRL-X and CTRL-C.

NOTE
The META key is usually labeled EDIT. If your keyboard doesn't have a META key, use the ESC key. META-A, a one-stroke command, would then be entered as ESC-A, a two-stroke command.

You can page around the file by using CTRL-V to move forward a screen, META-V to move backward a screen, and CTRL-L to refresh the screen. In a single screen, you'll need to use the cursor control commands. Table 5-2 provides you with a few basics. (The emacs documentation contains the complete list of commands.)

COMMAND	DESCRIPTION	COMMAND	DESCRIPTION
CTRL-F	Moves forward a character	CTRL-A	Moves to beginning of line
CTRL-B	Moves backward a character	CTRL E	Moves to end of line
META-F	Moves forward a word	META-A	Moves back to beginning of sentence
META-B	Moves backward a word	META-E	Moves forward to end of sentence
CTRL-N	Moves to next line	META-<	Goes to beginning of file
CTRL-P	Moves to previous line	META->	Goes to end of file

TABLE 5-2.   *Cursor Movement Commands*

Versatile Commands

Richard Stallman, the author of emacs, has thought of everything including a few time-saving steps. Nearly all the commands in the utility accept command arguments. Probably one of the most useful of these is to have emacs automatically execute a command a specific number of times without having to re-enter it. Here's how this is done. Let's say you want to move the cursor back 10 characters. Of course, you could press the CTRL-F command ten times. But wait! We said there is a faster way. Just type CTRL-U10, CTRL-F; and emacs will do the rest. The CTRL-U command can be used with any command. All you need to do is specify the number of times the command is to be executed as an argument to the CTRL-U command, then enter the command itself.

Get Me Out Of Here! All right, you've used the CTRL-U command to enter a numeric argument to another emacs command but you've entered 1000 instead of 10. Like all good UNIX utilities, emacs follows your directions and repeats the next command a thousand times. You can shout and scream, "Stop!" at the computer to no avail. What next? Just press the CTRL-G command and emacs will come to a safe stop.

Whoops! I Made a Mistake

Emacs is very forgiving, a feature that you'll treasure the next time you make a change you wish you hadn't. You can undo the change and have emacs bring the text back to its original state by typing CTRL-X, **u**.

The CTRL-X, **u** command restores the text that is affected by the latest command. However, you can restore changes that were made through other commands in the session by repeating the CTRL-X, **u** command several times. A word of caution! Commands that just move the cursor are ignored by the CTRL-X, **u** command. An insertion of text is considered to be a single change. This means that to remove it, you'd only have to execute the CTRL-X, **u** command once.

Okay, you're probably saying to yourself that typing CTRL-X, **u** several times is difficult. Instead of having a session of finger gymnastics, there is an alternate set of keystrokes that accomplishes the same task. This is CTRL-_ (underscore). The CTRL-_ command is usually easier to type and has the same effect as the CTRL-X, **u** command. So why not just use the CTRL-_ command? On some keyboards, it is not obvious how to type CTRL-_.

Information Always on View
You're always kept informed of the current status of your work. Emacs displays critical information in the *echo area,* which is the name given to the bottom of the screen. Right above the last line on the screen is the mode line. The *mode line* contains information such as the file name and the percentage of the file that is above the top of the screen. In place of the percentage, the mode line will state TOP or BOT if you are at the top or bottom of the file and ALL if the entire file is displayed on the screen.

You'll see asterisks at the beginning of the mode line if you changed text in the file but haven't saved the changes. The asterisks are changed to dashes as soon as the file is saved. The mode line also displays the current mode within parentheses. The emacs documentation contains the details about the emacs modes.

Let emacs Search for You
If you're looking for a pattern within your document, just sit back and let the emacs utility do all the work for you. We'll, you really can't sit back because the method of searching is different than what you'll find in other utilities. The search begins as soon as you type the first character of the search pattern. Here's how this is done. First, you must decide if the search will be conducted forward from the position of the cursor to the end of the document, or backward from the cursor to the beginning of the document. Press CTRL-S to search forward and CTRL-R to search backward through the document.

Now enter the search pattern, one character at a time. Each time another character of the search pattern is entered, emacs moves the cursor to the next occurrence of the pattern that you typed. You'll hear a beep if emacs doesn't find a match.

Let's say you started the search in the wrong direction. Don't be concerned. Reverse direction by pressing CTRL-S or CTRL-R; emacs will automatically search in the other direction without your having to retype the search pattern. When you are finished searching, just press ESC to terminate the search and return to your document.

Help Is On-Line

Heard enough about the emacs utility? Probably not, but we're just trying to whet your appetite so that you'll explore emacs yourself. The place to start is with the documentation files that come with the utility. Once you've sifted through those files, you can work through emacs' tutorial, which should have you up and running in no time.

Hold on! There's a lot to learn about emacs; more than you could ever memorize. Don't worry, Stallman has thought of everything, including an on-line help feature that will come to your aid in a pinch. So, if you're lost in emacs, just press CTRL-H and let emacs provide the answer.

For example, suppose you want to know the function of a command character such as the CTRL-P command. Press CTRL-H, C, then press CTRL-P. The first two characters tell the help feature that you want assistance with a character command. The last keystroke specifies the character command. Emacs returns a brief description of the command. In this case, you'll learn that the CTRL-P command will put the cursor on the previous line.

There are a few more help options available. We'll let you review the documentation files for a complete listing of these options.

Compiling and Debugging at a Keystroke

As we said, emacs is more than a text editor. You can compile a program without leaving the utility. Suppose you are editing a program and want to compile it. Just press META-X compile. The first time within your emacs session you will be given a standard make line in the mini-buffer for you to modify: "make -k". Edit the line and press ENTER. A new buffer named *compilation* will be created to hold the output of the compilation.

If you get errors and your compiler produces standard UNIX C-style error messages with file names and line numbers, you can use the CTRL-X,' (left quote) command to position the cursor at the source line referred to in the error message. This works even if you have not been editing the file in question. You can go to the next error message by repeating the CTRL-X' command.

Sometimes you might have to recompile a program after fixing one or two errors. If you edit a source file containing several errors, emacs is smart enough in most cases to compensate for the addition or removal of lines when computing where to position you to the next error. This allows you to fix more errors with fewer compiles.

Another nice feature is that you can start finding errors and fixing them even before the compile is finished! This is possible since emacs uses UNIX's multitasking, allowing you to find and fix the first error with the compile still running.

Still another helpful feature is the "make -k" default setting. The -k switch tells make not to stop building after the first compile failure. Instead, make will continue to compile any other sources that do not depend upon the one with the error. All you need to do is press CTRL-X' to get to the next error. You will be amazed at how your productivity improves.

So you have successfully built your program's executable file. Now you run your program and there it is, a bug. You can return to emacs and run the gdb debugger from within emacs! Here's how it's done.

Press META-X, type **gdb**, then press the ENTER key. Emacs will prompt you for the name of the executable to debug. You're now in the debugger. Look for our discussion about the gdb utility in this book.

Here is the best part. The debugger's output appears in one window and your source code is in another window. As the debugger steps you through the executing code, you can easily switch to the source code window and correct the bug. Again, emacs is smart enough that even if you have not been editing the source code file, emacs will display the file for you. Once the bug is fixed, recompile without leaving emacs.

And There's More...

Yes, there is a lot more that we could talk about, but we'll leave you with just two additional features that are available in emacs, the flexibility of viewing and reading files. emacs can be used to view more than one file at the same time. That's nice but not earth-shattering. Hold on! Each of these files is in its own window that can be split multiple times both horizontally and vertically.

This provides you with nearly any view of the file you may want, especially if you are using a large X Windows xterm. You can actually have the screen divide into four quadrants, allowing you to view four parts of the same file at the same time—a very handy feature for programmers. And if you make a change in one of the quadrants, emacs automatically copies the change to the other three quadrants, so that all four copies of the program are always up-to-date.

Now for the best news. Emacs doesn't care what type of data is contained in the file. This means you can use emacs to view or edit binary files or files that have very long lines. These are the kinds of files that will choke vi and other editors. Even non-printable characters are displayed. For example, ^M indicates a carriage return and a NULL is represented by a ^@.

Want to learn more? Unpack and install the emacs utility, then read the man pages.

The ispell Utility:
A Spelling Checker

Many of us have a problem with splling. Whoops! I mean *spelling*. Fortunately, Pace Willisson has come to our aid with the ispell utility. Now we don't have any excuses for misspelled documents. In addition to pointing out possible spelling errors in a document, Willisson has incorporated a feature that you'll find indispensable. The ispell utility will actually make an attempt to provide you with the correct spelling.

What else could you ask for? There's more! Not only will ispell identify incorrect spellings and suggest correct spellings for suspected words, the utility will even replace the misspelled word with the correct word. Now all you need is find a utility that will write the document for you.

Willisson's ispell has a long history. Willisson found it on the TOPS-20 system at MIT. It was first used at the MIT AI lab in the late 1970s. Apparently, it was originally written in assembler, and in the early 1980s Willisson rewrote the spelling checker in the C programming language. Shortly thereafter, the utility branched out in two directions. While Willisson was working on the present version, others made their own modifications, which can be found in many places, including */u/public/ispell* on *celray.cs.yale.edu*. As you can imagine, there are many who contributed to the ispell utility and they're given due credit in the ispell documentation files.

Enough history—Willisson's version has particular interest for users of the emacs utility. He made a special effort to create a seamless interface between ispell and emacs. This means that you can check the spelling of an emacs document without leaving emacs.

And there's more! If you're a programmer, you realize how difficult it can be to find misspellings in your source code. Sure, the compiler will usually find programming errors, but how do you check the spelling of text that your program displays on the screen? It is almost useless to run the program through a spelling checker since nearly all your commands will be marked as misspelled.

Even the ispell utility will have a problem deciphering program code from misspellings; however, you can add those commands to the ispell dictionary. The next time ispell encounters the command, the utility will recognize the command as a correct spelling. Therefore, ispell will spend nearly all its time searching for spelling errors in the text that your program displays.

Is there anything wrong with the ispell utility? Well, the utility is missing one thing—the Soundex capabilities; ispell can't suggest correct spellings of words based upon words that sound alike.

Installation Is a Snap

You'll find the ispell utility at various locations on the Internet. Here is just one: */gnu* on *csvax.cs.caltech.edu.* Copy the files to an empty directory on your system. The utility comes with a configure shell script, which attempts to guess the correct values for various system variables that are used during compilation. It is this script that creates a makefile. The configure shell script also creates a file called *config.status* that you can run in the future to recreate the current configuration.

The configure shell script takes about two minutes to run. After it has finished, you can type **make install**, which will place the necessary files into the appropriate directories. (For example, */usr/local/bin, /usr/local/lib, /usr/local/man.*) Finally, type **make** to compile the utility.

The documentation files that come with ispell explain in detail how to properly install the utility. You'll even receive a few tips if you have problems during the installation. If you experience serious problems with ispell, you may want to let Willisson know about them. He can be reached at *pace@ai.mit.edu* or at *pace@hx.lcs.mit.edu.*

Up and Running in No Time

Once the ispell utility has been installed, all you need is a document file to examine. At the prompt, type **ispell** *filename* and the utility does the rest. Keep in mind that like all spelling checkers, the ispell compares each word in the document against words contained in its dictionary. If a match isn't found, the word in your document is reported as a misspelling. Actually, the word might be correctly spelled but simply isn't in the dictionary.

A word that is considered a possible misspelling is displayed at the top of the utility's screen. The utility then searches for what Willisson calls near misses. These are words that differ only by a single letter, a missing or extra letter, or a pair of transposed letters.

When the ispell utility settles down, you'll see the suspect word displayed at the top of the screen, a list of suggested spellings in the center of the screen, and text of the document that contains the word at the bottom of the screen. The word itself is highlighted within the text if your terminal supports reverse video.

Now it is up to you to make a decision. You can accept the word as it appears in the document, select one of the suggested spellings, enter a replacement for the word, quit the utility, or type **?** for on-line help.

The ispell utility offers you three ways to accept the current spelling of the word. You can press the SPACEBAR to accept the word this one time, or you can press A to accept it for the rest of the file. This means that the word won't be flagged as a misspelling until you run ispell on a different file. Another way to accept the spelling of the word is to press I, which will also place the word in your private dictionary.

CAUTION
Unwanted punctuation must be removed from the word before you add the word to your private dictionary. You can leave in apostrophes, but other non-alphabetic characters should be removed. Keep in mind that any character you leave in will be used to determine if a word is correctly spelled and when to suggest spellings.

Willisson has given you two ways to correct the spelling of words. You can replace the word with a suggested spelling by pressing the number that corresponds to the replacement word on the list. Ispell will automatically erase the current word and place the new word in its place within the text. You can also press R to have ispell prompt you to enter the replacement word.

TIP
If you just want to quickly check the spelling of a word, you can start the ispell utility without specifying a file name. The utility will read words from the standard input (the keyboard). Enter the questionable spelling at the keyboard, press ENTER; ispell now checks the spelling. Figure 5-3 shows you a sample session. Table 5-3 contains a list of helpful commands.

Running from the emacs Utility

The ispell utility is especially useful for emacs users. Remember that emacs is an editor that has the capability of invoking other programs while it is running. (You can read more about emacs earlier in this chapter.) One of the utilities that can be executed from within emacs is ispell. This means that you can check the spelling in a file just as if you were using an integrated word processor.

For example, suppose you need to check the spelling of a single word while you are running emacs. First, place the cursor under the word that you want to check. Next, enter the emacs command META-$ (or on some terminals ESC, $). The META represents the META key, which is sometimes marked as EDIT.

```
% ispell
word: independent
how about: independent
word: CTRL-D
```

FIGURE 5-3. *Checking spelling interactively with ispell*

COMMAND	DESCRIPTION
?	Prints a help message
Q	Quits. Accepts the rest of the words in the file and exits
X	Exits. Abandons any changes made to this file and exits immediately
!	Shell escape. The shell command that you type is executed as a subprocess
CTRL-Z	Suspends ispell on systems that support job control
CTRL-L	Redraws the screen

TABLE 5-3. *The ispell Help Commands*

The ispell utility will crank away for a few seconds and if the word is found in the dictionary, a message is displayed in the echo area of the emacs' screen. If the word isn't found, ispell begins searching for suggested spellings.

Any guesses that ispell makes appear in a separate window. Each guess is preceded by a digit. Enter the corresponding digit on the keyboard and ispell automatically replaces the original word with the guess. There are, however, times when even the best spelling checker is stumped. Table 5-4 contains the options you have when this occurs with the ispell.

TIP

Don't be afraid to make a spelling change. If you make a mistake, just use emacs' undo command to restore the previous word.

Checking the spelling of your emacs document a word at a time can become very time consuming. You can direct emacs to check the spelling of all the words in the buffer by executing the META-X ispell command. Ispell will scan the entire buffer and create a list of all the potentially misspelled words.

When the ispell utility has finished, it automatically positions the cursor on the first word in the list and displays the list of options that are contained in Table 5-3. Once you've made a decision about the word, ispell continues this process with the next word on the list.

Here's another helpful hint. You can type the Q command to exit the ispell utility. This will usually leave you with other potentially misspelled words remaining in the document. However, you don't have to start over when you return to the document. Just type CTRL-X, $ and ispell will pick up right where you left off.

OPTION	DESCRIPTION
I	Inserts the word in your private dictionary
A	Accepts the word for this editing session. Doesn't put it in your private dictionary
SPC	Leaves the word alone
R	Replaces the word. This command prompts you for a string
L	Displays words from the dictionary that contain a specified substring
G	Stops the command without changing anything

TABLE 5-4. *Options When ispell Has No Suggestions*

Restrictions

You'll find that ispell is truly free software. You can use it and distribute it without charge, although the utility isn't in the public domain and free doesn't mean that there aren't any restrictions associated with its use. Ispell is copyrighted by the Free Software Foundation. However, the fine print in this case has a positive effect on the distribution of this utility.

Basically, the only thing you can't do is prevent others from sharing any version of the ispell utility that you distribute. This even applies to modifications that you make to your copy of the utility; so if you modify ispell, you must make it available to others without charge and without restrictions.

As with all the utilities mentioned in this book, ispell is distributed without any warranty. You can read more about the restrictions in the ispell documentation.

The groff Utility:
Text Formatting Software

Nowadays, since UNIX has been unbundled, your computer may not have the standard UNIX text processing utilities such as nroff. Need to write a man page? Need to read a man page that came with the package you just installed? Now what are you going to do? Get a full-featured, free replacement for nroff!

We're talking about the groff utility, which was created by James Clark (*jjc@jclark.com*). Clark has to be thanked for taking the time to develop a utility that so many of us can use every day. The groff utility is a front-end to the groff document formatting system and a post-processor for selected devices, including ps for PostScript printers, TeX .dvi format, X75 for a 75-dpi X11 previewer, X100 for a 100-dpi X11 previewer, ASCII for typewriter-like devices, and latin1 for devices that use the ISO Latin-1 character set.

The groff utility is a replacement for the standard UNIX nroff utility. Some nroff users have found it to be somewhat outdated since it doesn't support modern output devices such as PostScript printers. Another reason for using groff is that you can print nroff documents such as man pages. With groff, you print the man pages using a PostScript laser printer. This is something you can't do with the nroff utility. And be sure to keep groff in mind as you start to use utilities that are reviewed in this book. Nearly all the utilities that we talk about come with nroff-formatted man pages.

Now you have another powerful utility at your disposal. Just create your document, format it with groff, then let the groff post-processor convert your document format commands into commands that will give you the maximum output quality from your favorite device.

Installation

Here's just one place where you'll find a release of the groff utility: *prep.ai.mit.edu* in the *pub/gnu* directory. However, before attempting to copy the utility's files to your system, be sure that you have a C++ compiler installed to compile groff's source code. All the source code files have the '.cc' suffix. This means the C++ compiler that you use must be able to read such a file. Clark suggests that you use gcc 2.3.1 or a later version of the same compiler.

Create a directory on your system to store the groff files, then copy the files from the remote system. Once all the files are in place, you're ready to build the binary files. Type **configure**. This is a shell script that attempts to set various system-dependent variables that are used to create groff.

TIP

You might run into a little problem if you are using csh on an older version of System V. Try executing **sh configure** instead of **configure**. This should take care of the problem.

Besides creating the proper settings for the compile, the configure script also examines your C++ compiler for potential compatibility problems with the groff source code. If any problems are detected, the configure script prints a warning message, then stops running. You'll need to correct the problem before rerunning the configure script.

Now you're ready to create the binary version of groff. And this step isn't difficult at all since an install file is included with your copy of the utility. This means all you need to do is type **make install** at the prompt. Among other things, the install file creates a makefile for you. Just type **make** and your make utility will do the rest. When make stops running, groff's binary files are ready to run on your system.

Will groff compile just as easily as we described here? That all depends on your system. Don't worry; groff comes with details on how to install the utility on practically any system. Just read the installation instructions before you attempt to compile the source code.

Once the utility has been successfully installed, you'll need to set a few environment variables that groff uses to find its way around your system. A sampling of these variables is contained in Table 5-5. Check the utility's documentation for a complete listing of these critical environment variables.

Restrictions

The groff utility is covered under the Free Software Foundation's General Public License. You can read all the fine print in the utility's documentation. However, the gist of it is that you can't prevent anyone else from using the groff utility. You can copy, distribute, and modify it to your heart's content without any worry that Clark or the Free Software Foundation will complain.

Here's a point that you should keep in mind; groff is provided warranty free. This means that Clark makes no claim that the utility is fit for any purpose and makes no claim that the utility will work on your system.

In fact, you may want to take Clark's lead and place the "without any warranty" claim in every copy of the utility that you modify and distribute. This will help you

VARIABLE	DESCRIPTION
GROFF_COMMAND_PREFIX	If this is set X, then groff will run xtroff instead of gtroff
GROFF_TMAC_PATH	List of directories in which to search for macro files
GROFF_TYPESETTER	Default device
GROFF_FONT_PATH	List of directories in which to search for the devname directory
PATH	Search path for commands executed by groff
GROFF_TMPDIR	Directory in which temporary files will be created

TABLE 5-5.   *A Sampling of Environment Variables Used by groff*

ward off any complaints that may arise out of a possible malfunction due to your modifications.

If, after reading the restrictions in the utility's documentation, you still have questions about how you can and cannot use groff, contact the Free Software Foundation. They can be reached at this address:

Free Software Foundation
675 Massachusetts Ave.
Cambridge, MA 02139

Known Problems

Of course, nothing is perfect, including groff. There could be a few of those little creatures crawling around in the code that just want to spoil all your fun. If you're experiencing the presence of these guys, don't rush off and send in a bug report. At least not right away. Here are a few tips that can help you.

First, reread the documentation, especially the installation instructions to be sure that you haven't overlooked a step. You'll also find a listing in the documentation of some common bugs. Next, read netnews. You can read the latest news about groff along with problems other groff users have had with the utility. You might also find a few fixes listed.

If, after all your research you still have a problem, it's time to send in your own bug report. The utility's documentation contains a standard form that you need to complete. If you are experiencing more than one problem, you'll have to submit a separate form for each bug. Send these reports to *bug-groff@prep.ai.mit.edu* or to *jjc@jclark.com.*

Up and Running

You can execute groff by typing **groff** at the prompt and specifying on the command line the name of the file you want to format. You can read about how to format your file in the utility's documentation. Our brief review of groff is not intended to replace the step-by-step instructions that you'll find in the man pages that come with the utility.

Some of the features of the utility can be controlled by specifying one or more command-line options. Table 5-6 contains a sampling of these options, but the complete list is contained in the utility's man pages. Here's a hint for using options. Each option that contains an argument must be preceded by a hyphen. However, you can group options that don't require an argument behind a single hyphen.

OPTION	DESCRIPTION
-h	Prints a help message
-e	Preprocesses with geqn
-t	Preprocesses with gtbl
-p	Preprocesses with gpic
-s	Preprocesses with gsoelim
-R	Preprocesses with grefer
-v	Makes programs run by groff print out their version number
-V	Prints the pipeline on stdout instead of executing it
-z	Suppresses output from gtroff
-Z	Doesn't post-process the output of gtroff
-Parg	Passes arg to the post-processor
-l	Sends the output to a printer
-Larg	Passes arg to the spooler
-Tdev	Prepares output for device dev
-X	Previews with gxditview instead of using the usual post-processor
-N	Doesn't allow newlines with eqn delimiters

TABLE 5-6.   *A Sampling of groff Options*

So you've read about how groff is going to make a world of difference in your next report. We told you how straightforward it is to install on your system. You even learned that you are practically free to do with it whatever you want, without having to acquire prior permission or pay a royalty. What's next? Connect to the Internet and get your own copy of groff right now.

CHAPTER 6

Game Software

Are you ready for some football? We hope you're not because we can't offer you football software. However, we can provide you with some of the best game software that we could find on the Internet. These games are just waiting for you to copy them over to your system.

We begin with an extremely challenging game of chess. This is gnuchess, which is able to play like a beginner or like a pro, or at every level of expertise in between. The opponent that every chess player dreams of, gnuchess can perform at the same degree of skills you possess and is ready to play at a moment's notice. In fact, gnuchess has a special feature for the serious chess player. This is the capability of setting up the chessboard to depict a particular game that you want to study. Something for everyone!

Next we explore two very popular adventure games, moria and nethack. In both games, you find yourself exploring dungeons. We must warn you that these are not arcade games where the only challenge is to see who can press computer keys the fastest. There's a lot of thinking that goes into playing moria and nethack. For example, you have to decide what equipment you'll need for your journey. Bring the wrong equipment and there's no telling what you'll do once you arrive miles below the earth. You can read more about strategies in our review; however, we must warn you that both adventure games are addictive and can take hours—even days—to complete a single journey.

We'll finish this chapter with a look at two different types of software. The first is called xroach, which is really a novelty rather than a game. Starting xroach is like opening a box of roaches in daylight. You know how they scamper and hide under the nearest object that they can find. In this case, they hide beneath any X Window that is opened on your screen. Move the window and they'll find another window to hide under. Talk about a buggy program ...

The last game we'll review is called xtetris. The name should sound familiar. It is the public domain version of one of the best arcade games ever designed. As each block falls from the top of your screen, you must maneuver the block so that it fills out a row of blocks that are already on the game board. You'll find this both a challenge and an addiction. You'll even be seeing xtetris blocks falling in your dreams. The box that follows lists the programs presented in the chapter.

gnuchess: A Chess Game
moria: An Adventure Game
nethack: An Adventure Game
xroach: Novelty Software
xtetris: A Block-Dropping Game

gnuchess: A Chess Game

Don't expect Battle Chess! You won't see a knight lock swords with a pawn. But you will experience a challenging game of chess when you run gnuchess. Stuart Cracraft and a whole host of other contributors (all them are listed in the utility's documentation) have volunteered their time to create a game that provides a high resolution display and executes numerous strategies that will give most chess enthusiasts a good workout.

When gnuchess started out, it wasn't considered as a competitive game. Cracraft categorizes the older version as a class D in the utility's documentation.

But those were the old days; today's version is of master strength. Now it can beat the Fidelity Mach 3 (USCF 2265) in a blink of an eye when gnuchess is running on a Sparc-1.

How did Cracraft and his colleagues achieve such a goal? They used a hybrid of the Shannon Type-A and Type-B methods. The game conducts a full-width search to a fixed depth. Once this level is reached, the game starts a quiescence search for many more ply. This technique helps it find positions which can be evaluated safely. You can read the details of this technique in the utility's documentation.

You'll notice that special care has been given to strategy. For example, gnuchess will sacrifice pieces in order to win the game. This is possible since Cracraft and the other developers have given gnuchess the logic of easier-end games. And to keep you on your toes, they constructed the game to think of moves during your turn!

Installation

You'll find gnuchess at various locations on the Internet. Here's just one of them: */pub/gnu* on the *labrea.stanford.edu* host. Create the appropriate directories on your system, then copy the gnuchess files to those directories. You may have to modify the makefile that is supplied with the utility. In most cases, you only need to make sure that the LIBDIR and BINDIR make variables contain the right values for your system. Then type **make install**. Next, run the make utility in the src directory to create all the necessary binary files for gnuchess.

If you experience any problems, read about gnuchess on netnews in the *gnu.chess* and *nrec.games.chess* groups. You might be able to pick up a few tips that will help you with the installation. If there isn't a posting that will help you, post your problem. Keep in mind that you're going to receive volunteer support. No one is guaranteeing that your problem will be resolved.

And if all else fails, you may want to contact Cracraft directly. He can be reached several ways. His email address is *cracraft@wheaties.ai.mit.edu* or write him at this address:

Stuart Cracraft
P.O. Box 2841
Laguna Hills, CA 92654-2841

Another away to contact Cracraft is through the Free Software Foundation, Inc., which licenses the utility. They can be reached at this address:

Free Software Foundation, Inc.
675 Massachusetts Ave.
Cambridge, MA 02139

Restrictions

Available free of charge, gnuchess is distributed by the Free Software Foundation, Inc., and is covered by their licensing agreement. You have the right to distribute and modify the utility without having to pay the authors or the Free Software Foundation, Inc., a royalty or fee. The only catch is that you can't charge anyone for this utility nor prevent anyone else from using the utility.

No one guarantees that the utility will work on your system. The utility is distributed "as is" without any warranty. There is no obligation on the part of the author or the Free Software Foundation, Inc., to support this product. This means that you must rely on the informal network of gnuchess users to lend you a hand if you get into trouble.

The game's documentation contains a complete listing of these requirements and other restrictions that might apply to the utility.

Up and Running

Just type **gnuchess** and press the ENTER key to find yourself confronted with a master chess opponent. You can have gnuchess challenge you to a game or you can see how it will do against a real chess master—itself!

The chess pieces are displayed on a traditional board where each square is identified as an alphanumeric coordinate. It also understands notation like "nf3" which means "knight to F-3". The game actually offers several graphics versions of the game board. Table 6-1 contains alternate ways of starting the game. Each will provide a different display of the game board.

Although you'll find gnuchess a real tough competitor, you do have some control over how the utility plays the game. For example, you can specify the amount of time that the game has to make a move. You do this by entering the time factor as a command-line argument.

Let's say that you want a move to be made at least every 15 seconds. Start the game by entering **gnuchess** (or one of the alternate commands) with the number **15** as the argument. You can also specify time in minutes and seconds by using the

COMMAND	DESCRIPTION
gnuchess	Simple curses-based version
gnuchessn	Fancy version using curses and inverse video
gnuchessr	ASCII-based version
gnuchessc	chesstool compatible version
gnuchessx	xboard compatible version

TABLE 6-1. *Ways of Starting the gnuchess Utility*

colon as a separator. For example, 2:30 will cause the game to make a move a minimum of every two and a half minutes.

If you're a tournament chess player, you know that a simple time setting isn't sufficient. You usually establish a time parameter for a specific number of moves. Well, gnuchess isn't lacking in this feature. By entering two arguments on the command line, you can establish the tournament time limits. Here's how it works. The first argument specifies the maximum number of moves that are permitted. The second argument sets the time limit for making the moves. The following shows you the command-line arguments for specifying 90 moves in 10 minutes.

```
gnuchess 90 10
```

The game's documentation contains more tips on setting the game clock, including a way to decrease the amount of time for each move as the game progresses. And if you decided not to enter a command-line argument, the game will prompt you to set the level of play.

On the Move

Once you've determined the level of play, you're ready to enter your first move. There are a few ways to enter a move. Probably the easiest way is to use the alphanumeric coordinates of the board. For example, suppose you want to move your queen's knight to queen's bishop 3, you would enter **b1c3**.

Another way to move pieces is by using the first letter in the name of the piece (p,b,r,q,k), except for "knight," which is moved by entering **n**. Here's the command that you would enter for the same move of the queen's knight: **nc3**. The game's documentation contains other ways of moving pieces on the board especially when you want to castle and make other special moves.

And for the true chess buff, the gnuchess game allows you to set up the board. This means that you can recreate an interesting situation and see how the gnuchess game reacts. First, you'll need to have a board layout in mind. Next, use the setup command to create the initial board position. Enter the one character name for the piece that you want to position on the board. This is followed by the coordinate of the location of the piece on the board. Remember to use uppercase, one-character names to refer to black pieces and lowercase, one-character names for white pieces.

When you have completed the layout, enter the **save** command. You'll be prompted for a file name. You can use the **get** command to restart the game.

moria: A Dungeon Game

It's dark and dreary and cold. You enter the dungeon with trepidation. Who's in there? No one. And yet you're sure you're wrong...there's someone in the dungeon just waiting for you—and it isn't with a warm greeting. But you're prepared. At least you think you have the proper equipment to handle anything. Only time will tell.

No, this isn't a poorly written sci-fi novel. Instead, it's an adventure game that's addictive. The game is called moria and has the same flavor as the famous Dungeons & Dragons games. If you've never played Dungeons & Dragons, you're in for a treat.

The adventure game moria requires you to think as if you were in a fathomless dungeon yourself searching for a hidden treasure. You begin by choosing your character, then outfitting him or her with equipment that you think will be needed to wander around the dungeon. Oh, we should mention that you have to purchase the equipment from the moria game store. (Don't worry—this isn't a real store but only part of the game.)

Now you're ready to enter the dungeon. There are monsters just waiting to attack you and fellow adventurers who might try to eliminate the competition for the treasure. You're the competition! But your objective isn't just to find the treasure—it's to kill the Balrog who resides 2,500 feet underground on the 50th level of the dungeon. That's 2,500 feet of dead silence with terror stalking around every corner.

Sound exciting? You bet it is—and plenty of intelligent fun. Jim Wilson of the University of California at Berkeley wrote this version of moria. Robert Koeneke, Jimmey Todd, and Gary McAdoo wrote the original version at the University of Oklahoma years ago. You can read all about the history of moria in moria's documentation.

But enough about history. It's time for you to prepare yourself to enter the dungeon, find the treasure, and eliminate Balrog. A word of caution! Many before you have entered and none have reach Balrog—and lived to tell about it.

Installation

One of the places where you'll find the moria files is in the */pub/games* directory on *qiclab.scn.rain.com*. Before copying the files to your system, create a directory called source, then copy the moria files to that directory. You'll have to edit the *config.h* file that comes with moria to uncomment the appropriate lines for your system. (The moria documentation explains this step in more detail.) The game comes with a prepared makefile—just type **make** and the binary files of moria will be created for you.

TIP

You can control the hours during which moria can be played by editing the files/hours file. This is especially useful if you intend to install the game in the work environment. The game has a built-in scoreboard; however, moria needs to be installed setuid for the scoreboard to work. The documentation shows you how to do this.

Table 6-2 lists a sampling of the environments where moria has been compiled successfully. The documentation contains a complete list of these systems.

Restrictions

There are a few restrictions for using moria but nothing that won't prevent you from having fun with this never-ending adventure game. Koeneke and Wilson hold the copyright to moria, but this doesn't mean that you have to pay any money. The authors give you permission to freely copy and modify moria without receiving prior permission.

However, if you intend to sell or market moria in any form, stop! You'll need written permission from Koeneke and Wilson. Furthermore, they still retain the copyright to moria, even if you modify the game.

You can read the fine print about these restrictions in moria's documentation. You'll also notice that Koeneke and Wilson have no liability or responsibility if the game causes damages. You can reach Wilson at *wilson@ernie.berkeley.edu*. The documentation contains several land addresses in case you can't connect with him on the Internet.

Known Problems

The game isn't without a few problems, but these are nothing that will stop you from searching the dungeons. For example, the CTRL-Z command, which is used to suspend the game, isn't working properly. The movement commands become lost when moria is brought back to the foreground after being suspended. This is important to remember because a suspended game that receives a hang-up signal will die without creating a save file. There are other problems with moria which you can read about in the errors file in the source distribution.

Here's a reminder for fans of Umoria 4.87. Wilson recommends reading the file *doc/features.new* before installing the upgraded version on your system. Wilson doesn't want you to send him any bug reports until after you read this file. For more information about problems with moria, connect to either *games.moria* or *comp.sources.games* groups on netnews.

UNIX 4.2 BSD	IBM-PC (MSC 5.0, Turbo C 2.0)	Amiga
UNIX 4.3 BSD	Mac	VMS
UNIX SYS V	Atari ST	

TABLE 6-2. *A Sampling of Environments Where moria Has been Compiled*

Up and Running

You start your adventure by typing **moria** at the prompt. moria is a single player game so you'll be playing against your system. The first step is to select your character. No, this isn't like a game of Chutes And Ladders, the game pieces of which are colored pieces of plastic. We said this is a thinking person's game.

There is a host of characters available to you. Each one has a specific statistical profile and ability. A sampling of these is contained in Table 6-3 and Table 6-4. Next, you'll determine your character's race and class. (Don't think of race and class in earthly terms; they are more like Star Trek characters.) Choose your characters carefully because their characteristics will determine how well you succeed in the game.

The adventure begins in town where your character visits shops and barters for supplies, weapons, armor, and magical devices. Only the proper combination of these items will allow your character to successfully confront all that lurks in the dark caverns of the dungeon.

Seems too complicated? So did programming a computer until you invested time and patience to learn the ropes. The same is true with moria. The more you read rules in the documentation and practice playing the game, the more enjoyment you'll receive.

Your games are automatically saved and restored from a file called *moria.save*. You'll find this file in your home directory. There are two other ways to specify the game file. Since moria will read the environment variable MORIA_SAV, you can assign the name of the game file as the value of this variable. Another way is to specify the name of the file on the command line.

The command line can also be used to control how the game is played. Table 6-5 contains a sampling of command-line options, but the documentation contains a complete listing of options and their use.

QUALITY	DESCRIPTION
Strength	Important in fighting with weapons and in hand-to-hand combat
Intelligence	Increases a mage's chances of learning spells
Wisdom	Increases the chances of receiving new spells from a priest
Dexterity	May allow a character to deliver multiple blows at a time
Constitution	Character's ability to resist damage to his body
Charisma	Receives better prices from store owners

TABLE 6-3. *A Sampling of Character Statistics*

ABILITY	DESCRIPTION
Fighting	The ability to hit and do damage with weapons or fists
Throwing/Bows	The use of ranged missile weapons and throwing objects
Saving Throw	The ability of a character to resist the effects of a spell
Stealth	The ability to move silently about
Disarming	The ability to remove traps safely
Using Magical Devices	Using a wand or staff requires experience and knowledge
Perception	The ability to notice something without actively seeking it out
Searching	Actively look for secret doors, floor traps, and traps on chests
Infravision	The ability to see heat sources

TABLE 6-4.   *A Sampling of a Character's Ability*

Once you begin the game, you can easily recall the list of commands to the screen by typing a question mark (?). There are numerous commands to move your character throughout the dungeon and even to battle the monsters. We've supplied you with a very brief sample of commands in Table 6-6. This is just enough to whet your appetite for more.

Now the moment of truth has arrived. It's time to forget about your earthly ways and don the mantle of your character. The dungeon is open. The treasures and Balrog are waiting for you. It's time to begin moria.

OPTION	DESCRIPTION
-n	Creates a new game
-r	Moves the same way you do in the game, rogue
-s	Prints all of the scores in the score file and exits
-S	Prints only those scores belonging to you then exits
-w	Starts up in wizard mode, intended for debugging the game

TABLE 6-5.   *A Sampling of Command-line Options*

COMMAND	DESCRIPTION	COMMAND	DESCRIPTION
a	Aims and fires a wand	@ B~	Bashes (object/creature)
b	Browses a book	C	Changes name
c ~	Closes a door	@ D~	Disarms a trap/chest
d	Drops an item	E	Eats some food
e	Equipment list	F	Fills lamp with oil
f	Fires/Throws an item	G	Gains new magic spells
i	Inventory list	L	Locates with map
@ j ~	Jams a door with a spike	M	Map shown reduced size
l ~	Looks in a given direction	@ R	Rests for a period
m	casts a magic spell	S	Search mode
@ o ~	Opens a door/chest	@ T~	Tunnels in a direction

TABLE 6-6. *A Sampling of moria Commands*

nethack: an Adventure Game

You may claim that you're an adventurer. But you're not until you've proved your worthiness to the masters of your local adventurer's guild. And the test is to enter the bowels of the dungeon to recover the Amulet of Yendor, an artifact that will bring you honor and full guild membership—and immortality granted by the gods.

The dungeon where the Amulet of Yendor lies is called the Mazes of Menace. And to reach the dungeon's entrance you must gather all the gear and food you'll need for your journey, then embark on a several day trip to the ancient ruins. Camp outside the entrance of the Mazes of Menace for an evening. Now the adventure—and danger—begins.

Sound exciting? It is and is a formidable challenge for anyone who thinks of himself as a master of adventure games. A word of warning! Don't start playing nethack an hour before you plan to go to bed. You'll find yourself staying up all night searching the Mazes of Menace.

The game has a long history with the original version developed years ago by Jay Fenlason with help from Kenny Woodland, Mike Thome, and Jon Payne. They modeled nethack after the Berkeley UNIX game called rogue. Since the first generation of nethack, there have been countless other developers such as Andries Brouwer, who rewrote the original nethack game.

You'll find nethack a very user-friendly game to play. Unlike earlier adventure games, nethack doesn't require you to use pseudo-English sentences to interact with the game. All nethack commands are one or two keystrokes. In addition, nethack is screen oriented. This means that the results of your command are displayed graphically on the screen.

The time has arrived. The time to show your guild master that you can prove your capability of taking your rightful place in the guild. It's time to enter the Mazes of Menace.

Installation

After creating a directory called nethack on your system, one of the places where you can copy the nethack files from is */pub/gnu* on *qiclab.scn.rain.com*. The nethack documentation contains all the instructions that you'll need to install nethack on your system.

Before you attempt to build the binaries, you must run the makedefs program. This will create the configuration files for the nethack game. Once makedefs has been run, you're ready to compile the nethack source files. You'll find that the distribution contains several makefiles. Each one is system dependent. Use the makefile that is designed for your system.

The game has been successfully compiled to run on various systems, so you shouldn't expect to have any difficulty getting it to run on your system. A complete listing of these systems is available in the nethack documentation.

However, if you can't get nethack to work, connect to netnews and read the *rec.games.hack* group. Post your problem if you can't find a solution that has already been posted. And you may want to report your problem to *nethack-bugs@linc.cis.upenn.edu*.

Restrictions

The nethack game comes with the standard set of Free Software Foundation restrictions. For example, you can use it and copy it freely and distribute copies to your friends without receiving prior permission from the authors. In fact, the only major restriction is that you can't prohibit anyone else from copying and distributing nethack.

In the nethack documentation, where you can read all the fine print about these restrictions, the authors even give you the right to modify the game. However, you must let everyone who uses the modified game know that the version isn't recognized as an official distribution by the authors.

Another restriction is that you can't charge anyone for the game. However, you can charge a distribution fee for transferring the nethack files and you can offer warranty protection for a fee. (The game is made available without a warranty.)

Up and Running

Just type **nethack** at the prompt and you're ready to enter the world of adventure. Your objective is to locate the Amulet of Yendor which is housed deep in the dungeon below the 20th level. Well, it's a little more involved than that. You must also take it to the surface and this isn't easy. Many have tried and most have died trying. The game ends when you quit, escape the dungeon alive—or when your die.

While the main objective is to return with the Amulet of Yendor, the secondary objective is to achieve a high score so your name can be included on the list of top scores. Scoring points is a little tricky. Most of the points are given to you for taking amounts of gold from the dungeon and bringing them to the surface. You're awarded points on the basis of the amount of gold that you acquire, multiplied by your real experience level playing the game. The nethack documentation explains this formula in greater detail.

You can control some of the behavior of nethack by using command-line options. Table 6-7 contains a sampling of these options. Review the documentation for a more complete list of options and tips on how to use them.

The nethack game uses a graphic interface as the game board. This is a great improvement over those old adventure games that describe the scene in text rather than show you a picture of the situation you're in. The nethack screen is divided into several sections. At the bottom of the screen are two lines that describe your current status. These lines tend to be a little cryptic and frequently extend beyond the width of your screen. Table 6-8 shows you a sampling of the items that you'll find in this section of the screen. You can read the documentation for a detailed explanation.

Nearly everything that you need to know to play nethack can be displayed graphically. Those things that can't are described in messages that appear at the top of the screen.

OPTION	DESCRIPTION
-s	Prints the list of your scores
-n	Suppresses printing of any news from the game
-D	Starts the game in debugging mode
-X	Starts the game in a non-scoring discovery mode
-d	Supplies a directory that is to serve as the playground
-u	Supplies the answer to the question, "Who are you?"

TABLE 6-7.   *A Sampling of Command-line Options*

TIP
If you see the word More on the top line, it means that there is
another message to be displayed besides the message already on the
screen. Press the SPACEBAR to see the next message.

The remainder of the screen is a map showing the layout of the current level of
the dungeon. You'll notice that the map contains strange symbols. These represent
various items. Table 6-9 contains a sampling of the symbol definitions. You'll also
find a complete listing of these symbols in the nethack documentation. Here's a
hint that will help you quickly find the meaning of a symbol on the map. Type a
forward slash (/) and nethack will display a list of map symbols on the screen.

Now that you understand the game board, we'll take a brief look at how you
begin your adventure. All you need to do is to respond to prompts by entering the
proper command. Table 6-10 contains a sample list of commands. You can read
the documentation for the complete listing of commands or enter a question

ITEM	DESCRIPTION
Rank	Your character's name and professional ranking
Strength	A measure of your character's strength
Dexterity	Affects your chances to hit in combat
Constitution	Affects your ability to withstand injury
Intelligence	Affects your ability to cast spells
Wisdom	Affects your magical energy
Charisma	Affects how certain creatures react toward you
Alignment	Influences how monsters react toward you
Dungeon Level	How deep you have gone into the dungeon
Gold	The number of gold pieces you have
Hit Points	Indicates how much damage you can take before you die
Power	How much mystic energy is available for spell casting
Armor Class	How effectively your armor stops blows from unfriendly creatures
Experience	Your current experience level and experience points
Time	The number of turns elapsed
Hunger status	Your current hunger status

TABLE 6-8. *A Sampling of Status Items that Are Displayed on the Screen*

mark (**?**) in response to the prompt—nethack will then display a list of available commands.

Let's see how this is done. As you explore the dungeon, you'll find yourself having to perform various tasks that require you to use tools you've taken along on your trip. All the belongings that you have on your person including the tools are called your *inventory*. You assemble your inventory before you venture into the dungeon.

For example, you might have given nethack a command to turn over a rock. nethack might respond with a question: "What do you want to use?" You'll then be prompted to enter **a-zA-Z**. These letters refer to objects that you are carrying in inventory. If you type a question mark (**?**), a complete list of your inventory is displayed on the screen, along with a command letter for each item. It is the command letter that you enter when prompted with the question, "What do you want to use?"

If you pick the wrong object, you won't be able to complete the task. For example, selecting a flashlight to move a rock just won't work. You can always change your mind and return the item back to inventory by pressing the ESC key.

The dungeon is a scary place where you'll find rooms and corridors that are sometimes lit and sometimes not. You'll be able to see lit areas since they are

SYMBOL	DESCRIPTION	SYMBOL	DESCRIPTION
- and |	The walls of a room or an open door	[	A suit or piece of armor
.	The floor of a room or a doorless doorway	%	A piece of food (not necessarily healthy)
#	A corridor, or possibly a kitchen sink or drawbridge	?	A scroll
<	A way to the previous level	/	A wand
>	A way to the next level	=	A ring
+	A closed door or a spell book containing a spell you can learn	!	A potion
@	A human (you, usually)	(	A useful item such as a key
$	A pile of gold	"	An amulet or a spider web
^	A trap (once you detect it)	*	A gem or rock
)	A weapon		

TABLE 6-9. *A Sampling of Map Symbols*

displayed on the screen. But you'll be staring at a darkened screen if you enter an unlit area of the dungeon.

Not all of the corridors are on the map. Some are hidden and you must search for them using the **search** (s) command. It's a strange place down there. Doorways connect rooms with corridors. Some rooms have no doors while others have locked doors. You can try the **open** (O) and **close** (C) commands on the doors. But don't be surprised if you have to pick the lock with the **apply** (A) command or just break down the door with a strong kick using the **kick** (CTRL-D) command.

 TIP
The door can be your lifesaver if you're attacked by a monster. Most monsters can't open doors. The only exception to this is a ghost—it can breeze through any door that is shut in its face.

Don't become complacent in the dungeon. Always be on your guard! The map can't always be trusted. You can easily make a wrong turn and get snared by a trap. You can find yourself falling into a darkened pit. If you do, you'll miss a few turns, but be sure to remember the location of the trap. It might come in handy if you're being chased by a monster. Lead the monster to the trap, then quickly move away and let it fall prey to the pit.

Monsters are everywhere in the dungeon. Some you can see on the screen while others come upon you out of the darkness. Here's a hint. Be sure to take a

COMMAND	DESCRIPTION	COMMAND	DESCRIPTION
?	Help menu	a	Uses a tool
/	Tells what a symbol represents	A	Removes all armor
&	Tells what a command does	c	Closes a door
<	Goes up a staircase to the previous level	CTRL-C	Panic button—quits the game
>	Goes down a staircase to the next level	d	Drops something
.	Rests; does nothing for one turn	CTRL-D	Kicks something

TABLE 6-10. *A Sample List of Commands for nethack*

few magic items. These can help you locate a hidden monster before the monster finds you.

CAUTION
Not all monsters will attack you. Many will leave you alone as long as you don't bother them, but once provoked, all monsters can be deadly.

The object of nethack is to pickup the Amulet of Yendor and pieces of gold. Nearly any item that you see can be picked up by walking over the object, assuming that the automatic pickup option is turned on. You may want to turn off this feature and manually pick up items if you are carrying too many. The nethack documentation shows you how to do this.

Now that we've piqued your interest, don't you think it's time for you to test your skills and play nethack? The dungeon is waiting for you.

The xroach Utility: Novelty Software

Remember when you walked into a dark basement in an old house? You got that creepy feeling that with each step you knew you weren't alone. You turned on the lights and there they were—hundreds of little creepy crawlers scrambling for cover in all directions.

Well, these same bugs—or a computer representation thereof—are in your system when you install xroach. Now, don't become excited. These aren't the bugs you find in your programs and they have no connection to viruses. They are computer roaches created by J.T. Anderson, the author of xroach, that scamper just like their relatives who visit dark, damp basements, except they do all their running on your screen.

You really have to see it to believe it. After you launch xroach, images of roaches appear to run from the exposed areas of your screen and hide beneath your windows. Don't be surprised if you forget that xroach is running when you move an open window. Watch out! You'll see all of the roaches who had made their home beneath the window run in all directions to find a safe haven under another window.

You can stir a little excitement in the office by starting xroach, then let someone borrow your system. Just don't be too close when he moves a window and is greeted by your little friends.

Installation

Create an xroach directory on your system, then copy the xroach files from */pub/Linux/X11/games* on *sunsite.unc.edu* or from one of the other locations on Internet. Installation is rather straightforward. You can find step-by-step instructions in the xroach utility's documentation. You shouldn't experience too much trouble installing the xroach utility. If you do, you can drop J.T. Anderson an email note at *jta@locus.com* and report the bug. You can read about the xroach utility by reading the *comp.sources.x* netnews group.

Restrictions

The xroach utility is protected under a 1991 copyright held by Anderson. But don't be too concerned. Anderson has given permission to use, modify, and distribute xroach royalty free. You can read all the fine print about the restrictions in the xroach utility's documentation.

Up and Running

You start xroach by simply typing **xroach**. These creepy crawlers will run around your screen until they find a window to hide under. The utility can be started with one of three options. Each of these options, listed in Table 6-11, gives you control over the activities of your family of roaches.

OPTION	DESCRIPTION
-display display_name	Drops the roaches on the given display
-rc roach_color	Uses the given string as the color for the bugs. The default is black
-speed roach_speed	Uses the given speed for the insects instead of the default 20.0
-roaches num_roaches	This is the number of the little critters. Default is 10
-squish	Enables roach squishing. Point and shoot with any mouse button
-rgc roach_gut_color	Sets color of the guts that spill out of squished roaches

TABLE 6-11. *Command-line Options for xroach*

The xroach utility isn't really a game; however, if you set the right option you can spend your days stamping out those little guys with your mouse. Anderson decided to add a little realism—computer style that is. When you stamp on one of the creatures, its guts will splatter all over your screen.

Just thinking of that can make you queasy. Then again, the roach probably isn't enjoying it either. And if that isn't enough gore for you, how about setting the color of the guts! Yes, Anderson has even given you control over the color of the guts that spill out of the roach when the little guy is squished. Anderson recommends yellow-green.

xtetris: A Block-Dropping Game

Bet you can't walk away from playing this game. Try it once and you're addicted. You'll keep playing and playing in an attempt to beat the highest score. In fact, it has been known that the game pieces even enter your dreams. Sounds strange? Maybe, but let it be known that you've been warned.

The game that we're talking about is xtetris. Does the name have a familiar ring? It should—xtetris is the public domain version of the very popular game, tetris, that requires quick reflexes and a sharp eye to fit falling blocks into the correct position on the game board. As the block moves down your screen, you use direction keys on the keyboard to rotate the block into a snug fit among the blocks that have fallen to the bottom of your screen. Once you've competed a row of blocks, the row disappears, lowering the blocks above it one level.

Sound difficult? Probably not, but wait until you try it. Dan Greening, Didier Tallot, Phill Everson, and Martyn Shortley are the authors of xtetris. They carefully designed the game so that it seems easy to play at first but gradually becomes more difficult—without you realizing it! Unless you react fast, you'll become victim to the squeeze play.

The blocks fall slowly at first along the full length of the screen. As you fail to complete rows of blocks, the level of blocks increases, shortening the length of the fall of the new blocks. This reduces the time you have to place the next block into position. If you don't move quickly, there won't be any room for new blocks to fall—you lose the game!

Are you ready to meet the challenge? Remember, play your first game and you'll find it nearly impossible to stop playing.

Installation

You'll find xtetris files located at /archievs/mirror1/X11R5/contrib on cs.columbia.edu. (There are other locations where you can find xtetris.) Create an xtetris directory on your system, then copy the xtetris files. The xtetris documentation contains all the instructions that you'll need to create the binaries for the game. We'll just provide you with a few tips that will get you started in the right direction.

There are two key points that you'll need to remember. First, you must have X11 release 5 installed on your system, otherwise forget about installing xtetris. Next, you should make sure that the xmkmf file is on your path. The authors hint that you might find this file at */usr/bin/X11/xmkmf* or */usr/X11R5/bin/xmkmf*.

Although the xtetris files contain an Imakefile, take a few moments to review the switch settings in this file. You'll probably have to reset a few switches so that the Imakefile conforms to the setup of your system. The xtetris document provide hints on resetting switches.

Now, you're ready to begin building your personal copy of the xtetris game. Run the xmkmf script first, then type **make depend**. Once the make utility has settled down, run make install. The authors suggest that you may have to log in as root before running install.

After the install has finished running, xtetris is ready for your first game. If you have difficulties getting xtetris to run properly, read the known bugs section of the documentation. Another place to look for known problems is the *comp.sources.x* group on netnews. You might even want to post your own problem. And as a last resort, drop an email about your problem to *xtetris@cs.ucla.edu*.

Restrictions

There is practically no restriction on your use of the xtetris game. Greening, Tallot, Everson, and Shortley still hold the copyright to the game. However, they give you permission to use, copy, modify, and distribute the game for any purpose without a fee. The only catch is that you'll need to provide the proper copyright notice and permission notice on all copies of the game. You can read the fine print about this restriction in the xtetris documentation.

And here is another catch. You cannot use the names of the authors in any advertising or publicity about the game without their permission. Keep in mind that you're on your own when you choose to build and run the game on your system. No one is guaranteeing that the game will work. Likewise, no one can be held liable if during the creation of the game your system should be trashed.

Known Problems

Here's a very common problem that you can avoid by setting an environment variable. If, after installing the game in your local account, the game crashes the first time that you try to run it, you'll see an error message such as "Widget has zero height" displayed on the screen. This an indication that the application defaults files have not been installed.

Don't panic. Here's the fix. Set the following environment variable if you're in the C Shell: **setenv XUSERFILESEARCHPATH=./%N%C.ad:./%N.ad**. For Bourne

Shell, bash Shell, and K Shell, enter the statements shown below. Once these variables are set, try running xtetris from its build directory.

```
XUSERFILESEARCHPATH=./%N%C.ad:./%N.ad

export XUSERFILESEARCHPATH
```

Up and Running

Begin xtetris by typing **xtetris** at the prompt. You can control some of the behavior of the game by passing a command-line option. (A sampling of these options are shown in Table 6-12.) You'll find a complete list and tips on how to use them in the xtetris documentation.

The object of xtetris is to move a falling block so that it lands on the stack of existing blocks in such as way as to complete a row of blocks. As a row is filled, the row is automatically removed from the screen. This causes the stack of blocks above the row to drop down, leaving more room for the next block to fall. As the game progresses, the blocks begin to fall faster, giving you less time to find the proper spot on the stack for the block. The game is over when the stack of blocks reaches the top of the screen, thereby preventing another block from falling.

Each time you complete a row, you receive points that register on the screen's scoreboard. After the game is completed, xtetris determines if you should be inducted into the xtetris hall of fame. The hall of fame is actually the names and the scores of the players who have the ten best scores on your installation of xtetris.

OPTION	DESCRIPTION
-boxsize	Specifies the width of the square blocks that compose the falling objects
-noscore	Runs xtetris without recording your score
-score	Runs xtetris using the scorefile
-speed	Sets the game's speed
-color	Uses color display
-bw	Uses black-and-white display

TABLE 6-12. *A Sampling of Command-line Options for xtetris*

As a block falls, you can use the left or right mouse buttons to move the block in the corresponding direction. Pressing the SHIFT key while pressing a mouse button causes the block to rotate. The SHIFT-right mouse button combination sends the block rotating clockwise while the SHIFT-left mouse button moves the block in the reverse direction. And you can score more points if you press the middle mouse button to quickly drop the block into position.

Okay, you may not have use of a mouse. Don't worry, the authors have anticipated your dilemma. You can use the H key to move left, L to move right, J to rotate clockwise, and K to rotate counterclockwise. The SPACEBAR is used to quickly drop the block onto the stack of blocks.

Another way to control the blocks is to use the direction pad that is available on some keyboards. The LEFT ARROW moves the block to the left, the RIGHT ARROW moves the block to the right, the DOWN ARROW rotates the block clockwise, and the UP ARROW rotates the block counterclockwise. The SPACEBAR quickly drops the block.

CHAPTER 7

Communication Utilities

Internet applications allow us to transfer information across the globe at computer speed. In this chapter we'll explore some of the best communications utilities that we were able to locate on the Internet. All of these are yours for the taking and free of charge.

The initial step is to be able to connect your terminal to an Internet host. We found two utilities that are just perfect for the job: pcomm and sliplogin. Both of these are at the top of our list. Just kick start either process and it'll manage all of your communications traffic for you.

Once you're connected to the Internet, you'll find yourself needing to transfer files, and we have a few utilities that will make your life easier: gzip, kermit, and zmodem. First, we'll look at gzip, a nifty little software package that decreases the time it takes to transfer files (the secret lies in the data compression algorithm that it uses). We will also look at kermit and zmodem. Although you can use the FTP service to move files over the Internet, you may also need to transfer files via modem, and this is where these two utilities come into play.

And those files that you transfer should also be professionally maintained. As we all know, there is a danger in working with multiple copies of the same file. So stop worrying. We found a software, called zoo, that manages your files for you. It's well worth a look.

We covered most of the basic communication needs but we wanted to find something special, something that would make you say, "Wow! Guess, what?" We found two such software packages. When we looked at xtv, we said that it must be included in this book. Xtv is a teleconferencing utility that enables more than one person on the Internet to connect to the same process. This means that you can run your demo software on your system and have others from around the world see your creation on their screens. It gets better. Anyone who is part of this teleconference can interact with your software. You have to see it.

And talking about a must have, here is one software package that goes beyond the top of the list. The package is a hypertext browser for the Internet, called mosaic. Well, it's really a lot more than just a browser. It can handle sound, movies, graphic images—a truly multimedia window on the Internet. Don't pass this up! Note that mosaic is not included on the enclosed CD because it can be downloaded free-of-charge only from **ftp**.

The gzip Utility: Data Compression Software
The kermit Utility: File Transfer Software
The pcomm Utility: Teleommunications Software
The zmodem Utility: A File Transfer Utility
The sliplogin Utility: A Network Interface
The xtv Utility: Teleconferencing Software
The zoo Utility: Archival Software
The mosaic Utility: An Internet Hypertext Browser

The gzip Utility: Data Compression Software

Transferring large files over telephone lines is time consuming and expensive, but gzip dramatically reduces the size of the file. A smaller file means a shorter telephone call and reduced expense.

If you never used a data compression utility before then you are in for a treat. The utility gzip consists of two parts. First, it shrinks a file without losing any data, and later, after you transmit the file, you can use it to expand the compressed file back to its original size.

The GNU Project, the authors of gzip, designed the utility to replace the compress utility. The gzip utility uses the improved LZ77 algorithm by default, however, several compression algorithms are available. This means that you can use gzip to uncompressed files that were compressed using the ubiquitous **compress** command and the zip utliity. All this power in one utility and it's yours for the taking.

Installation Is Straightforward

Create a directory and copy the files for gzip in */pub/gnu* on *prep.ai.mit.edu*. The utility comes with a shell script called configure, which determines various system-dependent variables and creates a makefile that you can use to compile the utility's source code. It only takes a couple of minutes for the configure script to run, during which status messages are displayed on the screen.

Once the configure script is finished running, create the binary files by running make. Type **make install**. The gzip utility's documentation explains this in detail.

TIP
If you want to be sure that all the necessary files are available to the make utility, you can run it with the check file, which is supplied with gzip. Just type **make check** and make will do the rest.

Running Is a Snap

You can use one of three programs to compress or uncompress a file: gzip, gunzip, and zcat. Each of them accepts the name of the file to compress or uncompress as an argument. The gzip program compresses a file using the Lempel-Zivoding (LZ77) algorithm to compress the file. The compressed file is automatically given the extension .gz. All ownership and access permissions for the compressed file are the same as for the uncompressed file.

Both gunzip and zcat uncompress files; however, zcat sends the contents of the uncompressed file to stdout, rather than creating a new file.

CAUTION

Do not compress a device file using the gzip command; errors might occur in the compressed version of the file. Another point to keep in mind is that if a file name is too long, gzip automatically truncates the name, but it keeps the original file name in the compressed file. You can read more about this in the documentation files that are supplied with the utility.

Okay, you're probably wondering how much this utility reduces the size of the file. There isn't a straightforward answer, since the compressed size depends on the distribution of common substrings in the original file. Here is a good rule of thumb: a file that contains English text or typical source code can be reduced by about 70%.

TIP

Whenever you need to transmit more than one file to the same address, don't send individual files! Instead, let gzip compress and combine multiple files for you. The following example shows you how to do this. Notice that the append redirect symbol (>>) is used in the argument to the gzip program.

```
gzip -c source1 > foo.gz
gzip -c source2 >> foo.gz
```

After the file is transmitted, gzip automatically separates the files during the uncompressing process. This is illustrated here:

```
gunzip -c foo
```

And here is the best part. Even if one of the files is corrupt, the gzip program will make every attempt to recover the files that have not been corrupted.

You can set various options when you use gzip. Table 7-1 contains a few of these options. You can read more about how these and other options are used by reviewing the man pages that are supplied with gzip.

And When It Doesn't Work...

Yes, you might experience some problems with gzip. For example, on NeXT computers, the gzip program appears to work properly but the compressed files are too large. The gzip utility documentation suggests a few tips to resolve this problem.

You'll also find a list of other known bugs and available solutions. Review this information before reporting your own bugs. But if you still have problems, you can

OPTION	DESCRIPTION
-a	ASCII text mode
-c	Writes output on standard output and keep the original files unchanged
-d	Uncompresses a file
-h	Displays the help screen
-q	Suppresses all warnings
-S .x	Uses suffix .x where x can be any suffix
-t	Checks the integrity of the compressed file
-v	Displays the percentage reduction

TABLE 7-1.   *Options for gzip*

send the bug along with any comments that you might have to Jean-Loup Gailly at *jloup@chorus.fr* or to *bug-gnu-utils@prep.ai.mit.edu.*

The kermit Utility:
File Transfer Software

Now you have your own copy of a very popular file transfer program, called kermit. You won't find Miss Piggy alongside this Kermit, but you *will* be able to transfer files between all types of computers. Frank da Cruz and Christine Gianone are the authors of kermit and are also the authors of *Using C-Kermit,* which is a must-have book if you become a serious user of the kermit utility.

In the early 1970s, da Cruz and Gianone developed kermit at Columbia University to enable different hardware architectures to communicate with each other. This may sound obvious but a problem existed. Each incompatible system (workstations, personal computers, mini-computers, and mainframes) had their own set of rules for data communications. Then came kermit—the first utility that accommodated these differences.

Does this sound like the perfect solution? Almost. The kermit utility still should be in your collection of data communications utilities, but be aware of its limitations. Although kermit provides you with versatile data communications, it is generally regarded as a low throughput utility. But try kermit and find out for yourself. You may be very happy with its performance.

Getting kermit Ready to Run

You'll find the kermit files in the */kermit* directory on *src.honeywell.com*. Copy these files into an empty directory on your computer. The kermit utility comes with a makefile that is ready to run. Just use the make utility to create the binary version of kermit. For historical reasons, the binary that gets built is called "wermit," which you rename to "kermit."

The kermit utility should run problem free; however, you might not be so lucky. Unfortunately, one of kermit's downfalls is that very little documentation is provided with the utility. You won't find volumes of man pages or tips on installation.

So what do you do? Well, this is a case where the software is free but the documentation isn't. You'll have to purchase a copy of da Cruz and Gianone's book *Using C-Kermit*. In 514 pages, da Cruz and Gianone tell you everything you ever wanted to know about kermit. You can contact Digital Press in Burlington, MA, for a copy or call them directly at 1-800-344-4825. The book is also available at Columbia University's Academic Information Systems in New York City.

If you still have problems using kermit after reading the book, you may want to contact da Cruz and Gianone via email at *kermit@columbia.edu*, or at the following address:

Watson Laboratory
Columbia University Academic Information Systems
612 West 115 Street
New York, NY 10025

The Fine Print...

Columbia University holds the copyright to kermit. Although you can freely use it, there are a few restrictions that are imposed by Columbia University. One of the key restrictions is that you can't distribute the kermit utility for profit—even if you have incorporated kermit within your own com- mercial application.

Generally, you can modify and distribute kermit freely as long as you are not charging others to use the product. But before you embark on such an activity, read the restriction notice that is contained in the kermit files. You may also want to contact Columbia University and get their permission before combining kermit with your application.

Kick Starting kermit

Type **kermit** to open kermit in the command mode. Before beginning your first session, you'll need to set a few parameters: the line, speed, modem, file type, and the telephone number of the remote computer.

The line is typically set to */dev/tty00* or whatever communications line is appropriate for your computer. Likewise, the speed is set at 9600 baud or whatever is the maximum transmission speed for the other computer. Hayes is a frequent setting for the modem parameter, and the file type setting is either text or binary, depending on the kind of file that your are transferring.

After kermit connects to the remote computer, issue the connect command to connect your keyboard to the communications line. Your first session is underway. Although both computers are connected, you must run kermit on the remote computer. To do this, log into the remote computer, then type **kermit** without entering any parameters.

Next you'll need to have the remote computer enter the server mode by typing **server**, then pressing CTRL-\ to return to the kermit that is running on your computer. You are now ready to send a file by typing **send**, followed by the file name. Once the file is transferred, the prompt returns to the screen. Type **finish** to tell the remote kermit to end the server mode. Connect to the remote kermit by typing **connect**, then type **quit** to exit the remote kermit utility. Log off the remote computer, then press CTRL-\ and type **quit** to exit your copy of kermit.

The pcomm Utility: Telecommunications Software

Data communication was never this easy—and free! Well, the software is free. You'll still have to pay for the telephone call. The software that we're talking about is pcomm, which converts your system and modem into a powerful tool that can reach around the world.

The pcomm utility is truly a great find. It is designed to operate similarly to Datastorm Technologies, Inc.'s DOS ProComm software. The pcomm utility walks you through the complete communication cycle from dialing the telephone through transferring files. All you need to do is to respond to menus.

This is an all-in-one utility that combines basic communication features with file transfer capabilities using one of the many protocols that pcomm recognizes. And if you're only interested in capturing an interactive session, the pcomm utility is just what you need. You can create screen dumps or, for longer sessions, use a log file to capture every character that is displayed on the screen. If you're not sure how to use pcomm, all you have to do is use the online help feature.

You've heard the saying, "All that glitters is not gold." Well that's also true with pcomm. You won't find a script language (a feature that is available in its DOS cousin), but don't be too concerned—you can use the UNIX shell script to automate the communications process. The pcomm man pages show you how to do this.

Installation Is Uncomplicated

You'll find all the pcomm files in the */pcomm* directory on *ftp.cecer.army.mil*. Before moving the files over, create an empty directory. Build the program here. After that we suggest you install it in */usr/local/lib/pcomm*. Now you're ready to copy the sample support files. These are *Pcomm.dial_dir*, *Pcomm.extrnl*, *Pcomm.modem*, and *Pcomm.param*. Once these files arrive, change the uppercase P in all the file names to lowercase 'p' and make sure these files are writeable by only those users to whom you trust to modify the pcomm environment.

Next, you'll have to copy the manuals to the proper */usr/man* directory. These files are *Pcomm.1*, *Waitfor.1*, *Matches.1*, and *Modem_break.1*. And be sure to change all the uppercase letters to lowercase. Don't bother asking why the author named these files with caps—we haven't the vaguest idea.

You can expect the installation of pcomm to be almost flawless. However, here are a few facts that can spoil your installation. If you're using a Berkeley flavor of UNIX, you'll have to make some changes in the makefile that is supplied by pcomm. The following shows the necessary changes:

```
#for old curses(3) or Berkeley systems
CURSES = -lcurses -ltermcap
TERMLIB = -ltermcap
#CURSES = -lcurses
#TERMLIB = -lcurses

#for System V or Berkeley worlds
BSD = -DBSD
TTY = tty_ucb.o
#BSD =
#TTY = tty_att.o
```

All the default settings are for AT&T style of UNIX. A few other modifications are required, depending on the UNIX that you are running, so be sure to review the pcomm utility's man pages before you create the binary files. Creating the binary files is as easy as executing the make utility.

If you have a particular problem with pcomm, you may want to contact Emmet Gray, who wrote pcomm man pages. Emmet can be reached via email at *.!uunet!uiucuxc!fthood!egray*, or at the following address:

US Army
HQ III Corps @ Fort Hood
Attn: AFZF-DE-ENV
Directorate of Engineering & Housing
Environmental Management Office
Fort Hood, TX 76544-5057

But keep in mind that pcomm is a public domain telecommunication program. This means no one is compensated for helping you answer your questions.

Running pcomm Is a Snap

To launch the power of pcomm, type **pcomm** at the prompt and press ENTER. You can then take advantage of pcomm's large dialing directory, auto login shell scripts, automatic redialing, data logging, printer logging, and the administrative features that log phone calls and limit long distance access.

Once pcomm is up and running, the status line keeps you completely informed of the following data:

- The name of the TTY device that is currently being used

- The duplex mode status

- The current line settings

- The data logging and printer logging status

- Incoming and outgoing transmission status

- A reminder of which key displays online help

CAUTION
Don't try to run pcomm on terminals that display less than 80 columns and 24 lines. pcomm requires this minimum display size. It also requires a terminal that has cursor movement. You don't need arrows keys. The pcomm utility recognizes U for uploading and N for downloading files.

All the utility's commands are accessible by pressing CTRL-A followed by a letter. You can substitute you're own favorite key in place of the CTRL-A hot key by using the terminal setup menu. See the utility's man pages for details. Table 7-2 contains a sampling of the commands that are used to control pcomm.

You can choose of one of the following seven file transfer protocols when you're ready to send or receive files: xmodem, xmodem-1k, modem7, ymodem, ymodem-g, ASCII, and zmodem. And if none of these suits your needs, you can add your favorite protocol on to the utility's list of protocols—well, it's almost that easy. You have to provide the external file transfer program, such as kermit, then add the name of the program to the pcomm protocol list. Once on the list, all you need to do is select the external file transfer program from the menu.

COMMAND	DESCRIPTION
0	Help Screen
D	Dialing Directory
M	Manual dial
L	Print. Sends the dialing directory to the printer or a file of your choice
R	Automatic redial of selected dialing directory entries
P	Adjusts the current communication line settings
X	Exits from pcomm
I	Displays the program information screen
S	Displays a choice of setup screens
B	Changes the current working directory
C	Clears the local screen and brings the cursor home
E	Toggles the duplex mode from full to half, or from half to full
H	Hangs up the phone. Disconnects the phone, but remain in pcomm
<Up>	Displays a menu of file transfer protocols to be used to send files to a remote system
<Down>	Displays file transfer protocols to be used to receive files from a remote system
G	Dumps the contents of the screen to a specified file. Special graphics characters may not be represented accurately in the file
1	Begins data logging. Prompts the user for the name of the file that will be used to collect a complete record of the terminal session

TABLE 7-2. *A Sampling of pcomm Commands*

The Special Pass Through Mode

Nothing beats a versatile communications program, and pcomm is right up there with the best of them. For most of us data communication is straightforward. Dial up another computer and begin "talking." However, a few of us require a more complex arrangement called *daisy chaining*. This is when two systems communicate with each other through another system.

Complicated? Maybe so, but not for pcomm. Here's how it works. Suppose two personal computers need to communicate through a UNIX system. The first personal computer calls the UNIX system, as does the second personal computer.

The UNIX system, using pcomm, passes all communications between the two personal computers while appearing completely transparent. You won't find this feature on every communications program.

Auto Login the Easy Way

The pcomm utility allows you to incorporate UNIX shell script languages used by the Bourne, C, and Korn Shells to perform the necessary login dialog that occurs when signing onto a remote system.

The shell scripts are run outside of the utility, so you can't use any pcomm commands in the script. For example, the script can't dial a telephone number. This means that you'll have to use the utility to make the initial connection with the remote computer.

The pcomm utility does contain several smaller programs that help bridge the gap between pcomm and the shell script language. These programs are waitfor, matches, and modem_break. The waitfor program pauses the shell script and polls the communication port waiting to see the login string that you specify in the command.

The following shows a simple login script.

```
waitfor -5 "ogin:"
if [ "$?" -eq 0 ]
   then
      echo "bob"
fi
```

Here, the waitfor program is looking for the characters "ogin:" to appear at the communication port. The -5 argument sets the time limit for the waitfor program. In this example, the program will poll the communications port for five seconds. Once the "ogin:" string is received, the login script uses the shell language's echo command to respond to the login prompt with the user ID, "bob".

The matches program is a little different from the waitfor program since matches doesn't read the communications port. Instead, it reads from standard-in. The matches program compares two strings and returns a zero if the second string is contained in the first string otherwise a one is returned. The next example shows how the matches program is used to determine if the login has failed.

```
read junk
matches $junk "login failed"
if [ "$?" -eq 0 ]
   then
      exit
fi
```

The modem_break program sends a break signal to the modem which, in many cases, tells the remote system to switch to another baud rate. This is a standard for connecting to a UNIX system. If you connect at the wrong baud rate, the convention is to send a break signal. The getty (the utility that allows you to sign on to a UNIX system) understands a break signal to mean try the next baud rate in the loop. The loop is usually specified in the /etc/gettydefs file.

You'll find this to be a handy feature, especially if you must synchronize the baud rate with the remote system. Here is an example of how the modern_break program and shell programs can come to your aid.

```
echo ""
try=0
# loop until done
while true
    do
        # wait 5 seconds for the login prompt
        waitfor -5 ogin:
      # test the exit code of the waitfor command
      if [ "$?" -eq 0 ]
         then
      # send my user ID and exit the loop
      echo "bob"
      break
        fi

        # increment the number of attempts
        try=`expr $try + 1`
        # test to see if we should give up
        if [ "$try" -eq 5 ]
          then
            exit 1
        fi

        # send a modem break and loop again
        modem_break
        echo ""
done
# wait 5 seconds for the password prompt
waitfor -5 assword:
# test the return code from waitfor
if [ "$?" -eq 0 ]
    then
```

```
      # send my password
      echo "abcdefg"
   else
      exit 1
fi
# return to pcomm
exit 0
```

The zmodem Utility: A File Transfer Utility

Here is one of the most economical utilities that you'll ever find to transfer and receive files. It's called zmodem. This utility isn't the typical communications software that you've come to know—it is a file transfer program. This means that you'll have to dial up and connect to the remote computer yourself before invoking zmodem, but this is about the only limitation that you'll find.

The zmodem utility uses the proper error correcting protocols to receive files over a dial-up serial port from a variety of programs. This allows you to receive files from programs running under DOS, CP/M, UNIX and nearly any operating system that you can imagine.

The zmodem utility actually consists of two executable programs, sz and rz. The sz program is used to send a file to a remote computer using the zmodem protocol, while the rz program is used to receive files.

Installing the zmodem Utility

First create a directory for zmodem, then upload the *rzsz.arc* file from the */pub* directory on *ucsd.edu*. Once these files arrive, you take over. Type **make** to create the binary versions of the rz and sz programs. The makefile for zmodem is already provided for you. If you have problems compiling the utility, you can contact Chuck Forsberg, who is one of its authors. He can be reached by email at *!tektronix!reed!omen!caf*, or at the following address:

Omen Technology, Inc.
17505 V Northwest Sauvie Island Road
Portland, OR 97231

Known Problems

Athough you probably won't run into problems using zmodem, there are a few limitations that you should be aware of. Neither sz nor rz is intended to be called from another communications program. The rz program does not support zmodem

Crash Recovery, or other zmodem features. YAM can be used to support these features. Another limitation is that pathnames are restricted to 127 characters.

Sending a File Is a Breeze

You can use the sz program to send one or more files to a remote computer using the zmodem protocol. You'll find that the sz program greatly simplifies file transfers since it has a very friendly user interface. The sz program includes AutoDownload, which automates file downloading.

Once you begin sending the file, the sz program displays individual and total file lengths and transmission time estimates. All the default settings in the sz program are sufficient for sending most files; however, the authors of the sz program allow you to modify these settings through command-line options. Table 7-3 contains a sample of the options that are available to you.

OPTION	DESCRIPTION
+	Instructs the receiver to append transmitted data to an existing file
a	Converts NL characters in the transmitted file to CR/LF
b	Binary override: transfers file without any translation
d	Changes all instances of "." to "/" in the transmitted pathname
f	Sends full pathname
k	Sends files using 1024 byte blocks rather than the default 128 byte blocks
n	Sends each file if destination file does not exist. Overwrites destination file if source file is newer than the destination file
p	Skips transfer if the destination file exists
q	Suppresses verbosity
r	Resumes interrupted file transfer
v	Causes a list of file names to be appended to /tmp/szlog
y	Instructs a receiving program to overwrite any existing file with the same name
Z	Uses ZMODEM file compression to speed file transfer

TABLE 7-3. *Command-line Options for the sz Program*

Here's how you send a file. In this example, we'll send all the files that have a "c" extension to the remote computer. Remember, we're already connected to the remote computer. The proper command sequence is:

```
% sz *.c
```

This single command transfers all the "c" files that are found in the current directory. You can read more about how to send files in the man pages that are supplied with zmodem.

Receiving a File Is a Snap

Receiving a file using zmodem is almost as easy as sending a file. Type **rz** on the command line and press ENTER. The rz program then waits to receive the file from the remote computer. The file name of the incoming file is specified by the remote computer which is used by the rz program.

The rz default settings are probably sufficient to receive most files, however, you can use a host of command-line options to modify these settings. Table 7-4 contain a sample of these options. You'll find the complete listing of options in the zmodem utility's man pages.

Here's how to receive a file. Connect to the remote computer and type **rz** at the command line. Use the remote computer's zmodem software to begin the file transfer. It's that simple.

OPTION	DESCRIPTION
a	Converts files to UNIX conventions by stripping carriage returns and all characters beginning with the first <Ctl> Z (CP/M end of file)
b	Binary file transfer override
p	Skips file if destination file exists
q	Suppresses verbosity
v	Causes a list of file names to be appended to /tmp/rzlog
y	Yes, clobber any existing files with the same name

TABLE 7-4.   *Sample rz Command-line Options*

The sliplogin Utility:
A Network Interface

The sliplogin utility is a driver that handles the link between your system and your gateway into the Internet. The authors describe it as a serial line link to a network interface. This sounds rather abstract but it is really a valuable utility for anyone who is looking to connect to the Internet.

The concept is rather easy to understand. Let's say that you don't have an Internet connection. You search around for access through your local university but unless you're a student or a faculty member, they probably won't listen to you. Next, you turn to a commercial firm who offers an Internet connection for a monthly fee. Although the firm supplies you with an IP address, you still must connect to the firm's host. This is where sliplogin comes into play. It is a simple piece of software that you can't live without!

It is also drastically different from the other utilities we review in this book. The sliplogin utility is operating system dependent, which means that you can't simply search the Internet using another system to locate a copy of it. So you must use the version of sliplogin that is specifically designed for your system.

The best way to find the correct version of sliplogin for your system is to contact the firm who supplied you with your system. Ask them for a copy of sliplogin. Don't worry—you won't have to pay for it. You'll probably receive a copy on disk, or be told where your can find your version on the Internet.

Installation

We really can't provide you with tips on installing sliplogin, since each version could have a unique installation procedure. Your best bet is to create a sliplogin directory on your system then copy your version of the software onto your system.

The utility's documentation files contain specific installation procedures. Just follow each step carefully and you'll have the utility operational in no time.

CAUTION
Each version of the sliplogin utility has its own bugs, which are usually listed somewhere in the documentation. Read them before sending in a bug report.

Another place to look for help is the *comp.protocols.tcp-ip* group. Here, you'll find general discussions about sliplogin and more specific tips on the version that is designed for your system.

Restrictions

The Regents of the University of California hold the copyright to the sliplogin utility. However, you'll find that there are very few restrictions on its use. For example, you can use and distribute the source and the binary files without prior permission from the University of California. You are even allowed to modify the source code, although do this at your own risk.

There are a few minor restrictions that you can read about in the utility's documentation, but keep in mind that there are no warranties provided with the utility. If you lose critical data because of a failure with the sliplogin utility's link, don't call on the University of California to reclaim your loses. All of the legalese about this limitation is contained in the documentation.

Up and Running

Type **sliplogin** *loginname* at the prompt to begin sliplogin. The utility runs quietly, so you may not even realize that it is running. However, under the hood sliplogin turns your terminal line on your system's standard input into a serial line IP link to the remote host.

Here's how it works. The utility searches for the *slip.hosts* file. This file contains login names that are used for entry matching, and is located in */etc/sliphome*. Once a match is found, the standard input line of your system is then configured.

Next, a shell script is invoked that initializes the utility's interface with your local and remote IP address. This script is usually located in */etc/sliphome/slip.login*. You can read in the utility's documentation about various command-line arguments that are used to control the behavior of the script.

Once the connection is made, you are free to roam the Internet. Sliplogin continues the connection with the remote host until either the remote host disconnects or until sliplogins process is terminated.

The xtv Utility: X Windows Teleconferencing Software

You're ready to demonstrate the software package that you've worked months preparing. It works fine but you must show your work to five end-user groups who are spread out over many locations. You could take your show on the road and visit each location giving each group their own presentation, but now you have an alternative. You can teleconference all the users providing they are accessible via TCP/IP.

We're not talking about a video conference—we're talking about a networking conference that allows a single-user application to be shared among many end users. This means that you can start your application on your system and use the xtv utility to conference in each end user group.

Through a telephone line, you can talk a participant through the steps that are necessary to use your software. Since all the groups are viewing the same instance of the application, they can hear your directions and watch the results on the screen.

We're not talking about pure ASCII applications. The xtv utility can handle almost any application, including graphics, without having to use special coding techniques to prepare the application for teleconferencing. And there are no special hardware requirements either.

The xtv utility is a time saver that can also let you dazzle your users with the latest in teleconferencing techniques. You can't beat it, especially when you hear what it costs—nothing! It's free for the price of a connection to Internet.

Installation

After creating an xtv directory on your system, you're ready to copy the files to your system. You'll find xtv on various hosts throughout the Internet. One location that you can try is *pub/graphics/utils* on *shark.cse.fau.edu.*

The xtv utility comes with an Imakefile that makes building the binaries a breeze. We suggest that you review the Imakefile to assure that all variables and paths match your environment. Once you're satisfied with the settings in the Imakefile, type **xmkmf**, and this script will create the makefile for you. Next, type **make** to start the make utility.

The xtv utility should compile error free. However, if you discover a problem, review the utility's documentation to make sure that you covered all the installation steps. If you still have a problem, read the *comp.sources.x* group on netnews and see if other users have some tips that will help you. As a last resort, send an email message to *wahab@cs.odu.edu* or *jeffay@cs.unc.edu* and report your possible bug.

Restrictions

Old Dominion University and the University of North Carolina at Chapel Hill hold the copyright for xtv. As you'll read in the utility's documentation, both institutions give you free use of the utility without having to ask for prior permission. You can also copy, modify, and distribute xtv at your leisure without having to pay a fee for the privilege.

You still must include the official copyright notice found in the documentation in all copies of xtv that you modify and distribute. Also, keep in mind that neither institution makes any warranty. You can use the utility as is.

Known Problems

We're not saying that xtv is bug free but we couldn't find any reports of known problems in the utility's documentation. We suggest that if you run into any problems with your distribution of the utility that you connect to netnews and see if anyone else has a problem. You might also find bug reports posted to this group.

Up and Running

Don't rush to start xtv. You must be sure that your DISPLAY environment variable is set to screen zero on your system before the utility will run properly. This is assuming that your system will be running the application. In this case, you're called the *chairman* of the teleconference, which gives you ultimate control over the conference. Now you're ready to begin your first teleconference using xtv.

At the prompt, type **xtv &** and press ENTER. The xtv utility becomes a background process. Others who want to join the conference are called *participants*. Participants must know two pieces of information to join the conference: the chairman's machine name and the session number. The chairman of the conference can easily supply this information. Just type **xtv** *machinename session#* at the prompt on a participant's system. Press ENTER to make the participant a part of the conference. You have some control over the behavior of xtv by using command-line options. Table 7-5 contains a sampling of these options. The utility's documentation contains a complete listing.

If launching xtv is successful, the control panel will be displayed on the screen. The control panel can easily be relocated by pressing the left mouse button and dragging the control panel into the new position on the screen. Participants will also see a set of active tools appear, which can be repositioned in the same fashion.

The control panel contains three sections: Participants, Tools, and Message. The Participants section contains a list of all the participants who have joined the conference. Each one is identified by his or her login name and system name. The Tools section contains a listing of the tools that are available for use during the conference. One of the tools allows you to begin your application. Just place the cursor on the tool that you need and press the left mouse button to grab the tool. You'll find all the information that you'll need to know to use the various tools in the utility's documentation.

OPTION	DESCRIPTION
-v	Verbose mode on
-h	Displays a help message without invoking xtv
-j	Disables the dynamic joining feature
-p	Disables pop-up menus from tools

TABLE 7-5. *A Sampling of Command-line Options*

The Message section is used to display messages sent by xtv and is used to respond to queries that you make about the conference. The Message section also contains the Exit xtv button. Press this button to leave the conference if you are a participant, or close the conference if you are the chairman.

When you consider the capability to share the same instance of an application among users, and xtv's ease of use, you'll come to the same conclusion that we did about this utility: it is a must-have for any serious software developer.

The zoo Utility: Archival Software

Here you go again. The MIS auditors are loose and going over your project with a fine-tooth comb. We're not just talking about the budget—we're talking about every aspect of the project, including the proper storage of the source code. Let's face it. You're a professional and have all the necessary backups of the source in place. Enough backup copies so you can easily recover from a mishap and retain your job.

However, when the MIS auditors get a hold of a project, those precautions that you take never seem enough to satisfy their need for a perfect audit. You don't have to face this problem again if you use the zoo utility. In fact, you'll even invite the MIS auditors to examine your next project—and to show off your new tool.

The zoo utility safely stores and retrieves your most valuable files. And it does so without interfering with your style of operation. There are many factors about this utility that make it a must-have for serious developers. The first one that comes to mind is the ease of operation.

Rahul Dhesi is the author of this utility, and has built easy-to-use commands into it, so that you don't think twice about saving and retrieving files. He also built in a complex set of commands that give you nearly full control over the behavior of the archive. You can choose your own level complexity when working with zoo.

Another factor is efficiency. Zoo stores your files in a compressed format, which can release nearly 80% of the space that your source code now consumes on the disk. Just enter a single command line and the zoo utility restores your source code—and any other type of file—to its full size.

And now for a major reason for acquiring zoo. It can save your job by recovering damaged archives. Any archival software can lose track of information that it stores in the archive, including zoo. However, Dhesi has given you another tool that will recover data that is stored in a damaged archive—the fiz utility, which comes with zoo.

The zoo utility is easy to use, efficient, and a way to recover damaged archives. What else could you (or the MIS auditors) ask for?

Installation

You can find zoo on various hosts throughout the Internet. One location where the source code and other files reside is at *garbo.uwasa.fi/unix/arcers/* on *garbo.uwasa.fi*. Copy the files to your system, and then open the documentation files and find the step-by-step installation guide that is provided for you.

The utility comes with a nearly ready-to-run makefile. We suggest that you take a few moments and display the makefile in an editor in order to examine path names and variable settings. These factors may prevent you from having a clean compile on the first try. Another file that you should review before compiling is the *options.h* file. This file contains definitions of preprocessor symbols for various systems. You should be able to locate symbols for your system. Make sure that these definitions are uncommented in this header file.

If you have problems building the binaries, we suggest that you review the settings in the *machine.h, machine.c*, and the *portable.h* files. These contain machine-dependent code and definitions. Modify these files as needed.

Even after making all the necessary modifications to the utility's files, you may stumble across a few bugs. If these bugs aren't listed in the documentation or on netnews, prepare a bug report. The utility's documentation shows you how to prepare the report and where to send it.

Restrictions

You're free to use, copy, and distribute zoo. In the utility's documentation, Dhesi gives you permission to use, copy, and distribute free of royalty and without prior permission. Dhesi also gives you permission to modify the utility, but with three restrictions:

- The copyright notice for the original source code must be included in your distribution

- You must be sure that your modification maintains downward compatibility with existing versions of zoo

- Once you've completed your distribution of the utility, you are asked to send a copy of your source code to Dhesi

As with most of the utilities that we review in this book, Dhesi requires that you don't prohibit anyone from using the utility free of charge. In addition, zoo doesn't come with any warranties. It is made available to you as is. You can read the fine print of these restrictions in the utility's documentation.

Known Problems

And yes, the zoo does have a few little problems. For example, in the filter mode, you may notice that the utility properly compresses and uncompresses files, even though an "uncompression error" message is displayed on the screen.

Here's another serious concern. The utility has a glitch that causes it to fail to check space on the disk when you are adding files to an archive. The utility doesn't detect an out-of-disk-space condition.

The documentation reports another bug that occurs very rarely, but can cause you a sleepless night or two when it happens—a problem with random byte patterns being incorrectly recognized as tag values. This means that the utility might lose track of data. Don't be too concerned—the data is undamaged in the file and can be extracted using a little trial-and-error technique. The documentation talks more about this solution.

The zoo utility assigns generation counts automatically, which allows you to retrieve previous generations of the same file. However, there is a slight problem when the counter reaches 65,535. At this point, the utility should automatically reset the counter back to one. Not so! You'll have to reset the counter manually with the **gc -65000** command.

These are just a few of the potential pitfalls that we'll bring to your attention. You can read more about these and other bugs in the utility's documentation. You'll also be able to read about potential problems by connecting to the *comp.compression* group on netnews.

Up and Running

The zoo utility is designed to create and maintain your archive files. It's like having your own librarian inside your system. Type **zoo** *command* **archive** *filename* at the prompt and the utility will compress the file and place it into the archive. The utility uses the Lempel-Ziv compression algorithm so you'll being freeing 20% to 80% of disk space. The amount of space that you actually save depends on the type of information that is contained in the file that you are placing in the archive.

Once a file is archived, you can use zoo to extract the file by issuing the **zoo** command followed by the appropriate command-line argument. You'll find that the utility has two degrees of commands—novice and expert. Yes, finally someone has remembered that some users of the utility don't want to master complex commands to store a file in an archive.

The *novice* commands are especially designed for someone in a hurry. Table 7-6 contains a sampling of these commands. The *expert* commands are for those who want to fine tune zoo's operation. We'll let you read about these commands in the utility's documentation.

COMMAND	DESCRIPTION
-add	Adds the specified files to the archive
-freshen	Adds a specified file to the archive if an older file already exists
-delete	Deletes the specified files from the archive
-update	Adds a specified file to the archive
-extract	Extracts the specified files from the archive
-move	Deletes the source file after it is added to the archive
-print	Sends extracted data to standard output
-list	Gives information about the specified archived files

TABLE 7-6. *A Sampling of Novice Commands*

Nearly every command that is used to control the behavior of zoo can be altered by using a command modifier. Don't be concerned about having to learn one set of switches for each command—there is only one set of modifiers and they work with all of the utility's commands. Table 7-7 contains a sampling of these modifiers.

You've probably used archive software before and have discovered two frustrations that can leave you looking for another solution to your problem. One of these is the difficulty of using wildcards to store and retrieve multiple files that have similar names. Let's say that you have ten source files for the same project, each with the same first four characters in the file name. This identifies the files that are associated with the project and makes it easy to copy them. Just enter the first four

MODIFIER	DESCRIPTION
c	Prompts user for a comment for each file added to the archive
d	Makes commands act on both normal and deleted files
f	Causes fast archiving by adding files without compression
q	Suppresses listing the name of each file

TABLE 7-7. *A Sampling of Command Modifiers*

characters followed by a wildcard, and all the files can be copied on a single command line.

Unfortunately, some archive utilities require you to enter each file name individually—a time-consuming and frustrating task to say the least. Not any more, thanks to the foresight of Dhesi. Dhesi built in a variety of wildcards that you can use to speed the archival process. We've provided a sampling of these in Table 7-8. The rest of them you can read about in the utility's documentation.

The other major frustration found in some archival systems is that you're always exposed to damaged archives. Remember those ten source files for your project that you archived? Now it's time to retrieve them, and the near-fatal message is displayed on the screen. The archive is damaged. Not that the file is corrupted—it's just that the archival utility lost track of the data in the archive. Besides looking for another job, what do you do? We can't help you with other archival software, but if you're using zoo, you have no need to worry. This is because zoo comes with the fiz utility, which recovers your data from damaged archives. No, it's not magic. Fiz simply skips the damaged portion and moves to the undamaged data.

The fiz utility doesn't make any assumptions about the structure of the archive. This is important since a lost byte can play havoc to the offset of other bytes in the archive. Fiz searches the entire archive looking for archival tag values that are used to determine the locations of directory entries and file data. A directory entry contains information such as the names of the archived files, whether or not the files are compressed, and their timestamps.

Once the search is completed, fiz prints the location of the archive along with the directory path and the names of the files that are contained in the archive. Now, here is the key point: the utility also identifies if the directory entry seems to be corrupt. It also prints the value of the pointer to the file data that is found in this directory. This means that you'll know where the block of file data begins, which is truly a lifesaver. You can read more about how fiz functions in the documentation.

WILDCARD	DESCRIPTION
*	Matches any sequence of zero or more characters
?	Matches any single character
c-c	Two characters separated by a hyphen specify a character range
: and ;	Separates a file name from a generation number

TABLE 7-8. *A Sampling of Wildcard Characters*

The mosaic Utility: An Internet Hypertext Browser

You've heard all the hype about Internet becoming the electronic highway of tomorrow. Sometimes these futuristic images seem a little oversold, especially when you are experienced with the Internet of today. Technology is moving toward special effects, complete with sound and movies coming across your display. The question posed by many experienced Internet users is: Can the Internet keep up with these changes?

The answer is yes! We say this with confidence, because we've seen the software that is breaking new ground by giving you the capability of using graphics, sounds, video, and text to make it easier to poke around the Internet. We're talking about the mosaic utility, which we found to be a cut above all the other Internet browsers that we've used in the past. We'd like to underscore the word "past", because once you've downloaded and built the utility's binaries, you'll never return to using your previous browsers. Yes, mosaic is *that* powerful, without a doubt.

This program differs from others reviewed in this book in that it only can be gotten free by downloading from an **ftp** site. Its use, otherwise, requires a paid license. It is, therefore, not on the enclosed CD. Still, it is worthwhile and can be gotten free, so we've decided to include it here.

Eric Bina and Marc Andreessen of the National Center for Supercomputing Applications are the parents of mosaic. Through their efforts, they have created a utility that takes away all the pain and confusion that is sometimes experienced when browsing the Internet. With mosaic, you can point the mouse and click to move freely through the Internet. This is by far the interface of choice to the Internet.

At the heart of mosaic is hypertext. Hypertext isn't new. We've all used software at one time or another that incorporated it into help documentation—key words in the text are highlighted on the screen, and by clicking on these words, the software searches for pages that give you more information about the keyword.

The mosaic utility provides the same feature for finding your way through the Internet. All you need to do is to select the highlight text from the mosaic utility's display and click the mouse button. Mosaic will then hunt around the Internet for the information that you selected. When the utility returns, you'll have a new screen filled with additional text.

Where are the movies? Don't worry about the movies. Mosaic will take care of displaying movies, graphics, sounds, and anything else that the software developers can come up with. Mosaic is truly the latest in Internet browsers and will give you tomorrow's technology on your system today.

Installation

You can get ahold of your own copy of mosaic for X Windows by copying the files in */mosaic* on *ftp.ncsa.uiuc.edu*. There you'll find both the source code and some binary files for the most common systems, including Sun, SGI, IBM RS/6000, DEC Alpha OSF/1, DEC Ultrix, and HP-UX. We recommend that you try the ready-to-run binaries before you go through the trouble of making your own binaries from the source code.

TIP
You don't need to have Motif installed on your system to run the mosaic utility as long as you use the pre-compiled binaries. However, if you compile mosaic source code yourself, you'll also need to have Motif 1.1 installed on your system. You'll find all of the installation instructions that you'll need in the utility's documentation.

Mosaic has been ported to a variety of systems. Table 7-9 contains some of the names and the locations where you can find copies of the utility that are specifically setup to run on those systems. The National Center for Supercomputing Applications' FTP server has source and binaries for the systems listed.

```
NeXT
VMS
DESQview/X)
Unixware
HP9000/3xx/4xx
HP 700
```

You'll probably be able to install mosaic without much difficulty. However, here are a few tips in case Murphy's Law is enforced. Reread the installation procedures that are found in the documentation. In addition, be sure you read the FAQ (most frequently asked questions) about the utility. These are also in the documentation.

If all else fails, start your text processor and write down your problem. Then send it to one of four email addresses that have been set up to deal with such a situation. The email address that you use depends on the type of system that you are running. Table 7-10 contains the list of proper email addresses.

Restrictions
The mosaic utility is a product of the Software Development Group of the National Center for Supercomputing Applications at the University of Illinois at Urbana-Champaign. They hold the rights to the utility. In the utility's documentation they give anyone the right to use the utility for academic and research purposes free of charge. The rest of the restrictions are contained in the utility's documentation.

VERSION	LOCATION
Sun 3	ftp.cs.ubc.ca in /pub/local/www
Linux	sunsite.unc.edu in /pub/Linux/system/Network/info-systems/
386bsd	gil.physik.rwth-aachen.de in /pub/xmosaic/
SCO ODT	sosco.sco.com in /TLS/
Apple A/UX	iraf.noao.edu in /iraf/v210/AUX3/auxbin/

TABLE 7-9.   *Locations for Versions of mosaic*

Known Problems

The mosaic utility is rather a new offering on the Internet, and as you might expect, it does have a few problems that still must be resolved. However, the authors of the utility have gone out of their way to include most of the known bug reports in the documentation. We found this to be a great help. For example, you can read the "frequently asked questions" section to find a comprehensive listing of problems and their solutions. Every problem that is listed has a step-by-step procedure that you can easily follow to resolve that problem if it occurs on your system.

Now, we're not talking about off-the-wall questions, but questions that you might raise yourself. For example, when I start the mosaic utility, I get all kinds of errors. Why? Read the FAQ and you'll know why, and you'll also learn how to resolve the errors if they occur on your system. You may not find the solutions to all of your problems in the FAQ, but you have a big safety net in the form of a comprehensive list of typical problems and their solutions, and email addresses of support groups that will do their best to help you.

SYSTEM	ADDRESS
X Windows	mosaic-x@ncsa.uiuc.edu
Mac	mosaic-mac@ncsa.uiuc.edu
Windows	mosaic-win@ncsa.uiuc.edu
All Others	mosaic@ncsa.uiuc.edu

TABLE 7-10.   *Send Your Problems to these Email Addresses*

Up and Running

The mosaic utility is truly at the cutting edge of the worldwide electronic highway that the government is trying to build. We've discussed the X Windows version of the utility, but there are also versions for the Apple Macintosh and for Microsoft Windows. It seems like the authors have all the bases covered.

Once you've installed the proper version of mosaic on your system, you're ready to take your first tour of the Internet in style. At the prompt, type **xmosaic**. The mosaic utility reads the startup file for the first display of hypertext. Some of the text is highlighted—either by underline or in a different color. These are the phrases that have hyperlink connections to other documents or information resources somewhere on the Internet. For example, the highlighted phrase might be "New Users." Point the cursor to this phase and click the mouse button. The utility will follow the hyperlink to the resource that contains information about new users. This information is then displayed on the screen with new phrases highlighted that are used to move further down the path that contains new user information.

The Back button, located at the bottom of the screen, is used to retrace your steps. For example, suppose you want to return to the opening screen, but you're currently one level down the new users path. Just press the Back button once and mosaic will take you one step backwards. The next step in a hyperlink might be on a host that is around the world, but you don't need to be concerned about that—you don't even need to know the address of the host. Mosaic handles all of this for you.

Mosaic can handle information in nearly any form, including graphic images, sound, and even movies. The utility successfully works with multimedia because it has a wealth of resources that it can use. For example, X Play Gizmo is used as the control panel for sound players and movie viewers; xv is the default viewer for graphic images; showaudio is used as the default sound player; and mpeg_play is the default movie player. The list of resources is too long to be covered here in its entirety, but all that you need to know about mosaic resources is included in the documentation.

Words can never do mosaic justice so we'll stop trying. All we can say is that if you don't take a few moments and explore it, you'll be missing out on a glimpse of the world to come on the Internet.

CHAPTER 8

Printing And
Spreadsheet Utilities

In this chapter, we review three very interesting and powerful software packages that any serious UNIX user needs to have in their UNIX toolbox. We're talking about Ghostscript, ps utilities, and the sc utility. Each one is different from the others, but together they can give you the power punch that you'll need for those tough jobs.

We begin with Ghostscript, which is a free re-implementation of the PostScript language. You probably know that PostScript printers can output very fancy graphics. PostScript documents can use fancy fonts and a complete range of type sizes. Also, with Ghostscript you can display PostScript files on a non-PostScript printer, on X Windows, and more. But let's not get ahead of ourselves.

From Ghostscript we move to a set of utilities that give you printing capabilities only found in expensive, professional publication software. The utilities are in a collection called the ps utilities and are designed to make paginating a document as easy as entering a few commands.

We're talking about real power. Sure any text processor can divide a document into pages, but there are very few that can paginate a document into signatures. A *signature* is the pagination of a document for complex printing. You'll learn all about this in our review. But take it from us, you don't want to be without the ps utilities if you plan on producing any kind of professional publication.

Finally, the sc utility is a public domain spreadsheet that is capable of handling your most typical spreadsheet chores. You'll find the sc utility loaded with built-in functions that take the pain out of formulating complex expressions. And at the price, you can't beat it. The box that follows lists the programs covered in this chapter.

The Ghostscript Utility: A PostScript Language
The ps Utilities: Pagination Software
The sc Utility: A Spreadsheet

The Ghostscript Utility: A PostScript Language

How would you like to print like the pros? Well, you can if you use the Ghostscript utility. Professional documents require the power of PostScript, a programming language that gives pizzazz to the traditional drab, single font style that is used to print most text documents. However, if you don't have PostScript, you do have ghostscript— and it's free!

The Ghostscript utility, created by L. Peter Deutsch, is a programming language similar to the Adobe Systems' PostScript (TM) language. Actually Deutsch's Ghostscript is a set of programs that provide an interpreter for the PostScript language, as well as C programming language procedures that implement the PostScript graphics capabilities.

Probably one of the best features of Ghostscript is its portability to many platforms. This is possible since Ghostscript is written entirely in the C programming language. It runs well on MS-DOS, Microsoft Windows, and OS/2 computers, as well as in the UNIX operating system and on VAX computers.

Up and Running Quickly

As with all the software you acquire, create a separate directory for Ghostscript. In fact, it is wise to create several Ghostscript directories for installation. Here's a directory layout suggestion that you should take:

- */usr/local/lib/ghostscript* for the startup files, utilities, and basic font definition files

- */usr/local/lib/ghostscript/fonts* for additional font files

- */usr/local/lib/ghostscript/examples* for the Ghostscript utility demo files

- */usr/local/lib/doc/ghostscript/doc* for the Ghostscript utility's documentation files

You'll find all the files that you'll need to run the Ghostscript utility at various locations on the Internet, but here's one to get you started: */pub/ghost* on *cs.wisc.edu.* Copy all the files into the Ghostscript directory. Ghostscript comes with a makefile, so once the files are in place, all you need to do is run the make utility to create the necessary binary files.

If you discover any problems with Ghostscript, post your question to *gnu.ghostscript.bug* on Usenet news. There are hundreds of Ghostscript user sites all over the world and often another user will be able to help you. But if this fails, you can always drop a line to Deutsch (*{uunet,decwrl}!aladdin!ghost ghost@aladdin.com*). He can be reached at this address:

Aladdin Enterprises
P. O. Box 60264
Palo Alto, CA 94306

However, don't contact Deutsch if you are using the Ghostscript utility on a Macintosh, Acorn Archimedes, Windows-OS/2, or the Atari ST. He had help porting the software to those operating systems and computers. Instead, you can contact the developers of those versions directly. Martin Fong (*mwfong@nisc.sri.com*) worked on the Macintosh version, David Elworthy *(David.Elworthy@cl.cam.ac.uk)* created the Acorn Archimedes version, Gershon Elber (*gershon@gr.cs.utah.edu*) and Jim Yang (*jyang@daedalus.caltech.edu*) developed the Windows-OS/2 version, and Tim Gallivan (*timg@landau.ph.utexas.edu*) handled the Atari ST version.

Cutting Through the Docs

You'll find that Ghostscript comes with a variety of documentation files. Don't sift through all the files. Here are a few tips that can help find your way through the information. Head for the *use.doc* file right away. This will help you get up to speed quickly.

Although you might be able to locate an executable copy of the utility, you'll probably find yourself needing to compile your own binary version. Stop! Read the *make.doc* first. This will give you hints on compiling and save you time and a lot of aggravation.

After you have Ghostscript up and running, you may want to skim through *font.doc* and *language.doc*. The *font.doc* file contains information about fonts that are distributed with the utility, as well as tips on how to add or replace fonts. The *language.doc* file discusses in detail the Ghostscript language and how this compares with the PostScript language.

The *drivers.doc* and the *xfonts.doc* files are a must-read for developers. The *drivers.doc* file contains information about how Ghostscript interfaces with device drivers. The *xfonts.doc* talks about how the utility interfaces with platform-supplied fonts. These are the fonts that are already on your computer. And if you intend to distribute the utility with your software, you'll have to read the *commprod.doc* which explains the circumstances under which Ghostscript can be distributed with a commercial product.

CAUTION
Ghostscript is not compatible with the DEC C programming language compilers, since those compilers interpret the ANSI C standard differently than other compilers.

Tips on Running

Once you've created the binary version of the utility, type **gs**, which is the name of the Ghostscript program. You can specify options and file names on the command line. Table 8-1 contains a sampling of these options. The gs program reads text files that you specified on the command line in sequence and executes them as Ghostscript programs.

Once all of the files have been read, or if you haven't specified any file names as a command-line argument, the gs program reads from standard input, which is normally the keyboard. Each line that you enter at the keyboard is interpreted separately by the gs program. After you have finished using the gs program, enter **quit** or the end-of-file character by pressing CTRL-C. The gs program will then exit gracefully.

In addition to command-line options, you can also set one of several switches on the command line. Table 8-1 contains a brief listing of some of the commonly used switches—they apply to all the files that are read by the gs program.

By now you're probably ready to jump in and create your first Ghostscript program. So where is the definition of the Ghostscript language? You won't find it on these pages, but you will find a complete description in the documentation that is supplied with Ghostscript. You'll also find on-line help by using the **-h** or **-?** commands when in the gs program.

And the Fine Print...

The Ghostscript utility is free for you to use; however, there are a few restrictions that you must follow. Aladdin Enterprises, of which Deutsch is the president, holds the copyright. Keep in mind that you're on your own; there are no warranties and no author or distributor will accept any responsibility for the consequences of using the Ghostscript utility.

You'll find that Ghostscript comes with more detailed information about these restrictions in the documentation files. Look for the heading "General Public License." The key point to keep in mind is that you can't restrict the use of the utility, even if you add your own modifications to it. This means that everyone is granted the same rights you have. Everyone has permission to copy, modify, and redistribute Ghostscript free of charge.

The ps Utilities: Pagination Software

Making your publication look sharp using your favorite editor can be a nearly insurmountable task. Most editors are not designed to be page-making tools.

OPTION/SWITCH	DESCRIPTION
-q	Quiet startup—suppresses normal startup messages
-Idirectories	Adds the designated list of directories at the head of the search path
-dDISKFONTS	Causes individual character outlines to be loaded from the disk
-dNOPAUSE	Disables the prompt and pause at the end of each page
-dNOPLATFONTS	Disables the use of fonts supplied by the underlying platform
-dSAFER	Disables the delete file and rename file operators

TABLE 8-1. *Handy Options and Switches (switches begin with -d)*

However, you won't have these problems any more thanks to Angus Duggan, the builder of a series of publication tools that he calls the ps utilities. Actually, Duggan had some help in creating these valuable utilities. He modeled some of them after works created by Chris Torek and Tom Rokicki.

The ps utilities is a group of programs that allow you to easily arrange PostScript pages into signatures, select pages and ranges of pages, rearrange pages, and print multiple pages on a single sheet of paper. Doesn't sound too impressive? Not unless you have to manually arrange pages for a publication.

Here's a simple test that illustrates this point. Assume that you want to print a booklet. Let's say you stack three sheets of 8 1/2 x 11 inch paper and fold them in half to give the appearance of the booklet. Next, number each page of the booklet. The first page is number one, the inside of the first page is number two. You get the idea.

Now for the final step. Unfold and separate the pages. Notice that the page numbers are not in consecutive order. This is because there is a difference between the way you view a publication and the way the publication is printed. Publications are printed in a signature format. Each 8 1/2 x 11 inch page is called a signature and must be printed separately from the other signatures. Your printer can handle this task as long as you position your publication pages in the proper place on the correct signature.

You can spend hours paginating your document or you can let one of Duggan's utilities do the work for you in a matter of minutes.

Installation
The ps utilities are available in */.2/usenet/comp.sources.misc/* on *gatekeeper.dec.com*. You can also find the ps utilities at other locations on the Internet. Create a directory for the ps utilities, then copy all the source files over your system. The utilities come with a makefile that might require editing to assure that the proper paths are the same as in your system. The ps utilities' documentation shows you everything you need to know about installing these utilities on your system.

Duggan reports that the utilities have been successfully compiled and run well on the Sun-3 and Sun-4 under SunOS 5.1 and Solaris 2.1, and earlier versions of the Sun operating system. They also run on VAX/VMS, DEC station, and a variety of IBM and HP systems. You can read about the complete listing in the documentation.

If you have problems with the installation, connect to the *comp.lang.postscript* news group and see if anyone else has experienced the same problem. If the problem isn't listed, post the problem and see if you receive any responses. And if that fails, report the possible bug to *ajcd@dcs.ed.ac.uk*.

Restrictions

Use all or any part of the ps utilities freely. Although Duggan holds the copyright on the source code, he has no problem with you using it for any purpose—even if you want to distribute it in your own commercial software package.

Duggan just asks that you clearly give credit to the original utilities and the author. This is necessary even if you modify or rename the utilities. He also wants you to provide the source code to the utilities free of charge. The only exception is a reasonable charge for distributing the source code.

And as with all the software that we review in this book, the ps utilities are provided to you 'as is' without any warranties. If they work for you, fine. If they don't work, don't complain to Duggan (unless you discover a new bug).

Known Problems

Here are a couple of problems that you might encounter with the ps utilities. You can read about other ps utilities problems on netnews and in the utilities' documentation.

An important factor to keep in mind is that none of the utilities checks for ps-Adobe-?.? conformance. The assumption is that the original documents conform to these PostScript standards. If your document doesn't conform, the output of your document will be in question.

Another problem that you might notice is that the utilities are in need of an extra save/restore around the whole document on a SPARCPrinter with NeWSPrint 1.0. It has been reported that the problem lies with bugs in the xnews server.

Up and Running

The ps utilities is actually a group of utilities. We'll take a closer look at a few of them and let you explore the others yourself. Probably the more useful of the ps utilities are psselect, pstops, psnup, and psbook.

The psselect utility is used to select pages from a PostScript file and is most useful when you need to build a new document from an existing one. Let's say that you have a set of book pages and you want to create an article from one of the chapters in the book. Instead of using an editor to copy and paste pages, you can use the psselect utility to copy just those pages that you need from the book file into a new PostScript file.

You can copy all the even pages, all the odd pages, a range of pages, or even reverse the order of the pages by using the proper command-line option. You can read about how each option is used in the utilities' documentation.

CAUTION
Page numbers that are used to specify the range of pages to copy into the new file refer to page numbers within the file. These numbers may be different from the actual page numbers that appear on the page.

The pstops utility is used to shuffle pages within a PostScript file. This is particularly useful when you are arranging pages for printing. You can setup your document to print 2-up, 4-up, in booklet form, reverse pages, and other interesting formats that are described in detail in the utilities' documentation. The pstop utility then copies the pages from the source file, places them in the new arrangement, and saves them into a new PostScript file.

The psnup utility is used to place multiple pages of your document on a single sheet of paper. When you save your document, the document is stored in logical pages. Once you specify the dimensions of the paper, the psnup utility transforms the logical arrangement of pages into a format that will use a single sheet of paper. Table 8-2 contains a sampling of command-line options that are used to control the output of the psnup utility.

OPTION DESCRIPTION

Option	Description
-w	Paper width
-h	Paper height
-p	Alternative to setting the paper size
-l	Pages that are in landscape orientation
-r	Pages that are in seascape orientation (rotated 90 degrees clockwise)
-c	Pages that are placed in columns down the paper
-m	Margins option
-b	Specifies an additional margin around each page on a sheet
-d	Draws a line around the border of each page
-s	Selects the scale
-nup	Selects the number of logical pages to put on each sheet of paper
-q	Suppresses the printing of page numbers

TABLE 8-2. *A Sampling of psnup Command-line Options*

The psbook utility is designed to rearrange pages of your document so that they conform to the pagination of book signatures. If you're not familiar with printing publication-quality documents, you may not realize the value of this utility.

As mentioned earlier, a signature is a sheet of paper that contains multiple book pages. When you look at a signature, the book pages seem to be placed randomly on the sheet. Page numbers are not in consecutive order. In fact, some pages might even appear to be printed upside down. However, when the signature sheet is folded, all of the pages fall in order. All that is necessary is to trim the borders of the signature sheet, freeing the individual pages of the book. Signatures sheets are then bound and nearly ready for reading.

As you can imagine, it is up to you to position the logical pages of the document into the proper position on the signature sheet. The psbook utility does this for you. All you need to do is supply the size of the signature using the -s command-line option. The psbook utility does the rest. You can read more about how to use this utility in the ps utilities' documentation.

The sc Utility: A Spreadsheet

If you're looking for a simple spreadsheet for doing your personal budgeting, then you're looking in the right place. Although the current version of the program is called pname, its roots lie deep. James Gosling started it all with his original spreadsheet program called vc, then Mark Weiser came along several years ago with enhancements and renamed the program sc. Jeff Buhrt and Robert Bond have come up with the latest version of sc and renamed the program pname. Although the latest version is called pname, we'll refer to it by its more common name, sc, throughout this chapter.

Whether it's called vc, sc, or pname, the results are the same—a powerful public domain spreadsheet that can handle nearly anything that you can throw at it. A word of caution: don't expect anything fancy. You wouldn't find a macro language or graphic capabilities. But you will find built-in financial functions that are perfect for budgets and mortgages—and a lot more.

The sc program starts up quickly and can be learned in a few minutes. Best of all, the sc program is portable to other systems since each spreadsheet is stored in the ASCII format. This allows you to transfer spreadsheets to run with the sc program on different architectures without any conversion.

How to Install the sc Utility

First, create a new directory for the sc program, then copy all of the sc program source files from */pub/database* on *qiclab.scn.rain.com* or another location on the Internet. Buhrt supplies you with the makefile; however, you should review the settings in the makefile before you build the source code.

Don't feel that only the authors of sc can change the program name! You can also rename the sc program by changing the name=sc and NAME=sc lines in the makefile to name=<new name> and NAME=<NEW NAME>. (You supply the <new name> of course.) Once you are satisfied with the makefile settings, type **make sc** or **make** <new name>, depending on whether or not you changed the name of the program.

Don't forget to also make the sc documentation if you've renamed the program. Do this by typing **make** <new name>**.man**; you'll then be able to use the man utility to view the on-line help facility for the spreadsheet program.

After you build the executable, the next step is to install the program. Run make install, and the make utility will create the directory specified by the makefile's EXDIR variable and place the binary there.

CAUTION
The makefile supplied by Buhrt changes the name in the nroffable man page. However, if you don't have nroff, you will have to change sc.man yourself.

Although we're providing you with the basic installation procedures, be sure to read the latest hints on installing the sc software in the *README* files that are supplied with the sc utility. You should also read the *comp.sources.unix* netnews group. If you experience any problems, you can contact Buhrt directly at this address:

Jeff Buhrt
Grauel Enterprises, Inc.
sequent!sawmill!buhrt

How to Run the sc utility
At the prompt, type **sc** or whatever name you used to rename the program. An empty table of cells organized as rows and columns are displayed on the screen. If you provided the program with the name of a spreadsheet file, the data contained in the spreadsheet is displayed. Type **q** when you want to exit sc.

The screen is divided into four regions. The top line is for entering commands and displaying cell values. The second line is for messages from the sc program. The third line and the first four columns show the column and row numbers from which are derived cell addresses (e.g. A0 for the cell in column A, row 0). Cell addresses are case-insensitive, so you can enter either **A0** or **a0**.

Each cell on the table may have associated with it a numeric value, a label string, or an expression called a formula. A *formula* evaluates to a numeric value or label string that is often based on other cell values. The program evaluates each formula by row and column, depending on the selected calculation order.

The total number of display rows and columns available is set by curses and may be overridden by setting the LINES and COLUMNS environment variables, respectively. For example, LINES=20 COLUMNS=15. As with all standard UNIX programs, sc uses *curses* to format the screen. Be sure to set your TERM environment variable to properly identify the terminal you are using.

There are two types of cursors used by the program, the cell cursor and the character cursor. The cell cursor is indicated by the highlighted cell and the less than symbol (<). The character cursor is indicated by the terminal. The cell and character cursors are often the same; they differ whenever you type a command on the top line.

Although we are only providing you with a brief overview of the sc program, you can use the on-line tutorial to learn how to use the various features of the program. Begin the on-line tutorial by typing **sc #LIBDIR#/tutorial.sc** at the prompt. Remember, #LIBDIR# represents the location where you installed sc.

How to Use the Command-line Options
You can override the default start up options by passing the program a command-line argument. For example, you can have the program recalculate the spreadsheet in column order by specifying the -c option on the command line (sc -c). Another useful command-line option is the -r option. This causes the spreadsheet to be recalculated in row order, which is the default setting.

And if you want to turn off the automatic recalculation feature altogether, you can use the -m option as the argument on the command line. This is a very common time-saving technique whenever work is performed on a large spreadsheet that contains many formulas. You can always manually recalculate by using the @ command.

How to Change Options
If you forget to set the appropriate option at the command line, you can always change these features while the program is running. There are three ways to do this: use the CTRL-T menu (toggle setting), S menu (set options), or make the changes interactively by using commands shown in Table 8-3.

You can display a menu list of options by pressing CTRL-T. Your selections are saved when data and formulas are saved. This ensures that you will have the same setup next time you recall the spreadsheet. Although we'll cover a few of the options here, you'll find a complete listing in the man pages.

The A menu item sets the status of the automatic recalculation feature of the program. By default, the spreadsheet will be recalculated each time a change occurs in a cell. The C menu item affects how the current cell is highlighted. If enabled, the current cell is highlighted using the terminals standard outmode, in addition to being marked by the cell cursor. If disabled, only the cell cursor is used (without the cell being highlighted).

Another time saver is the E menu item. This either disables (default) or enables the execution of external functions whenever the spreadsheet is recalculated. Disabling this feature allows you to change your spreadsheet without having to wait for each function to be recalculated.

The L menu item is used to set the auto-labeling feature. If enabled (default), labels will be displayed flush left in the cell, assuming the cell to the left is empty. Next, there is T menu item, which determines how the top line of the program is displayed. When the T option is enabled, the name and the value of the current cell is displayed on the top line. This is the default setting. When this feature is disabled, the top line is left blank.

Here is another time saver. Use the $ menu item to enable the dollar prescale if you are working with dollar figures. When enabled, all numeric constants (not expressions) are multiplied by 0.01 so you don't have to keep typing the decimal point.

The S command, called Set, displays a smaller menu list than the CTRL-T option. Some of the more notable options are the byrows/bycols menu item, which specifies the order of cell evaluation whenever an update occurs. These options also determine the order in which cells are filled and cleared. Another important option is the iterations menu item, which sets the maximum number of recalculations before the screen is displayed again. The default setting is 10. Other Set options are normally used only in sc data files.

How to Move Around the Spreadsheet

The sc program is very similar to other spreadsheet programs you've used before. First, you move the cell cursor via the cursor control commands to the cell where

COMMAND	DESCRIPTION
autocalc/!autocalc	Sets/clears auto recalculation mode
numeric/!numeric	Sets/clears numeric mode
prescale/!prescale	Sets/clears numeric prescale mode
extfun/!extfun	Enables/disables external functions
cellcur/!cellcur	Sets/clears current cell highlighting mode
toprow/!toprow	Sets/clears top row display mode

TABLE 8-3. *Interactive Setting Options*

you want to enter data into the spreadsheet. Here are a few of the cursor control commands to get you started; you can read the man pages for more information about them. The CTRL-P moves up one cell, the CTRL-N moves down one cell, the CTRL-B moves backward one column, and the CTRL-F moves the cell cursor forward one column. These should remind you of emacs-style movement.

However, if you are familiar with vi and find that the character cursor is not on the top line, you can use the vi cursor control commands as an alternative to the sc cell cursor control commands. Pressing letters **h**, **j**, **k**, and **l** will move the cell cursor left, down, up, and right respectively. Likewise, the uppercase form of these commands (**H**, **J**, **K**, and **L**) moves the cell cursor by half-pages left, down, up, and right respectively.

Your terminal's arrow keys provide another alternate set of cell cursor controls if they are supported in the appropriate termcap entry.

CAUTION
Some terminals have arrow keys which conflict with other control key codes. For example, a terminal might send CTRL-H when the LEFT ARROW key is pressed. In these cases, the conflicting arrow key performs the same function as the key combination it sends.

The caret symbol (^) moves the cursor to the top cell of the current column. Zero (**0**) moves the cursor to the left-most cell of the current row (except if you are in numeric mode, in which case the zero will be interpreted as entering a number into the current cell). Finally, the dollar sign (**$**) moves the cursor to the last column containing a value in the current row.

How to Use Enter and Edit in a Cell

When the cell cursor is positioned over a cell, you can enter data into the cell by typing numbers or letters from the keyboard. Anything that you type will appear on the top line of the program. In numeric mode sc assumes that if you enter a number, the value in the cell will be a numeric value. If you enter a letter, the assumption is that you are entering a label into the cell. Once you press the ENTER key, the current contents of the cell are erased and the new value is displayed in the cell.

You can enter an expression into the cell by typing an equal sign (=) as the first character of the expression. The sc program will accept standard spreadsheet expressions. Read the man pages for the sc program if you are unsure about how to create a valid expression.

When you place the cell cursor on a cell that contains data, the data is displayed on the top line of the program. You can then position the cursor on the line by typing **e** to edit numeric data, or by typing **E** for editing text. This places the cursor at the top of the screen at the value of the cell. Now use vi commands to edit the contents of the cell. When you have finished editing, press the ESC or ENTER keys.

How to Use the File Commands

The sc program offers several techniques for storing information into a file. For example, with the W file command, you can write a listing of the current spreadsheet in a file in a form that matches the appearance of the data on the screen. This means that you can display the file in a text editor and see the same information that you see using the sc program. Hidden rows or hidden columns are not shown.

Another way to save a spreadsheet to a file is by using the P file command called **Put**. This command stores files that are retrieved using the G file command (called **Get**), and are not designed to be viewed with a text editor. In addition, files saved using the P file command can be encrypted if the encryption feature of the sc program is enabled. The G file command decrypts the file before loading it into the spreadsheet. Read the sc man pages for the details.

A spreadsheet can also be saved using the T file command called **Table**. This causes the sc program to save the spreadsheet using delimiters. Such a file is then suitable for processing by other software. You can use the options commands to determine the characters that are used as delimiters.

You can specify a subset of the spreadsheet to be saved to the file by using the optional range argument with the P, W, and T commands. In addition, these three output commands can pipe unencrypted spreadsheets to a program rather than to a file. Refer to the man pages for more information on how to use the sc program's file commands.

How to Use the Row/Column Commands

As with any spreadsheet program, the sc program enables you to add and delete columns and rows on the fly. The **Append** (**ar** and **ac**) commands are used to add a new row or column immediately following the current row or column. The **r** and **c** determine if the command effects rows or columns. The same principle holds true for all the row and column commands. Another way to add a row or column is to use **Insert** (**ir** and **ic**) commands.

Deleting a row or column is just as easy by using the **Delete** (**dr** and **dc**) commands. However, if you make a mistake, you can always use the **Pull** (**pr** and **pc**) commands to undo the last deleted set of cells.

Using the **Remove** (**vr** and **vc**) commands allows you to remove an expression from affected rows and columns, leaving behind only the values that were in the cells before the command was executed. You'll find this a handy timesaving trick. You don't need to waste time by having to constantly reevaluate the expression. Simply replace the expression with its resulting value.

If you find yourself working on a spreadsheet that contains too much information to display on a screen, you can take advantage of the **Hide** (**zr** and **zc**) commands. This set of commands keeps the current row or column from being displayed, while maintaining the values of the cells in the spreadsheet. The **Show** (**sr** and **sc**) commands can then be used to display the contents of the hidden row or column.

Built-in Functions

Although sc isn't a fancy spreadsheet program, it does come with a host of built-in functions that can easily handle many tasks. Built-in functions fall within five groups: range functions, numeric functions, string functions, financial functions, and date and time functions. We'll leave a complex discussion on how to use each of these functions to the man pages that are supplied with the sc program. However, see Table 8-4 below to immediately appreciate some of the built-in functions that you'll find in the sc program.

RANGE FUNCTIONS	DESCRIPTION
@sum(r)	Sums all valid (nonblank) entries in the region
@prod(r)	Multiplies together all valid (nonblank) entries
@avg(r)	Averages all valid (nonblank) entries in the specified region
@count(r)	Counts all valid (nonblank) entries in the specified region
@max(r)	Returns the maximum value in the specified region
@min(r)	Returns the minimum value in the specified region
@stddev(r)	Returns the sample standard deviation of cells
@lookup(se,r)	Searches through the range r for a matching value
@index(e,r)	Uses the value of expression e to index into the range r

NUMERIC FUNCTIONS	DESCRIPTION
@sqrt(e)	Returns the square root of e
@exp(e)	Returns the exponential function of e
@ln(e)	Returns the natural logarithm of e
@log(e)	Returns the base 10 logarithm of e
@floor(e)	Returns the largest integer not greater than e
@ceil(e)	Returns the smallest integer not less than e
@rnd(e)	Rounds e to the nearest integer
@round(e,n)	Rounds e to n decimal places
@dtr(e)	Converts e in degrees to radians

TABLE 8-4.   *Sampling of Built-in Functions*

NUMERIC FUNCTIONS	DESCRIPTION
@rtd(e)	Converts e in radians to degrees
@sin(e)	Returns the sine of e
@cos(e)	Returns the cosine of e
@tan(e)	Returns trigonometric functions of radian arguments
@max(e1,e2,...)	Returns the maximum of the values of the expressions
@min(e1,e2,...)	Returns the minimum of the values of the expressions
@ston(se)	Converts string expression se to a numeric value
@eqs(se1,se2)	Returns 1 if se1 has the same value as se2; otherwise, returns 0
@nval(se,e)	Returns the numeric value of a cell selected by name

STRING FUNCTIONS	DESCRIPTION
@substr(se,e1,e2)	Extracts and returns a substring from a string expression
@fmt(se,e)	Converts a number to a string
@sval(se,e)	Returns the string value of a cell selected by name
@ext(se,e)	Calls an external function (program or script)
@coltoa(e)	Returns a string name for a column from the numeric argument

FINANCIAL FUNCTIONS	DESCRIPTION
@pmt(e1,e2,e3)	Computes the monthly payments for a mortgage
@fv(e1,e2,e3)	Computes the future value for monthly payments
@pv(e1,e2,e3)	Computes the present value of an ordinary annuity

DATE AND TIME FUNCTIONS	DESCRIPTION
@date()	Returns the system date in text
@now	Returns the UNIX time (seconds since 1970)
@year(e)	Returns the year
@month(e)	Returns the month
@day(e)	Returns the day of the month
@hour(e)	Returns the number of hours since midnight
@minute(e)	Returns the number of minutes since the last full hour
@second(e)	Returns the number of seconds since the last full minute

TABLE 8-4. *Sampling of Built-in Functions* (continued)

CHAPTER 9

Software Development Utilities

When we were planning this chapter, we asked ourselves what software utilities would make our job as software developers easier. Among other things, we were hoping to find a package that would accurately predict the stock market, but we were out of luck. Instead we found several handy utilities that most developers should have in their arsenal.

Our first considerations were function libraries. Were there any out there on the Internet that could improve our productivity? There are, in fact, plenty available on the Internet—but the two that caught our eye are InterViews and the Tcl utility. InterViews is actually a C++ class library; the Tcl utility is an embedded scripting language. Both have built-in, ready-to-use features that would take you days and even months to program yourself. Be sure you don't miss our reviews of these products in this chapter.

Next we looked for utilities that would help us better manage our source code. Three met this demand: the rcs utility, the GNU diff utilities, and the patch utility. The rcs utility is a source code manager that automatically tracks generations of source code, so you'll never have to wonder which file contains the latest version of your source. However, there might come a time when you need to compare two versions of the same source code. Which one is which? Don't wonder, just use the diff utilities; they will show you the difference between the two files. And once you know that, you can use patch to add the updated source code to the proper file. This set of software development utilities is a must for your arsenal.

The next step in the development cycle is to create a makefile and build the binaries for your application. The tool we found that makes this process easier is the makedepend utility. One of the trickiest parts of the creating a makefile is to locate all the dependencies between your .c and .h files. Just run makedepend, and your troubles are over. This utility collects all the dependencies that are necessary to reliably build the binaries for your application.

No matter how carefully you are writing source code, there are bound to be a few bugs in your application. We located a utility that will take the pain out of finding and removing those creatures from your program: the gdb debugger. You'll find it easy to use and a valuable asset for debugging your application.

Finally, we went looking for a utility that will let you show off your work, and we stumbled across xscope. This little helper allows multiple users to connect to your application. You'll find xscope a great way to demo your application.

The GNU diff, diff3, and sdiff Utilities
The gdb Debugger: Debugging Software
InterViews: A C++ Class Library
The makedepend Utility: A Software Development Tool
The patch Utility: Automatic Source Code Updating
The rcs Utility: A Source Code Manager
The Tcl Utility: An Embedded Scripting Language
The xscope Utility: Multiple Users on a Single Process

The GNU diff, diff3, and sdiff Utilities

So you've spent days working on a source code file. You've even worked on it at home. The boss should give you an award for your performance—but there is this little problem that you don't want to anyone to know about. It's like this: You copied the source code from your system at work to a floppy disk so you could work on it on your home system. Changes you made there were transferred back to the floppy and restored to your system at work. On some days, however, you left the floppy at home, so you created another floppy disk at work.

Now you're confused. Which of the three source files is up-to-date? The one on your system at work or the ones on the two floppy disks? If you choose the wrong one, you'll be days behind in your work. Sure, you know you should have been more careful, but that's not going help you now. Relax—the diff sisters are here to come to your aid. Don't expect the diff utilities to tell you which source code file is the latest; they can't. What they *can* do is show you where each source code file differs with the others. With that information, you will be able to easily determine the version of the source code that you should use to continue your work.

There are three diff sisters that will help you: diff, diff3, and sdiff.

- The diff utility compares the contents of two files and makes the differences available, line by line, in several formats. And we're not just talking about text files, either; diff can also compare binary files.

- The diff3 utility performs a function similar to diff, except the comparison is made among three files. The results of this comparison are sent to a merged file that contains all changes, and warnings about conflicts among the files.

- The sdiff utility functions similarly to diff, except that the source files are displayed side by side with markings to point out the differences. You can also have sdiff interactively merge two files.

Since all three of these programs are re-implementations of the standard UNIX utilities of the same name, why would you want yet another version? For two reasons: first of all they are faster, and second, on some versions of UNIX, diff3 is broken and dumps core, whereas GNU diff3, in our experience, is robust. You'll also appreciate the extra options available in the GNU version.

All the credit for these valuable additions to your UNIX toolbox must be given to Mike Haertel, David Hayes, Richard Stallman, Len Tower, and Paul Eggert—the authors of the diff utility. Additional thanks must be extended to Randy Smith, who wrote diff3, and Thomas Lord, who wrote sdiff.

You'll find plenty of ways to use the diff utilities. For example, the output from diff can be used to create an updated version of your software. Just take the diff output and use it as input to the patch utility (discussed later in this chapter). And here is another way diff can help you. Did you ever find yourself with mirror copies of a directory, and wondering if they're really mirrored? Don't guess anymore—the diff utility is capable of comparing directories. Just run diff against the allegedly mirrored directories to confirm how they differ.

Installation

We won't go into the details of installing the diff utilities. Their documentation contains all the information that you'll need to successfully install the utilities on your system.

You can locate diff, diff3, and sdiff at many locations on the Internet; here just one: */pub/Z* on *moxie.oswego.edu.*

If you do run into any problems with the installation, be sure to retrace your steps, and then read the *gnu.utils.bug* group on netnews. You'll find a large user group there, with folks who are more than willing to help you get these utilities up and running. Just post your questions and check back later to read the replies.

And if all else fails, email your potential bug to *bug-gnu-utils@prep.ai.mit.edu.* Be sure to include a precise description of the problem, including samples of the input files that produced the problem.

Restrictions

All three diff utilities are protected by GNU Free Software Foundation, Inc.'s license agreement. The specifics are discussed in detail in the utilities' documentation, but here is the brief version. You can use, modify, and distribute copies of diff, diff3, and sdiff without prior approval of the Free Software Foundation, Inc. The only limitation is that you can't restrict anyone else from using the utilities.

Known Problems

The authors of diff, diff3, and sdiff are still improving their work, so you might find a few problems when you use them. Following are a few that have been reported. You'll find a more complete list in the utilities' documentation.

The diff utility treats unusual files such as symbolic links, device special files, named pipes, and sockets as if they are regular files. However, the patch utility can't represent changes to such files. Another problem occurs when a file name contains an unusual character, such as newline or whitespace. In this case, diff generates a patch that the patch utility can't parse.

The foregoing isn't the only conflict between diff and patch. For example, though diff can analyze files that have long lines or end in incomplete lines, patch cannot patch such files.

Available memory can be a serious problem for diff. The utility reads both files into memory before doing the comparison, but no comparison can take place if insufficient memory is available to diff.

Up and Running

Running diff is rather straightforward. Type **diff**, followed by any command-line options, and then the names of the two files to be compared. File names must be separated by a space. Table 9-1 contains some of the command-line arguments that you can use to control diff. You'll find a complete listing in the utility's documentation.

The diff utility goes about its business and produces an exit status code of 0, 1, or 2. The 0 means that diff ran successfully and both files contain the same information. A 1 exit code means that diff found a difference between the two files. An exit code of 2 means that diff ran into trouble and did not operate properly.

If you receive an exit code of 1, you'll be able to see the conflicting lines on the display or in the file. These lines are marked appropriately, so you'll be able to identify which of the two files contains the difference. See the standard UNIX documentation for details.

TIP

If you discover that diff is running at a snail's pace, you can take a few steps to encourage the utility to increase its performance. The trick is to change the method diff uses to compare files. For example, try running diff with the -d or --minimal option. diff will use an alternative comparison algorithm that sometimes produces a smaller set of differences. You can read about other techniques in the utility's documentation.

OPTION	DESCRIPTION
-LINES	Shows lines of context; LINES is an integer
-a	Treats all files as text and compares them line by line
-b	Ignores changes in amount of blank and tab whitespace
-B	Ignores changes that just insert or delete blank lines
--brief	Reports only whether the files differ
-c	Uses the context output format
--ed	Makes output that is a valid 'ed' script to change file 1 into file 2
--ignore-case	Ignores differences in case

TABLE 9-1. *A Sampling of diff Command-line Options*

You execute the diff3 utility very similarly to the way you launch diff. At the prompt, type **diff3,** followed by any options, and the names of the three files to be compared. Each file name must be separated by a space. Table 9-2 contains a sampling of diff3 command-line options, and the diff3 utility's documentation contains a complete list. Diff3 returns the same exit codes as diff.

The proper format for comparing three files is

diff3 *file1 file2 file3*

You can also have diff3 take an original file plus two edited versions and output a file that contains all of the modifications combined. GNU diff3 pays special attention to ranges of lines that have been modified in both edited versions.

If you look at the ouput, you'll notice a few strange-looking symbols at the beginning of some lines. These are the *conflict markers*; they indicate the lines that are in conflict with the other files, as well as which files contain the conflicts. The diff3 utility's documentation tells you how to identify these markers.

To start up the sdiff utility, type **sdiff** and then specify any options. Table 9-3 offers a sampling of these options. You must then specify the name of the source file (referred to in the documentation as the from-file) and the name of the merge file (the to-file). Sdiff compares the contents of the from-file with the contents of the to-file. If you specify the --output option, sdiff pauses and displays it on the screen. You are then asked which line to use for the merged output. Say "l" to select the left line, "r" for the right line. See the documentation for a complete description.

OPTION	DESCRIPTION
-a	Treats all files as text and compares them line by line
-A	Incorporates changes from *file1* to *file2* into *file3* and identifies conflicts with brackets
-e	Generates an 'ed' script
--merge	Applies the edit script to the first file and sends the result to standard output
--text	Treats all files as text and compares them line by line

TABLE 9-2. *A Sampling of diff3 Command-line Options*

OPTION	DESCRIPTION
-a	Treats all files as text and compares them line by line
-b	Ignores changes in amount of blank and tab whitespace
-B	Ignores changes that just insert or delete blank lines
-H	Uses heuristics to speed handling of large files
-i	Ignores changes in case; considering upper- and lowercase to be the same
--output	Does an interactive merge and puts the output in FILE

TABLE 9-3. *A Sampling of sdiff Command-line Options*

The gdb Debugger: Debugging Software

Here comes another debugger. So what, right? Well, don't be too quick to jump to conclusions. The gdb debugger is a real time saver, and you should add it to your arsenal of tools. It lets you see what is going on inside your program while the program is executing. And gdb tells you what your program was doing at the moment it crashes. The gdb debugger's original authors Richard Stallman, Stu Grossman, John Gilmore, and a team of developers (all are listed in the documentation) have spent a considerable amount of time carefully planning this very efficient utility—and you benefit from their work.

Did you ever find yourself having to type the **step** command over and over again as you walked through your program? Not with the gdb debugger! Typing the RETURN key automatically repeats the last command, so you only have to enter the **step** command once.

Here's another time-saver: You no longer have to retype printed values each time you need to see the values. With gdb, every time you ask to have a value printed, the "m" is saved in a variable. Just use the variable instead of typing the value.

And then there is the **finish** command. This tells gdb to continue to run to the end of the current function and then enter a breakpoint. If you ever accidentally step into a function, this will get you back to the invocation point in a hurry.

Best of all, if you are a GNU emacs fan, you will love the way the gdb debugger is seamlessly integrated into emacs. You can look at your program—with an arrow pointing to the line you are currently debugging—in one window, and the debugger output in a second window. The program text is in an otherwise normal editing buffer, so if you see a bug you can edit it on the spot. A word of caution! You will still have to recompile the program in order to have the debugger see the changes.

Heard enough? Well, there is plenty more ahead when you step into the world of the gdb debugger. You can use it to debug programs written in C, C++, and Modula-2. Fortran support will be added when a GNU Fortran compiler is ready.

Installation Is Fast

Create a directory called *gdb*, and copy the gdb source files from the */pub/packages/gnu* directory on *ftp.cc.mcgill.ca*. We'll use gdb*. Then replace the asterisk with the verson number of the gdb utility that you copy to your system. Versions of free software change frequently, sometimes more than once a week. Use the uncompress or gunzip utilities, both described elsewhere in this book, to unpack the gdb debugger source files. Once you unpack the file *gdb-*tar.z*, you'll have the GNU include files, the BDF (binary files description) library, the readline library, and all the other libraries that you need, in their own directory beneath the gdb-* directory.

Once the files are unpacked, you're ready to create the binary files. The gdb debugger comes with a configure script that automates the process of preparing gdb for installation. After executing the configure script, you can use make to build the gdb debugger binary files. The simplest way to configure and build gdb is to run configure from the *gdb-*source directory. First switch to the *gdb-*source directory, and then run configure. As an argument, pass the identifier for the platform on which gdb will run. For example:

```
cd gdb-*
./configure HOST
make
```

where HOST is an identifier, such as sun4 or decstation, that identifies the platform gdb will run.

The configure script does not provide any query facility to list all supported host names or aliases. The script calls the Bourne shell script *config.sub* to map abbreviations to full names. You can read the script or you can use it to test your guesses on abbreviations for your HOST name.

Running configure HOST followed by make will build the *bfd, readline, mmalloc,* and *libiberty* libraries, and then *gdb* itself. The configured source files and the binary files are left in the corresponding source directories.

CAUTION
The configure script is a Bourne-shell (`/bin/sh`) script. If your system
does not recognize this automatically when you run a different shell,
you may need to run sh on it explicitly. For example, type **sh
configure HOST**. Also, if configure can't determine the type of
system you're running, you can specify your system as an
argument to configure—for example, ./configure sun4. If you
receive any compiler warnings, review the "Known Problems "
section under gdb debugger for help, and consult the man pages
supplied with gdb.

   Table 9-4 contains the command-line arguments that you can use to set various
configure options.
   After you have successfully installed the debugger, you can print the formatted
quick reference card on a PostScript printer and make the on-line help files. The
man pages show you how this is done.

Known Problems
The gdb debugger does have a few problems that still must be resolved.

- Watchpoints are very slow. They currently are implemented in software.
  Future versions of gdb may resolve this problem.

- Under Ultrix 4.2 on the DECstation-3100, there have been problems with
  backtraces after interrupting the inferior out of a **read( )**. This is caused by
  the **ptrace()** function returning an incorrect value for register 30.

- When using gdb on the DECstations, you'll experience warnings about
  shift counts being out of range in various BFD modules. None of the
  warnings is cause for alarm because they are actually the result of bugs in
  the DECstation compiler.

- Be careful if you are running gdb on the SPARC. There have been reports
  about incorrect values of struct arguments to functions. This occurs in the
  seventh and subsequent arguments.

- And on the Solaris, executing the **run** command when the program is
  already running will restart the program. It might also leave a core dump
  from the previous execution in the current directory.

   The gdb debugger is able to produce warnings about symbols that it does not
understand. By default, these warnings are disabled, but you can enable them by

ARGUMENT	DESCRIPTION
--help	Displays a quick summary of how to invoke configure
--prefix=DIR	Configures the source to install programs and files under directory DIR.
--srcdir=PATH	Makes configurations in directories separate from the gdb source directories
--norecursion	Configures only the directory level where configure is executed
--rm	Removes the configuration that the other arguments specify
--target=	Configures gdb for cross-debugging programs running on this target

TABLE 9-4.   *Command-line Arguments for Configure*

executing the **set complaint** command. This will point out problems that you may be able to fix. Warnings produced during symbol reading indicate some mismatch between the object file and gdb's symbol-reading code. In many cases, it's a mismatch between the specs for the object file format and what the compiler actually outputs or what the debugger actually understands.

If you have questions about these problems or encounter other problems with the debugger, you can contact the authors at *bug-gdb@prep.ai.mit.edu* or *ucbvax|miteddie|uunet}!prep.ai.mit.edu!bug-gdb*. Be sure to include your HOST name. You can also contact the authors via regular mail at the following address:

GNU Debugger Bugs
Free Software Foundation
545 Tech Square
Cambridge, MA 02139

Running Is Uncomplicated

The gdb debugger has many ways to help you catch bugs in the act. You can catch any signal that might affect your program's behavior. You can also set breakpoints that will stop your program. You can even set conditions on a breakpoint. Once your program is stopped, the debugger helps you examine what has happened with your program. You can then experiment and correct your program.

The gdb debugger is very easy to start: just type **gdb** at the prompt. From there, the debugger reads commands from the terminal until you tell it to exit. You can also run the debugger using a variety of arguments and options that allow you to specify more of your debugging environment when you launch the program. The typical way to start the debugger is with one argument specifying an executable program—for example, gdb PROGRAM, where PROGRAM is the name of the program to be debugged. Table 9-5 contains a list of command-line arguments. Refer to the manpages that come with the gdb debugger for more examples.

In addition to arguments, you can set various options from the command line to control gdb options. For example, the command **gdb -tty=/dev/tty3 PROGRAM** will use the specified terminal for input and output of the program you are debugging. All options and command-line arguments you give are processed in sequential order.

CAUTION
The order of arguments and options can have an effect on the operation of the gdb debugger. Be sure to read the man pages for more details. Table 9-6 contains a listing of the more commonly used options.

Once you have gdb running, you can control its operation by issuing the proper commands. Table 9-7 lists a few of the common commands that you'll need. You can also use the **help** command to learn how to use commands that are not found in this table. When you are finished debugging your program, enter the **quit** command to exit the debugger.

ARGUMENT	DESCRIPTION
-symbols=FILE or -s FILE	Reads symbol table from file FILE
-exec=FILE or -e FILE	Uses file FILE as the executable file to examine data in a core dump
-se=FILE	Reads symbol table from file FILE and uses it as the executable file
-core=FILL or -c FILE	Uses file FILE as a core dump to examine
-command=FILE or -x FILE	Executes gdb commands from file FILE
-directory=DIRECTORY or -d DIRECTORY	Adds DIRECTORY to the path to search for source files
-r or -readnow	Reads each symbol file's entire symbol table immediately

TABLE 9-5. *Common Command-line Arguments for gdb Debugger*

OPTION	DESCRIPTION
-nx or -n	Does not execute commands from any `.gdbinit' initialization files
-quiet or -q	"Quiet"; does not print the introductory and copyright messages
-batch	Runs in batch mode
-cd=DIRECTORY	Runs using DIRECTORY as working directory
-b BPS	Sets the baud rate of any serial interface used by gdb for remote debugging
-tty=DEVICE	Runs using DEVICE for your program's standard input and output

TABLE 9-6. *Common Command-line Options for gdb*

COMMAND	DESCRIPTION
c	Continues running your program after stopping (e.g. at a breakpoint)
next	Executes next program line after stopping; steps over any function calls in the line
step	Executes next program line after stopping; steps into any function calls in the line
help	Shows information about gdb
quit	Exits gdb
targets	Selects local files to debug at run-time
watchpoints	Stops execution whenever the value of an expression changes

TABLE 9-7. *Common Debugger Commands*

Consider the following buggy program:

```
bash$ cat foo.c
#include <stdio.h>

main (argc, argv)
    int argc;
    char *argv [];
{
  int i;

  for (i = 0; *argv [i]; i++)
    printf ("Word %d: %s\n", i, argv [i]);
}
```

Here is a debugging session that demonstrates gdb's power. First, we compile *foo.c* using the -g flag to include debugging symbols:

```
bash$ cc -o foo -g foo.c
```

Here is what happens when we try to run it:

```
bash$ ./foo
Word 0: ./foo
Segmentation fault (core dumped)
```

Oh, oh! Time to use gdb:

```
bash$ gdb foo
GDB is free software and you are welcome to distribute copies of it
under certain conditions; type "show copying" to see the conditions.
There is absolutely no warranty for GDB; type "show warranty" for details.
GDB 4.9, Copyright 1993 Free Software Foundation, Inc...
(gdb) run now is the time to
Starting program: /net/u/4/r/remon/foo/foo now is the time to
Word 0: /net/u/4/r/remon/foo/foo
Word 1: now
Word 2: is
Word 3: the
Word 4: time
Word 5: to
```

```
Program received signal 11, Segmentation fault
0x22b8 in main (argc=6, argv=0xeffffe1c) at foo.c:9
9    for (i = 0; *argv [i]; i++)
```

The gdb utility has identified the statement that failed. What was the value of i at the time?

```
(gdb) print i
$1 = 6
```

OK...what is the argv value we were about to print?

```
(gdb) print argv [i]
$2 = 0x0
```

Hmm...I'm confused...let's look at all argv values, using two valuable gdb features. The first is using what gdb calls a *convenience variable* (a variable known to gdb but not to the program), in this case $n, to help us index through the argv array. The second is repeating the last command by pressing the Return key. Notice the auto-increment syntax is understood by gdb, making it trivial to step through argv:

```
(gdb) set $n = 0
(gdb) print argv [$n++]
$3 = 0xeffffe7c "/net/u/4/r/remon/foo/foo"
(gdb)
$4 = 0xeffffe95 "now"
(gdb)
$5 = 0xeffffe99 "is"
(gdb)
$6 = 0xeffffe9c "the"
(gdb)
$7 = 0xeffffea0 "time"
(gdb)
$8 = 0xeffffea5 "to"
(gdb)
$9 = 0x0
```

OK, now the problem is obvious. The program should not be dereferencing argv [i]. The gdb utility has helped us once again.

Restrictions on Using gdb

Gdb is free software, which means you can copy and modify it. The only restriction is that you can't place any restrictions on the use of gdb, even if you distribute your modified version of the program. The Free Software Foundation holds the copyright for gdb. Typically, copyrights are used to limit your use of the software; however, the Free Software Foundation's objective is to assure that no one limits anyone's use of the software. Therefore, you'll have to include the Free Software Foundation's copyright and restriction notices with your modified or copied version of the debugger. You can read more about the restrictions in the man pages supplied with the software.

InterViews: A C++ Class Library

You're ready to develop a new application. You've met with the end-users, who are looking forward to your contribution to their efforts. Then they asked, "When can I have your system?"—and it's time to hedge. You don't want to disappoint them, but you want to have sufficient time to develop the system properly.

The specs are nothing unusual, just another simple database application. But the user interface? That can be tricky and time-consuming—unless you use InterViews. InterViews is a C++ class library that speeds the development of user interfaces. Its secret is that nearly all of the objects used to compose a typical application interface are available as part of the library. You simply use these classes as part of your application.

The InterViews library has special features that provide support for resolution-independent graphics, sophisticated document formatting, and graphical connectivity. Want more? You got more! InterViews runs on top of the X Windows system, and comes with a drawing editor, WYSIWYG document editor, and an interface builder all at your fingertips. What more could you want?

According to the InterViews documentation, the library works on systems by Silicon Graphics, DEC, HP, Sun, and IBM. In fact, the authors claim they haven't yet found a UNIX platform that InterViews won't run on. And if you adopt InterViews for your system, you'll be in good company. A few firms listed in the library's documentation as users of the library are NASA, Fujitsu America, Canon Information Systems, and Teknekron.

Installation

One of the many places on the Internet where you will find InterViews is *interviews.stanford.edu*. Copy the library files to your system. You'll find a file called *README* that explains how to build and install the library.

CAUTION
The uncompressed source files are about 8MB, and another 18MB will be used by the installed binaries on a MIPS system that doesn't have shared libraries. You'll need about 30MB of disk space for the building process; this excludes the space required for the binaries. Be prepared to spend about an hour installing the InterViews library.

It's unlikely you'll have any problems during the installation; however, something might go wrong. Before you panic, connect to the InterViews netnews group (*comp.windows.interviews*) and see if another user has a suggestion on how to resolve your problem.

Restrictions
InterViews is protected by the copyright laws, but, the authors of the library are very liberal in granting rights. According to the library's documentation, everyone has unrestricted rights to use, copy, modify, distribute, and even sell the InterViews library.

NOTE
There is no warranty. If you use InterViews and it doesn't work or causes problems with data that is generated by your application, you're on your own.

Known Problems
You'll find that InterViews is well worth the time you spend installing it, although there are a few minuses that you should know. InterViews doesn't fully support Motif or OpenLook. These are planned for the future, but no timetable is available. Also, InterViews 3.0.1 doesn't work with the g++ compiler, and it's unknown whether there are any plans to remedy this situation.

InterViews's documentation contains information about other problems with the library that have been reported by the user community. The documentation also recommends that you contact Mike Stump at *mrs@csun.edu* for more information about InterViews.

Up and Running
The InterViews library contains classes that enable you to easily build attractive and very functional end-user interfaces for your application. In fact, much of the work has been completed for you. All you need to do is use the classes and some of your own code to create the interface. Your application will truly be window based. The window to your application can contain various objects, such as

buttons, menus, pull-down menus, pop-up windows, text boxes, and an assortment of other widgets typically found in a professional application. The specific behavior of each of these is inherited from InterViews objects.

InterViews is based on a top-down input model, where the end-user responds to your application by pointing and clicking the mouse or by entering keystrokes at the keyboard. Each action is treated as an event, and the library has classes built to handle nearly every event that occurs in your application.

Each object in the current window has an associated handler that facilitates your application's response to the end-user's input. For example, there are classes that define the style and the behavior of a push button on the screen. When the end-user points and clicks on the push button, the event is recognized by an InterViews class, which passes the event to the push button's handle. From there, your code handles the response.

A key aspect of using InterViews is that objects are shared, which cuts down on wasted resources. In fact, the library has special routines that act as a "garbage collection service," keeping track of shared objects that are no longer being used by the application. These objects are then released and their associated memory freed for other resources.

Behind the scenes, InterViews is working hard to give you the latest window design features for your application, as well as features that will increase the application's performance. For example, objects on your interface frequently need to retrieve values very fast, as when displaying a character. The application must determine the value of the font before displaying the character on the screen. InterViews has routines built to handle these needs efficiently.

The InterViews library also allows your application to manage information easily. Let's say you want to manage text using a text object. The end-user can select text on the screen by either pointing to it with the mouse or using keyboard commands. A click of the left mouse button over the text object places the application in insert mode. The user can also use any of several control-character commands to execute common editing operations.

Another built-in feature of the library is to allow the end-user to highlight several characters and then replace them with new characters entered from the keyboard. This operation would take you hours to program, but with Interviews it can be a feature of your application within minutes. Nearly every text-editing technique that you find in the latest window-based application is available via InterViews, including the ability to scroll horizontally so you can display text that doesn't fit in the text object on the screen.

Why not take a few minutes right now and download a copy of the InterViews library. Once you've complete the installation process, you'll have a very powerful library handy for use in your next development project.

The makedepend Utility: A Software Development Tool

Programmers, stand back—for a blast that will give you a boost when you create your next C or C++ application. The makedepend utility will take all the hassles out of the dependencies in a makefile, and it's yours for the asking.

Let's face it. All of us know that a make speeds the compiling and linking of application files during development. Once the makefile is created, you let the make utility worry about compiling just the source code that you changed. However, there's a price to pay for this assistance: It's up to you to write the makefile! If you're like many programmers, you don't really *write* a makefile—you *borrow* someone else's and change it to suit your application. Then you have the tedious and error-prone task of specifying the dependencies. Not anymore! You can thank Todd Brunhoff, the author of makedepend. He built a utility that reads your source code and identifies all the dependencies that are required for your makefile.

Sure, you've heard about dependency generators before, and yes, the makedepend utility is another dependency generator. Brunhoff's approach, however, makes this dependency generator stand out from all the rest. He makes three assumptions that allow the makedepend utility run an order of magnitude faster than any other: First he assumes that all files compiled by a single makefile will be compiled with the same -I and -D options. Next, he assumes that most files in a single directory will include largely files of the same type. Third, he assumes that makedepend is called once for each makefile, with all source files maintained by the makefile appearing on the command line.

Confused? Don't be. You don't have to know makedepend's inner workings in order to use it. However, if you like to poke around under the hood, be sure to read the details in the utility's documentation.

Installation

You'll find the source code and documentation files for makedepend at various locations around the Internet; one is */pub/mnt/source/X11R5/mit/util* on *emx.cc.utexas.edu*. Create a makedepend directory on your system and then copy the files. We won't discuss installation procedures here; you'll find everything you need for the installation process in the documentation.

Once you have makedepend installed and running, you may want to read the *comp.sources.x* netnews group to find what the utility's user community is thinking about the software.

Known Problems

You can expect makedepend to be mostly bug-free. However, you might experience a slight problem if you don't have the source for the Berkeley C preprocessor on your system. The makedepend utility is automatically compiled so that all the #if directives are evaluated to True, regardless of their actual value. This means the wrong #include directives might be evaluated. makedepend should have its own parser written for #if expressions; you can read more about this problem and how to work around it in the utility's documentation.

Be sure to check the *comp.sources.x* netnews group for the latest information about new bugs.

Up and Running

You launch makedepend by typing **makedepend**, followed by the name of the source code files. (The example below shows you this command.) Behind the scenes, the utility looks for common dependencies among the source files. Every file included by a source file, directly or indirectly, is referred to as a *dependency*. Dependencies are automatically written to a makefile so that the make utility knows which object files must be recompiled when a dependency has changed.

Suppose each of the source files shown in the following example contains the *header.h* file, which is dependent on *def1.h* and *def2.h* include files:

makedepend *file1.c file2.c*

The makedepend utility parses the first source file and the three include files, determining that the dependencies for these files are *file1.o: header.h def1.h def2.h*. The next step is for makedepend to parse *file2.c*; however, in doing so, the utility recognizes the *header.h* file. Instead of parsing this file—along with the *def1.h* and *def2.h* files—makedepend just adds these include files to the dependencies for *file2.o*.

The makedepend utility places the output of its dependency search in the makefile only if a makefile exists. If the makefile doesn't exist and you don't specify a makefile on the command line, then the output is placed in a file called *Makefile*. (You can specify a specific makefile by using the -f command-line option.) Based upon the results of its source code analysis, makedepend inserts a line in the makefile for each source that is specified on the command line. The line begins with the name of the source file's object file, which is followed by the dependency files that are found in the file's #include directives.

You can control some of makedepend's features by using command-line options. Table 9-8 contains a sampling of these. Read the utility's documentation

OPTION	DESCRIPTION
-Dname=def	Places a definition for name in makedepend's symbol table
-Iincludedir	Prepends includedir to the list of directories to search
-fmakefile	Specifies an alternate makefile
-oobjsuffix	Object file suffix
-wwidth	Line width

TABLE 9-8. *A Sampling of Command-line Options for makedepend*

for a complete listing of options and tips on how to use them. And don't worry if you enter the wrong option. The makedepend utility ignores any option that it doesn't recognize.

The patch Utility: Automatic Source Code Updating

Larry Wall and his associates have come up with a utility to answer any UNIX programmer's dream. Ever try to update software? You probably have, many times, and you've probably discovered how frustrating and time-consuming this chore is. The patch utility changes all that; it takes the output of the diff utility (explained earlier in this chapter) and uses the results to update a program file. This eliminates the need to go line by line in the program file, identifying locations needing to be updated, and then copying the appropriate lines of code into the file. All this work is done for you, thanks to Wall's patch utility.

How does patch do this? You'll have to scan the utility's source code for the whole answer—but it's quite evident that Wall has built in routines that allow patch to make intelligent guesses about where to insert patches into the program file.

The most important benefit of patch is for you programmers who must maintain copies of the same program on various computers. Now, instead of writing your own update program, all you need to do is send the patch file—the output of the diff utility—and have patch do the work for you.

Installation
The source code for patch is located in the */contrib-source/dco/patch/src* directory on *decuac.dec.com*. Create a patch directory on your computer and then copy the

utility's files to that directory; patch comes with a makefile all ready for your make utility. Type **make** at the prompt, and the proper binary files will be created for you.

The patch utility should work without giving you any problems. It comes with a set of manpages to help you if you do uncover any difficulties. If you find a bug, you may want to contact Wall at *lwall@netlabs.com* directly to report your problems.

Watch Out!

The patch utility is almost perfect, but it still has a few problems. One is that it cannot tell if the line numbers are off in an ed script; it can only detect bad line numbers when diff finds a **change** command or a **delete** command. Generally, you needn't be too concerned with this, as long as the program file compiles without any errors.

Another problem occurs if the code within the program file has been duplicated and set off by the #ifdef statement. Consider this example:

```
#ifdef OLDCODE
 /* old code */
 #else
 /* new code */
#endif
```

Here patch is unable to patch both versions. In fact, you may think that the utility was successful, when in reality the wrong version received the update.

CAUTION
Don't apply the update twice. If you execute patch with the same set of files twice, patch will actually reverse the update and offer to remove the patch.

Jump-Starting the patch Utility

The patch utility is very easy to use. You'll need two identical program files. Make changes to the first program file; then the objective is to update the second program file with those changes.

- The first step is to use diff to create a patch file. This file contains the difference between the first and second program files—the changes that you just made to the first file.

- Now you're ready to put patch to work. At the prompt, type **patch <
patchfile**. The utility automatically determines the type of diff utility listing that is contained in the patch file.

■ The patch utility skips the leading and trailing garbage and applies the new lines of code to the second program file. This is a handy feature—it means you can feed an article that contains a diff listing directly into the utility, without having to strip away the article from the code. When patch is done, the new file will replace the original file.

In our earlier example, the new file will replace the second program file. Before this occurs, the original file is backed up and given either the *.orig* or the ~file name extension, depending on the system that you are using. (You can specify your own file name extension by using the -b option.)

Table 9-9 contains a sampling of command-line options that you can use. Read the patch utility's manpages for more information about all options that are available to you.

We mentioned that the patch utility has some intelligence; let's see how Wall implemented this. A typical problem for patch is detecting when line numbers are incorrect. The utility will intelligently attempt to find the correct place to apply the changes.

The patch utility first takes the line number that is mentioned for the change and adds an offset determined by the previous changes. For example, if the line number in the patch file is 110, but the previous change added 20 new lines, patch will operate on line 130.

If there isn't a match, patch scans forward and backward for a set of lines that match the context of the changes. Once a match to that is found, the changes are placed in the file. If no context match is found, patch repeats the scan, this time ignoring the first and last lines of the context of the changes. If again no match is found, the utility doesn't give up. Another scan is executed, this time ignoring the first two and last two lines of the context of the changes.

At this point, if no match is found, patch gives up and copies the failed changes to a file that has the same name as the program file but with either the *.rej* or the # extension, depending on your system. Keep in mind that the line numbers of the rejected changes reflect the approximate numbers in the *new* file rather than the *original* file. The patch utility will exit with a nonzero status if any rejection files are created. You'll have to manually update any lines that are contained in the rejection file.

The rcs Utility:
A Source Code Manager

Nearly every programmer has experienced this nightmare: You work on the program for days. You even make copies of your work in progress on tape, disk,

OPTION	DESCRIPTION
-c	Interprets the patch file as a context diff
-d dir	Causes patch to interpret dir as a directory
-D sym	Causes patch to use the #ifdef...#endif construct to mark changes
-e	Interprets the patch file as an **ed** script
-E	Causes patch to remove output files that are empty
-f	Hides prompts
-o filename	Specifies the output file name
-s	Makes patch do its work silently unless an error occurs
-S	Skips the current patch from the patch file, then looks for the next file
-v	Causes patch to print out its revision header and patch level
-t'	Always makes numbered backup files

TABLE 9-9. *Helpful Command-line Options for patch*

and in several directories. But which source code is the latest? Make the wrong decision, and you lose countless hours of work.

The rcs utility prevents this nightmare from becoming reality. The utility is actually six programs; together they take the pain and confusion out of managing your source code. As long as you faithfully use rcs, you'll never have to wonder which copy of the source code is the current version of your program. The utility acts as a librarian, requiring you or other programmers on your team to "check out" the latest copy of the source code. Once the file is checked out, no one else can retrieve it for editing until the original file is checked back in by rcs.

The rcs utility's six components are ci, co, ident, rcs, recdiff, and rcsmerge. When you use rcs, the first step is to save your source code, using either ci or rcs. The rcs component can also be used to change one of the attributes in an existing rcs file.

Once your source code is safely stored, you'll want to check out a copy of the program. Just call in the co component, which does all the leg work for you and retrieves a revision from an rcs file. Now, are you sure you are working with the correct rcs file? You can't leave anything to chance. You start up the ident component, which helps you identify an rcs file by searching for all occurrences of a keyword that you specify in a command-line argument.

You start making your changes, and in the process perhaps you walk away from your system without checking the source code back into the rcs utility. When you return, you may be unsure if rcs is up-to-date. But you needn't be—the rcsdiff component comes to your aid. It will compare the contents of your source with those of rcs; if you find a difference, you didn't check the file back in. Next, you use the rcsmerge component to incorporate the changes between two revisions into a single revision file.

What power! And it's all yours at no cost. You can thank Walter F. Tichy, Adam Hammer, Thomas Narten, and Dan Trinkle of Purdue for their work on rcs through version 4.3. The many other contributors who were involved in rcs's development receive due credit in the utility's documentation.

Installation

You'll find the source for the rcs utility in */pub/packages/gnu* on *ftp.cc.mcgill.ca*. Create the appropriate directories on your system and then copy the rcs utility files. Since the utility comes with a ready-to-run makefile, all you need to do is type **make**, and make will create all the necessary binary files for you. You can read more details about rcs installation in the documentation.

If everything doesn't go well after a few attempts, drop an email describing your problem to *rcs-bugs@cs.purdue.edu*. As with any free UNIX utility, there isn't any guarantee that your problem will be fixed, but there is an excellent chance another user might have a suggestion to place you on the right track.

The ci Component

The ci component saves new revisions to a specially formatted rcs with the rcs file name extension. Here's how it works: Type

ci *filename*

at the prompt. For *filename*, enter the name of the working file to be incorporated into the rcs file. Then press ENTER—it's that simple.

CAUTION

Before executing ci, make sure that your login ID is on the access list for the rcs file if the access list option is in effect for this file. The only exception to this rule is if you are the superuser or the owner of the file. Read the rcs documentation for more about the access list.

Before it saves the new revision, ci determines if the new revision is different from the existing revision. If it finds no difference, ci ignores the new revision.

Fortunately, ci informs you of the operation each step of the way, with messages that summarize the changes. If this is the first entry into the rcs file, ci creates the new rcs file, places the source code into the file, and identifies the source code as revision 1.1. Also, an empty access list is created in the process.

The ci component can be controlled with command-line options, a sampling of which are listed in Table 9-10. A complete list can be found in the utility's documentation.

The ci component might create a few temporary files, in the directory that contains your source code and in the system's temporary directory. In addition, the user of the rcs file must be able to search and write to the directory that contains that file. Access to rcs files can be controlled by properly setting the permission of the directory containing the files. Keep in mind that only users with write access can change the rcs files.

NOTE
You may want to let your systems administrator handle rcs file access control. In fact, the rcs utility's documentation contains several useful hints for systems administrators. Be sure your systems administrator reads this information before installing the utility on your system.

The co Component

The co component is used to retrieve a version of your source code from the specified rcs file. Just type

    co *filename*

where *filename* is the file you want to retrieve. Press ENTER, and co copies your source file to a working file, which you can browse and edit at your leisure.

OPTION	DESCRIPTION
-r[rev]	Checks in a revision, releases the corresponding lock, and removes the working file
-l[rev]	Immediately checks out the deposited revision and locks it
-u[rev]	Reads the working file immediately after check-in
-f[rev]	Deposits the new revision even if it is not different from the preceding one
-k[rev]	Determines the revision number, creation date, state, and author
-q[rev]	Initiates Quiet mode

TABLE 9-10. *Some Command-line Options for the ci Component of rcs*

Can someone else check out a copy of an rcs file while you have it? That depends on whether you locked the file when you executed co. You won't need to lock the file if you are not going to change the file; for example, if you'll just be browsing or compiling, don't bother locking the file. If you intend to change the file, however, place a lock on it when you check it out. This prevents two programmers from updating the same file at the same time. The utility's documentation shows you how to lock the file.

You can select a revision from the rcs file based upon a variety of key pieces of data, including the data and time the file was checked in, the author, and the state. Additional options are discussed in the documentation. Table 9-11 contains a sampling of these command-line options.

The ident Component

Searching for information within the rcs file is easy, thanks to ident. The ident component searches for all occurrences of the rcs-formatted keyword that you enter on the command line. Simply type

>   **ident** *keyword filename*

at the prompt, substituting the appropriate *keyword* and *filename* information, and press ENTER.

As ident cranks away, you might see warning messages displayed on the screen. You can suppress these messages by using the -q option on the command line (**ident -q**). The rcs documentation covers in detail how to use the ident component, including examples.

The rcs Component

The rcs component is used to the create new rcs files and to change the attributes of an existing rcs file. Along with the source code, the rcs file contains an access list, a change log, some descriptive text, and other control attributes—all of which

OPTION	DESCRIPTION
-r[rev]	Retrieves the latest revision equal to rev
-l[rev]	Same as -r, plus it locks the retrieved revision
-u[rev]	Same as -r, plus it unlocks the retrieved revision
-p[rev]	Prints the retrieved revision on the standard output
-q[rev]	Initiates Quiet mode

TABLE 9-11. *Some Command-line Options for the co Component of rcs*

can be modified by using the rcs component. For example, before anyone can check out source code, they must be registered on the access list for that particular rcs file. There are a few exceptions, which are discussed in the documentation. You can add a programmer's login ID to the access list by typing

    rcs -abook *filename*

and pressing ENTER. The **rcs** command invokes the rcs component; -a is the append option; and book is the login ID to be added to the access list. The *filename* is the name of the rcs file.

    Table 9-12 contains additional command-line options that can be used with the rcs component. You'll find a complete list and instructions for use in the rcs documentation.

The rcsdiff and rcsmerge Components

Whenever you are unsure whether two rcs files are identical, stop wondering and call on the rcsdiff component to answer your question. Just type

    rcsdiff -r *version one* **-r** *version two*

and press ENTER. You can also compare your working copy of the file with the latest file checked into rcs, by leaving out the -r flags; or compare your working copy with a specific older revision by using only one -r flag. If both files contain exactly the same characters, the rcsdiff component returns a 0 return code and prints nothing. A 1 is returned if there are any differences, and a 2 is returned if rcsdiff has a problem while making the comparison.

OPTION	DESCRIPTION
-i	Creates and initializes a new rcs file, but does not deposit any revision
-alogins	Appends the specified login names to the access list of the rcs file
-e[logins]	Erases the specified login names from the access list of the rcs file
-u[rev]	Unlocks the revision with number rev
-L	Sets locking to strict
-U	Sets locking to nonstrict
-orange	Deletes ("outdates") the revisions given by range
-q	Runs in Quiet mode.

TABLE 9-12. *Some Command-line Options for the rcs Component of rcs*

Once you have identified that the two rcs files are different, you can easily incorporate the differences by using the rcsmerge component—assuming that you want to maintain the changes and keep both rcs files up-to-date. Say you have two versions of the *hello.c* program. The first version is called revision 1.1, and the second is an unreleased revision that you call 2.1. Now you want to merge both files into a third file called *mergedfile.c*. Here is the command line you type:

```
rcsmerge -p -r1.1 -r2.1 hello.c >mergedfile.c
```

Table 9-13 contains a sampling of the command-line options available with the rcsmerge component. The rcs documentation tells you more about how to work with the rcsdiff and rcsmerge components.

Restrictions

The rcs utility is distributed under the license of the Free Software Foundation, Inc. The utility's documentation contains the official list of restrictions. You'll find that there are no warranties, guarantees, or even a statement that the utility will work on your system. Furthermore, you have the right to freely distribute and modify the utility.

The major limitation is that you can't prohibit anyone else from distributing or modifying the utility—even if you distribute your modified version. Basically, if you receive the utility free-of-charge, you can't charge anyone else for any version of it, nor can you prohibit anyone else from using it.

The Tcl Utility:
An Embedded Scripting Language

Anyone who has ever dealt with an end-user soon realizes the main objectives of developing software. End-users don't care what language you use or how

OPTION	DESCRIPTION
-p[rev]	Sends the result to standard output instead of overwriting the working file
-q[rev]	Runs in Quiet mode and does not print diagnostics
-r[rev]	Merge with respect to revision rev

TABLE 9-13. *Some Command-line Options for the rcsmerge Component of rcs*

efficiently you write the code. All they care about are three things: Will it do the job? Is it easy to use? And can you deliver it tomorrow, before lunch?

Considering all the years that you've worked at building your programming skills, these questions are almost an insult. But they are also the reality most application developers must face. So how can you meet such a challenge? One possible answer is to use the Tcl utility for your next development project. Tcl is an embeddable scripting language that has many of the features you need for a typical application. Consider it your "secret weapon" for combating typical—and sometimes unreasonable—requests made by the end-user.

John Ousterhout developed the Tcl language at the University of California at Berkeley. The principle behind this language is that a single interpretive language (Tcl) controls all aspects of an interactive application, including the application interface and communication between applications. This all sounds good, but what will Tcl do for you? It will make programming X Windows simpler and accelerate your development time about five to ten times. Yes, you read correctly. These are the latest in programming techniques—we're talking about using the Tcl utility to create a widget-based application in a minimum amount of time.

Does this sound too good to be true? It is true. If you don't believe us and you don't want to waste time loading Tcl on your system, we'll give you another option: In the documentation, Ousterhout offers a preview of his upcoming book about the Tcl utility. Just FTP to the Tcl directory on *sprite.berkeley.edu,* and download the draft of his book.

Installation

You'll find a copy of the Tcl utility in the */.0/BSD/UCB* directory on *gatekeeper.dec.com* on the Internet. Remember to use archie to find other locations that are closer to you. You should be able to build and run the binaries without much difficulty, as long as your system is compatible with POSIX, DSD, or System V.

Ousterhout reports in the documentation that Tcl works well on workstations from Sun, DEC, HP, IBM, and Silicon Graphics. It also runs on personal computers that have the SCO UNIX and XENIX operation systems.

Following is an overview of what it takes to install Tcl on your system. But in no way do these brief instructions replace the step-by-step ones that come with the utility. Be sure to read those instructions before you attempt to build the binaries.

- ◾ Execute the configure script that comes with the utility. This script allows you to customize Tcl for your system, and then creates a makefile for you. If you're not confortable with this process, read the *configure.info* file, in which Ousterhout offers tips on using the configure script.

- ◾ Once the makefile is created, type **make** at the prompt to execute the make utility. Two files will be built: The *libtcl.a* file is the Tcl utility library that you link to your C-language program so you can execute embedded Tcl commands from within your C program. The *tclsh* binary is used to enter Tcl commands interactively from the keyboard.

■ Type **make install**, which installs the Tcl binaries and the script files in the standard place on your system. However, before executing the make utility, be sure to grant write permission on */usr/local*. If you're interested knowing where the Tcl utility's files are installed on your system, just read the makefile, which was created in the previous step of the installation process.

■ Before you rush into invoking the utility, the final step is to set your tcl_LIBRARY variable to the full path name of the library subdirectory. If you leave out this step, the Tcl utility won't be able to find all the files it needs to execute properly.

■ When you're ready, type **tclsh** to start the utility.

Restrictions

The Regents of the University of California hold the copyright to the Tcl utility; however, all the freedom you need to use it is given in the utility's documentation. You can use, copy, modify, and distribute this software without prior permission from the university, and you don't have to pay any fees or royalties. The university also states that you can't hold it responsible for any liability as a result of using this software. They make no warranties that the utility will work on any system. Keep this in mind if you decide to incorporate Tcl into your own application.

Known Problems

We could find no bugs reports in Tcl's documentation, but this isn't to say the utility is bug free. Ousterhout is quick to fix any reported bug, however, so by the time a bug report finds its way into the documentation, Ousterhout probably will have eliminated it.

Probably the fastest and most reliable way of identifying problems with the Tcl utility is to connect to the *comp.lang.tcl* news group on netnews. There you'll find the exchange of general information and bug reports, along with possible workarounds for problems that arise. If you experience a possible bug, let Ousterhout know about it as soon as possible. Although you can drop him an email at *ouster@cs.berkeley.edu*, your best bet is to post your problem to the utility's netnews group. In this way, you'll be asking for help from Ousterhout *and* the very large community of Tcl users at the same time. Ousterhout states in the documentation that he is an avid reader of the news group. The user community will only provide you with tips and hints on solving your problem, as a favor to you; no one receives financial compensation for helping you out of a jam.

Sometimes the problem isn't with Tcl but rather with the programmer. If for some reason you find yourself in need of more hand-holding than is available on the Internet, Ousterhout reports a service that is ready and willing to come to your aid—for a price. The NeoSoft Corporation supplies commercial training and support for Tcl. If you're interested in this service, drop them an email at *info@neosoft.com.*

Up and Running

We've praised the Tcl utility, and now it's time to take you behind the scenes and show you a little of how to use it. (Underscore the word *little.)* We don't have enough space in this book to give you a complete tour, but you'll find a very fine set of documentation provided with the utility, which should answer nearly all of your questions. And of course you can also read the draft of Ousterhout's book, which you will find in the documentation.

Enough about what we're *not* going to tell you—let's look at some examples of the Tcl utility's language. The syntax of Tcl is similar more to a shell language than to C. Words are separated by spaces, commands are separated by newlines or semi colons, and all commands return a string result. There is a rich set of built-in commands and functions. Tcl even gives you access to UNIX files and commands. In addition to these value-added extras, you also get the features that you expect from any language, such as conditional and looping, procedures, and arithmetic expressions. Now on to the examples.

One of the major advantages of using Tcl is that you cut down on the programming time necessary to build a sophisticated user interface for your application. This is possible through Tcl's Tk Toolkit, which allows you to create simple commands that produce complicated screens.

Suppose you want to display a button on the screen that the end-user can press to exit the application. If you've developed applications in Motif or other windowing languages, you know that you'll need several lines of code to make this button a working part of your application. But with Tcl this isn't so. Here is the one line of Tcl utility code that you need in your program to create this functional button:

```
button .dlg.quit -text Quit -foreground red -command exit
```

Take a closer look at this example. Just by reading the syntax, you probably know what's going on with this statement. That's why it's easy to learn Tcl's language. The button is the name of a class of widget; widgets are the buttons, menus, scroll bars, and so forth that are used to build a Motif-like user interface.

Back to the button. It's located in the dialog widget called *dlg,* which itself is in the window called *quit.* This statement has three arguments: *text, foreground,* and *command.* Each argument is preceded by a hyphen and followed by a value. In this example, the word Quit is displayed inside the button widget, in red, and when the end-user selects the button, it executes the **Exit** command.

Now let's get fancy. This time you'll see three additional widget properties:

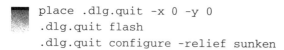

```
place .dlg.quit -x 0 -y 0
.dlg.quit flash
.dlg.quit configure -relief sunken
```

The first command, *place,* is used to position the dialog/window at screen coordinates 0, 0. Notice that the *-x* and *-y* arguments are used to define the upper-left corner of the widget. Tcl's geometry manager actually moves the widget into position.

Now, let's flash the widget. To do this we just tell Tcl the name of the widget and the command to flash. Finally, we want to dress up the appearance of the widget. Tcl has several built-in styles that will give any application a professional look. In this example, we'll give the widget a sunken, relief-style appearance. We identify the widget and then issue the *configure* command; then we set the *relief* value to *sunken.*

Is the Tcl utility really that easy to use? We think it is—and it will be a valuable addition to any programmer's UNIX toolbox. But you'll have to convince yourself. Connect to the Internet and download your own copy of Tcl. It's free!

The xscope Utility: Multiple Users on a Single Process

James Peterson has written a small but powerful utility that is perfect for keeping a watchful eye on a remote application. We're talking about xscope, which monitors the connection between an X11 window server and a client program. Admittedly, this sounds a little like Big Brother looking over your shoulder, but sometimes that's required fine-tuning for an application.

Let's say you delivered your application to an end-user. For a few weeks everything is working well, and then you receive a telephone call: There seems to be a problem with your software. And it's one of those bugs hated by end-users and developers alike—it's the bug that goes away every time you try to investigate the problem. "It didn't work. Believe me. When you're *here,* everything works fine..." You know they're not making it up, but you can't begin to fix the problem unless you can replicate or at least see it.

With xscope, you have another tool in your UNIX toolbox that is just right for this job. Launch the utility into action, and you'll be able to see every byte that travels between the X11 window server and your application. Besides showing you the input and output of your program, xscope prints information about the traffic and gives you performance and debugging information. What more could you ask for? This is a perfect tool for debugging your application in the field, as well as for tuning the application to its best performance.

Installation

As for most of the utilities reviewed in this book, the Internet has many locations where you can pick up xscope for free. One of those is */pub* on *qiclab.scn.rain.com*. Make an empty directory on your system and then copy over the files. You'll find complete installation instructions in the utility's documentation. Just follow each step carefully, and xscope will be running smoothly in no time. If you run into problems, you may want to read one of the *comp.sources.x*, *comp.windows.x* netnews groups and see if other xscope users have posted workarounds to your problem. If not, post the problem yourself and see if you receive any hints.

Restrictions

Peterson holds the copyright to the xscope utility. The fine print on any restrictions he has placed on his product is available in the utility's documentation.

Known Problems

You'll notice that xscope still has areas for improvement. For example, the utility may require additional modifications to handle byte swapping on architectures other than the Sun3 (it does work well on the Sun3). Another potential problem is with the Imakefile that is supplied with the utility; the file may contain incorrect code for some systems.

One of the concerns listed in the documentation is that there is no code in xscope to interpret typed commands from the keyboard. You can read all about these problems and a few others in the xscope documentation.

Up and Running

Start xscope by typing **xscope** at the prompt, followed by the appropriate options and the name of the X Windows server and the display. Table 9-14 contains a sampling of the available command-line options, and a complete list can be found in the utility's documentation.

Running the xscope utility involves three processes: X11, xscope, and the client program. Let's say that the X11 window server is running on machine A and will be displayed on display B. Machine A is actually the name of the server, and display B is the number of the display. This is how Peterson explains the xscope operation in the documentation.

The xscope utility operates between the X11 window server and the client program. For this to occur, you must identify the server and the display to the xscope utility, by passing this information on the command line. In the following

OPTION	DESCRIPTION
-d	Defines the display number
-h	Determines the host that xscope will use to find the server
-i	Specifies the port that xscope will use to take requests from clients
-o	Determines the port that xscope will use to connect to the server
-q	Runs in Quiet output mode

TABLE 9-14.   *A Sampling of Command-line Options for xscope*

example, the name of the server and the number of the display will replace the letter A and B:

    xscope -hA -dB

The final step in the process is to connect the client program to the xscope utility, rather than to X11. This isn't difficult because xscope listens on the same port as X11. In our example, the client program would connect to A:B, where A is the name of the server and B is the display number.

CHAPTER 10

Graphics Utilities

Nearly every application that you build or report that you generate requires the punch of graphical output. End users have come to expect and demand professional looking graphics as part of their software. However, including graphics in an application can be tricky and some developers seem to skirt the issue. If you're one of those developers, you don't have to run away from graphics any more.

Here are a few powerful graphics utilities that make it easy to incorporate graphics into your application. We're talking about the gnuplot, pbm, xfig, and xv utilities. The gnuplot utility will take your raw data from a file or from an expression and use it to plot a professional quality graph. We're not talking about just one kind of graph, but graphs that range from the simple to the three-dimensional. All you need is to specify the data and the style of graph, and gnuplot does the work for you.

After the gnuplot utility, you'll learn about the pbm utility, which is a 'must have' for anyone who works with bitmaps. Let's say that you found this perfect bitmap to use in your application. There are no restrictions on this bitmap and it's free for the taking. However, the bitmap format is incompatible with your application. Well, this is the last time you run into this problem. Now, just call on the pbm utility to convert the bitmap format into a format that is compatible with your application.

What happens if you can't find the right diagram for your application? Create it yourself. It isn't difficult at all if you have the proper tool in your UNIX toolbox. And you have it! The utility is called the xfig utility, and you'll read its review in this chapter. The final graphics utility that we'll talk about is the xv utility, which you can use to display and manipulate many types of images. The utilities discussed in this chapter are listed here.

The gnuplot Utility: Plotting Software
The pbm Utility: Bitmap Converter Software
The xfig Utility: Graphic Software
The xv Utility: An Image Viewer for X Windows

The gnuplot Utility: Plotting Software

In today's world of computing, very few users of applications want to deal with raw data. In fact, many of them want only to see a dramatic picture of the information in the form of a graph. Let's face it. There are simple graphs that can be programmed in a few minutes. And then there are those graphs that can take hours to develop. Of course, users almost always prefer—and sometimes demand—complicated graphs.

Next time this happens to you, don't duck. Instead, come out shooting because you'll be packing all the tools you'll need to produce the fanciest, most complicated graphics that you can image—within minutes.

The tool that we're talking about is gnuplot, which was originally created by Thomas Williams and Colin Kelley. Russell Lang, Dave Kotz, John Campbell, and Gershon Elber picked up where Williams and Kelley left off to give us the powerful utility that we know today.

What makes gnplot so powerful is that all you need to create a publication quality graph is to describe the graph using simple commands. In fact, gnplot has built-in functions that will even perform math for you. So instead of massaging the raw data into a plottable form, you can have gnplot do some of the massaging for you.

The gnplot utility can save you countless time. All you need to do is invest some of your time installing the utility on your system and learning how to use a few gnuplot commands. In return, you'll receive a powerful addition to your UNIX utility toolbox.

Installation

You'll find gnplot at many locations across the Internet, one being in the *pub/gnuplot/gnuplot3.2.tar.Z directory* on *dartmouth.edu*. Create a directory on your system and then copy all the necessary files to that directory. Be sure you set ftp to binary mode before bringing over the files.

Although installation of any software can be tricky, you'll find complete instructions provided in the utility's documentation files. Keep in mind that you're not the first to install gnplot. Others have successfully installed this utility on the Sun's 3 and Sun's 4, as well as the VAX 6410, IBM PC, and the DECStation 5000/200PXG. You'll find a whole list of other systems where installation has been successful in the utility's documentation.

The gnuplot utility comes with an almost ready-to-use makefile. The file is actually called *makefile.unx*, which you need to copy to Makefile. Each system is different, so the setup of the makefile might require a little tweaking before you can use it. Examine the Makefile and make any necessary changes. Be sure to review the settings of the HELPDEST and TERMFLAGS variables. These settings are probably the most common variables that you must change to suit your system.

Next, type **make**. After a few minutes make will finish creating the binary files. You're still not finished. You must type **make install** to complete the building process.

The gnuplot utility should compile cleanly. However, should you run into difficulty, reread the installation procedures to be sure that you haven't left out a step. If you're still having a problem, review the known bugs that are listed in the utility's documentation, then read the *comp.graphics.gnuplot* news group on netnews. If all else fails, you can send your bug report to:

bug-gnuplot@ames.arc.nasa.gov

Once you've successfully installed the gnuplot utility, join the utility's mailing list. Just send a note to :

info-gnuplot-request@ames.arc.nasa.gov

Restrictions

Simply stated, there aren't any real restrictions to the gnuplot utility. You can use, copy, and distribute the utility for any purpose without paying the authors a royalty. All you must do is assure that the copyright notice, as listed in the utility's documentation, appears in all copies that you distribute.

However, you must abide by one rule if you decide to include your own modifications to gnuplot. The authors don't have a problem with you modifying their work. In fact, explicit permission is given to modify the source code. The only catch is that you don't have the right to distribute your modified version. All modifications are distributed as patches to the current released version of the utility.

You can read all about the details of these restrictions in the utility's documentation. You'll also notice as part of the restrictions that the utility is provided to you as is. There isn't any expressed or implied warranty. Be sure to include a similar notice in the copies of the utility that you distribute.

Known Problems

The gnuplot utility is a powerful tool—once you have it up and running. However, there are a few known problems that can impede your success. For example, for all of you who are using ULTRIX X11R3, watch out for a bug that causes the X11 driver to display every other plot. The only solution is to upgrade the X11 libraries. You can get this upgrade from either DEC or MIT.

Up and Running

The gnuplot utility is a command-driven, interactive function plotting utility. Launching the utility is done by typing **gnuplot**. At the gnuplot prompt, type **plot**, followed by an expression and the name of the file that contains the data. Let's say that you want to plot a sine curve. You'd enter **plot sin(x)**. Next, you'd want to plot pairs of numbers from a file called *datafile*. Just type **plot "datafile"** and gnuplot interprets the data as XY coordinates, and plots them on a graph.

You can create several types of curves with gnuplot. Curves are nearly always planar and are assumed to be in the XY plane. In such a case, all you need to provide are the X and Y coordinates. The most basic curve that can be created is the explicit function. This is where for each given X, there is one and only one Y value that is associated with it.

At the heart of any gnuplot graph are the **plot** and **splot** commands. The **plot** command is used to plot two-dimensional graphs, while the **splot** command draws a three-dimensional surface of the data. Each of these commands accepts arguments that describe the graph that is to be built. These arguments are range, function, title, and style.

The range argument specifies beginning and end points of the data. Function is usually either a mathematical expression or the name of the data file. The title

argument is used to specify the names of the XY coordinates, and the style
argument defines the type of graph that is to be plotted.

The gnuplot utility will accept any mathematical expression that can be used
by C, FORTRAN, Pascal, or BASIC. The C programming language precedence table
is followed for each operator. You can, of course, use parentheses to explicitly
define the order of operation.

However, the utility's mathematical capabilities don't stop here. Gnuplot uses
the same built-in mathematical functions that are found in the UNIX math library.
In addition, you are able to use the logical operators and their shortcuts within an
expression in gnuplot. These are the same operators that you use in the C
programming language.

You'll find gnuplot filled with commands that allow you to create nearly any
graph that you can imagine. Table 10-1 contains a sampling of these commands.
The utility's documentation contains a full listing along with tips on how to use
each command. You'll also notice a full listing of editing commands that help you
describe the graph in gnuplot terms. We've provided a sampling of these in Table
10-2.

COMMAND	DESCRIPTION
cd "directory"	Changes the current working directory
clear	Erases the current screen or output device
comments	Comments are preceded by a pound sign (#)
help	Displays on-line help
load	Executes each line of the input file as if it had been typed in interactively
pause	Displays any text then waits a specified amount of time or a carriage return.
ranges	Specifies the region of the plot that will be displayed
print	Prints the value of an expression to the screen
replot	Repeats the last plot or splot command
save	Saves user-defined functions, variables, set options, and the last plot command
set arrow	Places an arrow on a plot

TABLE 10-1. *A Sampling of gnuplot Commands*

COMMAND	DESCRIPTION
CTRL-B	Moves back a single character
CTRL-F	Moves forward a single character
CTRL-A	Moves to the beginning of the line
CTRL-E	Moves to the end of the line
CTRL-H and DEL	Deletes the previous character
CTRL-D	Deletes the current character
CTRL-K	Deletes from current position to the end of line
CTRL-L and CTRL-R	Redraws line in case it is lost
CTRL-U	Deletes the entire line
CTRL-W	Deletes the last word

TABLE 10-2.   *A Sampling of Editing Commands*

We hope that your appetite is whetted and you're ready to go full steam into gnuplot. Now it's time to load the files, create the binaries, and beef up your knowledge of the gnuplot commands so you'll be ready the next time someone asks for a quick graph.

The pbm Utility:
Bitmap Converter Software

Here's a problem anyone who works with graphics can appreciate. You spend days looking for the ideal bitmap for your graphics project. Then you find it. But, wait! The bitmap is in a format that your graphics software doesn't recognize. You can't use the bitmap—until now!

Don't throw away a bitmap because your graphics software can't read the file. Instead, turn the problem over to pbm to convert the bitmap into a file format that is acceptable to your graphics utility. Now, practically any bitmap that you can get your hands on can be incorporated into your graphics project.

The pbm utility is actually a toolkit of several utilities, each of which is used to convert a particular type of file format. Once you've installed pbm, you can read about each of these in the utility's documentation. When you do, you'll find that this is a powerhouse of bitmap file reformatting tools.

With pbm in your toolbox, you can tackle conversion of simple bitmaps, gray scale images, and full-color images. What more could you ask for?

Installation

You'll find pbm in the */.9/X11/contrib* directory on *gatekeeper.dec.com*, as well as in other locations on the Internet. Copy the utility's files to an empty directory on your system. Once you've unpacked the files, you can use make to create the binaries. The pbm utility's documentation provides several useful hints on making the utility.

If all goes well, you'll be ready to convert your first bitmap in no time. And if you experience problems, drop an email to:

jef@well.sf.ca.us {apple, ucbvax}!well!jef

Be sure to include the details of your problem. You can also read the *comp.graphics* netnews group to read more information about pbm.

Restrictions

The restrictions on the utility are complicated—and simple. The problem stems from the number of software packages that make up the utility. A number of these packages have their own restrictions. You can read about these individual limitations in the utility's documentation files.

Although there might be a number of restrictions, most of them have the same limitations. That is, you can use, copy, modify, and distribute the utility and documentation for any purpose without paying the authors any fee. All you must do is include the author's copyright notice in your distribution. You must also make it known that the utility is provided "as is" without any expressed or implied warranty. Simply, no one is promising that the utility will work.

Up and Running

The key to using pbm is to find the proper converter tool to use. Table 10-3 lists some of the file formats that can be converted by the utility. Each format has its own converter tool. It is up to you to match the converter tool with the graphic file format.

At first, this might seem as an insurmountable task. But it isn't. The objective is to convert the source bitmap file to the utility's portable bitmap format. Next, convert from the portable bitmap format to the target bitmap format.

TIP

To find the proper commands for reformatting your bitmap, bring up the utility's *README* file using your favorite text editor, then use the text editor's search facility to locate the format command that you are interested in using.

FORMAT	READING	WRITING
BLACK & WHITE FORMATS:		
Sun icon file	X	X
X10 and X11 bitmap file	X	X
MacPaint	X	X
CMU window manager format	X	X
MGR format	X	X
Group 3 FAX	X	X
GEM .img format	X	X
Bennet Yee's "face" format	X	X
Atari Degas .pi3 format	X	X
Andrew Toolkit raster object	X	X
Xerox doodle brushes	X	
ASCII graphics		X
HP LaserJet format		X
GraphOn graphics		X
BBN BitGraph graphics		X
Printronix format		X
Gemini 10x printer format		X
Epson printer format		X
UNIX plot(5) file		X
Zinc Interface Library icon		X
GRAY SCALE FORMATS:		
Usenix FaceSaver(tm) file	X	X
FITS	X	X
Lisp Machine bit-array-file	X	X
raw grayscale bytes	X	
HIPS	X	
PostScript "image" data	X	

TABLE 10-3. *Formats That Can Be Converted Using pbm*

FORMAT	READING	WRITING
COLOR FORMATS:		
GIF	X	X
IFF ILBM	X	X
PICT	X	X
Atari Degas .pi1 format	X	X
XPM	X	X
PC Paintbrush .pcx format	X	X
TrueVision Targa file	X	X
HP PaintJet format	X	X
Abekas YUV format	X	X
MTV/PRT ray-tracer output	X	
QRT ray-tracer output	X	
Img-whatnot file	X	
Xim file	X	
Atari uncompressed Spectrum	X	
Atari compressed Spectrum	X	
NCSA Interactive Color Raster	X	
X11 "puzzle" file		X
Motif UIL icon file		X
DEC sixel format		X
MULTI-TYPE FORMATS:		
Sun raster file	X	X
TIFF	X	X
X11 window dump file	X	X
X10 window dump file	X	
PostScript		X

TABLE 10-3. *Formats That Can Be Converted Using pbm* (continued)

The xfig Utility: Graphic Software

You've heard lots about the graphical power of UNIX and X Windows. So how can you harness some of this power for yourself? Start with xfig. The xfig utility can help you transform those graphic images from your mind to your electronic canvas. And when you combine xfig with the TransFig package, which comes with TeX, you can make hard copies of those images.

Supoj Sutanthavibul of the University of Texas at Austin is the original author of xfig. However, the version that you have is the result of Sutanthavibul's work combined with that of many more contributors. The utility's documentation gives them their due credit.

So what does this utility do? Nearly everything in the way of charts. The xfig utility is menu driven, so you don't have to worry about looking up strange commands. In fact, it's totally intuitive. Well, almost. You'll still have to read the utility's documentation. And you'll find plenty to read to help you through those rough spots.

For example, you can create a graphic that includes text, then scale both to any size. You can have multiple graphics on the same image, then combine some of them so they can be treated as a single graphic. Worried about aligning objects on your canvas? With other graphics packages you might, but not with xfig. The xfig commands will automatically align objects on your canvas any time you select one of the alignment options.

In addition to being able to draw standard objects such as a box and circle, you can use xfig to rotate the object in nearly any direction. It's as easy as making an icon from a palette, then entering the degree of rotation—just like standard paint programs. There's a whole lot more to xfig, as you'll soon see.

Installation

First, create an empty directory on your system, then copy the files from the /contrib/R5fixes/xfig-patches/ directory on x.org or from another location on the Internet. One of the files that you copy is a Imakefile. This file is already prepared for the UNIX Imake utility.

Imake actually creates the makefile that you need to build the utility's binary files.

Next, execute Imake. Once it has completed its operation, you'll have a makefile that can be used by the UNIX make utility to create your copy of xfig.

Known Problems

There are a few known problems with xfig. For example, you'll notice that the image may not be redrawn automatically. Redrawing occurs by default for most operations. For those times when redrawing doesn't occur, you'll need to use the Redraw menu option.

Another reported problem is with scaleable fonts in OpenWindows. By default, xfig will not handle OpenWindow's scaleable fonts. However, you can add this capability to your version of xfig by compiling the utility with -DOPEWIN.

And there's another problem with running xfig under OpenWindows 2.0. You'll have problems with pixmaps in widgets unless you compile the utility using -DOPENWIN_BUG. The documentation shows you how to compile using both -DOPEWIN and -DOPENWIN_BUG.

A problem may occur when you pan an object or iconify/deiconify a window while in the middle of an operation. The xfig utility will become confused and will distort the image on the screen. But don't worry. Use the Redraw menu option to correctly display the image.

Keep in mind that xfig output isn't truly WYSIWYG. That is, if you rotate text and ellipses, they will be displayed horizontally on the screen but will be rotated when the image is printed using PostScript.

These are just a few of the common problems that users have reported with the xfig utility. The xfig documentation contains an up-to-date list of bugs. If you experience a problem other than what has already been reported, drop an email to Brian Smith at *bvsmith@lbl.gov*. You can also read information about the utility in the *comp.sources.x* netnews group.

The Fine Print

Sutanthavibul holds the original copyright for xfig. You have permission to use, copy, modify, distribute, and sell the utility and the documentation without any royalty or fee. All you need to include in your distribution is the copyright notice that appears in your copy of the utility.

But keep in mind that xfig is distributed without any warranty. No one is going to guarantee that the utility will work on your system. You should include this notice on any copy of xfig that you intend to distribute.

Although these are about the only restrictions that have been placed on xfig, be sure to read the documentation for further information about the utility's limited use.

Up and Running

Get started by typing **xfig** at the prompt, followed by any options you require and the name of the file that you want to edit or create. If you don't include a file name on the command line, you can name your file when the file is saved. Table 10-4 contains a sampling of useful command-line options. The utility's documentation has the full listing of them.

Once xfig has settled down, you'll see several regions on the screen. These are the command region, drawing mode region, editing mode region, message region, indicator region, mouse function region, and canvas region. We'll talk briefly about the command region and let you discover the other regionss for yourself.

The command region contains the command panel where you'll find all the menu selections. Just point and click the left mouse button to enter your choice. Don't worry about making a mistake, the Undo menu option is always standing by to undo the last object creation, deletion, or modification.

As you would expect, xfig has an assortment of traditional menu options. You can edit and delete objects, and copy or cut an object to a buffer, then paste the contents of the buffer onto a canvas.

You'll also find a few other helpful features on the menu. For example, the Export option displays a list of output file formats to choose from. This allows you to easily change the graphic into another common graphic file format. You'll have to dig into the xfile utility's documentation for a complete listing of these power-packed tools.

Adding Text and Shapes

Although xfig is a graphics package, you can use it to display text within your graphic image. There is an assortment of text commands that allow you to enter text, set the font, and change the size of the text. In addition, you can have the utility automatically justify the text to the right, left, or center of the text block.

Furthermore, the text capabilities of xfig don't stop here. You have true typeset style control over the spacing between lines of text. The authors call this *interline*

OPTION	DESCRIPTION
-ri	Moves to the right of the canvas window
-le	Moves to the left of the canvas window
-L	Displays in landscape mode
-P	Displays in portrait mode
-tr	Activates mouse arrows
-not	Deactivates mouse arrows
-inc	Uses inches as the unit of measurement
-me	Uses metric as the unit of measurement
-inv	Uses inverse video
-de	Activates debug mode
-startf	Sets the point size for text objects

TABLE 10-4. *Sampling of xfig Command-line Options*

spacing. The xfig utility allows you to set and change the amount of interline spacing. This means you can make those fine adjustments that separate professional publications graphics from traditional home publishing software.

You can produce the standard array of images such as a circle, box, arc, ellipse, polygon, and lines. In addition to drawing these objects, xfig gives you complete control over the details of each object. In the case of a line, you have a choice of line widths and styles. You can even place an arrow at the end of the line.

You need a box? Do you want square corners or rounded corners? It's your choice when you use xfig. Make the decision and xfig will draw the box in the style you want. It's really that simple.

For more complex images, you can turn to the polygon feature that will join lines to form any shape that you desire. Once you have the polygon just the way you want it, you can use the area fill option to color in the polygon. Don't be concerned if you're not using a color monitor. The xfig utility will use the gray scale to fill the polygon instead of color.

An important feature of xfig is the ease in which it allows you to work with complex graphic images. Although you build an image in pieces, you can have the utility glue together the pieces of your graphic. Glue? Sure, in fact, that's the name of the menu item used for this purpose.

For example, your image may call for a box to be drawn inside another box. By default each box is treated separately. But by using xfig's Glue Compound feature, you can tell the xfig utility to treat both boxes as one compound item. So, if you move the outer box, the inside box will move at the same time. If you later want to treat each box separately, simply use the Unglue option.

Moving Objects

Although you create an object on the screen, it doesn't have to remain stationary. You can always use the move option to relocate an object on the screen. But that's not all! The utility is ready and able to flip an object vertically and horizontally at the selection of a menu option. Just point and click, and xfig flips the graphic for you.

Well, maybe a flip isn't just what you had in mind. You only want to turn the object slightly. You can try to modify your graphic yourself or take the easy approach—let xfig do it for you. Just select rotate from the menu and enter the number of degrees that you want the image rotated. The xfig utility can rotate an image both clockwise or counterclockwise.

CAUTION
Boxes and arc boxes can only be rotated in 90 increments, and text objects cannot be rotated at all.

So you've flipped and reflipped the image. You've even rotated the image 360 degrees and it still doesn't look right. Don't walk away—at least not yet. Try the scale option. This allows you to increase and decrease the size of the image proportionally to the image aspect ratio. This means that no matter what size you make the graphic, xfig will make sure the image isn't distorted. All you need to do is select Scale from the menu, then use the mouse to change the size of the image.

The xfig documentation is loaded with tips and techniques for creating nearly any type of graphic that you can imagine. So, now it's time to load xfig onto your computer and read the documentation to learn how to unleash the entire power of this utility.

The xv Utility: An Image Viewer for X Windows

You can't open a magazine or watch a story about computers on television without seeing an assortment of dramatic images appear on the screen. All of us know that computer images are really bitmaps of photos or art that were scanned into computer memory. In fact, there are countless bitmaps available on the Internet or from commercial sources.

But the bitmap is just half of the story. You still need software that will read the bitmap, display the image on the screen, and send the image to the printer. Where do you find such software? Right here! We're talking about the xv utility, which can transform an image file into an attractive display on your computer screen.

John Bradley (*bradley@cis.upenn.edu*) and his team at the University of Pennsylvania's GRASP Lab developed xv. You'll find xv a very worthwhile utility to add to your collection because it does nearly everything you could ever dream of with a bitmap. Let's begin with the basics. The xv utility displays an image in a window on your screen—or on the root window. This allows you to have a backdrop for all your child windows.

But wait! It does a lot more than simply displaying an image. Execute the proper commands and you can have xv stretch or compress the image; rotate the image in 90 degree steps; flip the image around the horizontal or vertical axes; and even crop a rectangular portion of the image.

Could you ever want more? Sure! And xv is not going to disappoint you. You can magnify any portion of the image by any amount up to the size of the screen. You can adjust the image brightness and contrast. And when it comes to color, well you'll find the utility extremely versatile.

Regardless of how the image was created, you can apply different red, green, and blue color components to correct for non-linear color response. You can adjust the global image color saturation. You can even reduce the number of colors in an image. All right, you may not like the colors that are in the utility's color map, but that shouldn't limit your creative juices; xv allows you to edit the color map.

We could go on about the advantages of using xv, but we won't. We would need the entire book to fully describe these features. Instead, we'll leave it to you to poke around the utility's documentation—and you won't be disappointed.

Unpacking and Installing

Create an empty directory on your system, then copy the xv utility files from the */mirror2/x-contrib* directory on *cs.ubc.ca*. (It is available elsewhere on the Internet.) The utility comes with a *makefile.std*, which is in the old style minimalist makefile. You'll have to copy this file to makefile, then run make to create the binary version of xv.

Building the binaries should run smoothly if you are on a Sun running SunOS, a DECstation running Ultrix, or an IBM RS/6000 running AIX. You can ignore any warnings you receive from the optimizer on DECstations.

Running on a SVR4-based system can give you a few compiling problems. You'll probably have to edit the makefile. The xv utility's installation instructions provide hints on modifying the makefile.

Watch out for the JPEG library that comes with the utility. This library was prepared independent of Bradley and his team, which means the JPEG library isn't integrated into the xv makefile. You may have to edit the JPEG library makefile found in the JPEG subdirectory before building the binaries. The installation documentation contains the details.

Once the executable files are created, copy the programs and the man pages to appropriate directories. The documentation recommends specific directories. Besides using the on-line man pages for help, you can also print the *xvdocs.ps* file that contains the ready-to-print PostScript manual for the xv utility. Bradley reports that you might experience problems printing the manual; however, he does provide fixes in the installation documentation files.

The xv utility was developed on Sun 4/280 running SunOS 4.1, using both the normal 'cc' and gcc-1.37 compilers. Bradley has successfully compiled and tested the utility on the following systems: Sun4 running SunOS 4.1, VAXstation 3500 running Ultrix 3.0, MicroVAX II running Ultrix 2.0, DecStation 3100 running UWS 3.0, and IBM RISC System/6000 running AIX 3.1.

Restrictions

Bradley and the University of Pennsylvania hold the copyright to xv. However, you are granted permission to use, copy, and distribute the utility for non-commercial purposes without having to pay a fee. In fact, you can even modify the utility for your own purposes. But hold off before you distribute your modifications! You'll need Bradley's consent. And as with nearly all the free software on the Internet, xv comes without any expressed or implied warranty.

Although the utility is freely available on the Internet, Bradley hopes that you will help toward future support and development of the utility. He'd like you to drop him an email that includes your name and the full name of your organization if you should decide to become an xv user. He'll add your name to a long list of folks who are currently using the utility.

In addition, Bradley would appreciate a $10 donation if you find xv to be, as Bradley puts it, "nifty, useful, generally cool, and of some value to you." Keep in mind that those donations are not tax deductible. And for a donation of $25 or more, Bradley will throw in a bound copy of the xv manual printed on a 600 dpi laser printer.

Sounds a little like public television's fund drives. Maybe so, but a lot of uncompensated time and effort went into creating a utility that might save you time and money. You can reach Bradley directly at either of the following addresses:

John Bradley
1053 Floyd Terrace
Bryn Mawr, PA 19010

or:

GRASP Lab, Room 312C
3401 Walnut St.
Philadelphia, PA 19104

Known Problems

Bradley reports that there are known problems with xv running on certain window managers. For example, there is a problem with the twm window manager that creeps up if you have title bars turned off. When xv tells the window manager to make a window a specific size, the twm automatically adds enough room to place the title bar at the top of the window. But twm doesn't draw the title bar since this feature is deactivated.

You'll also have to be aware that there are color map installation problems with using xv on the twm and tvtwm window managers. Bradley goes into more detail about this problem in the documentation.

There are also known problems with running xv with the dxwm window manager. Bradley's recommendation is to abandon the dxwm for the mwm window manager. This will save you a lot of headaches if you intend to run the utility often.

Besides the problems with some window managers, xv also has problems with certain displays. For example, it will not work on displays that aren't 1-, 4-, 6-, 8-, 16-, 24-, or 32-bits deep. However, don't be too concerned. The utility still should work fine on nearly every display that is out there. The *comp.sources.x* netnews groups contains additional information about xv.

Up and Running

You can open your world to computer images by typing **xv** at the prompt. The xv utility displays an opening window filled with a logo, credit, and revision date. You can get a feeling for the way xv handles images by resizing the opening window. You'll notice that the logo, which is a bitmap, is automatically stretched to fit the new size of the window.

You interact with xv by using control options, menus, and your mouse. For example, the Display Modes popup menu lets you determine how the image will be displayed in the window. It won't take you long to become completely at home with the utility's menu system.

Of course, the first task is to display a list of image files. Each image is in a separate file and by selecting the proper menu item, all the file names in the list appear in a scrollable window. The current selection is shown in reverse video. Just double-click on the image you want (or use techniques described later in this chapter), and xv displays the image in the current windows.

You'll notice that if you place the cursor on the image and press the left mouse button, xv displays a strange looking set of numbers on the screen. The numbers represent information about the pixel that is pointed to by the cursor. The following contains typical pixel information:

```
196, 137 = 191,121,209 (287 42 81 HSV)
```

The first set of numbers (196,137) represent the x and y positions of the cursor within the image coordinates. The next set of numbers (191, 121, 209) are the numerical representation of the red, green, and blue color values of the pixels. The value for each color has a range from 0-255. The next set of numbers (287, 42, 81) are the HSV values.

Although this pixel information might seem useless at first, it will become important when you perform serious modifications to the image, such as cropping and recoloring. You can even cut and paste the information into other utilities.

We've shown you just the tip of the iceberg. Table 10-5 provides a sampling of commands that you can use to work with the image. However, it is strongly recommend that you read either the on-line or printed manual for the information about how to use the xv utility. It is well worth your time.

Load and View Images Interactively

The xv utility permits you to load images either as a command-line argument or interactively from within the utility. Once xv is running, open the load window. The load window displays the contents of the current directory.

COMMAND DESCRIPTION

n	Returns the image to its normal size
m	Makes the displayed image the same size as the screen
M	Makes the image as large as possible while preserving the aspect ratio
>	Doubles the current size of the image within the size of the screen
<	Halves the current size of the image
.	Increases the current size of the image by 10%
,	Decreases the current size of the image by 10%
4	Resizes the image with a width to height ratio of 4 to 3
a	Applies the default aspect ratio to the image
t	Rotates the image 90 degrees clockwise
T	Rotates the image 90 degrees counterclockwise
h	Flips the image horizontally
v	Flips the image vertically
s	Smoothes out distortion when an image is expanded or shrunk
c	Crops the image to the current cropping rectangle
u	Returns the image to its normal, uncropped state
A	Crops off any constant borders that exist in the image

TABLE 10-5. *Helpful xv Commands*

File names are sorted alphabetically, and you can scroll the list to view additional file names.

You can use the UP ARROW and DOWN ARROW keys and the HOME, END, PAGE UP, and PAGE DN keys to move around the file list. In addition, you can click the scroll bar with the mouse, which will also move the contents of the list. You'll notice that the file name you highlight is automatically placed in the Load file text box. Just press the Ok button or the ENTER key, and xv will try to load the file.

The load window will disappear and the image will be displayed if the image is loaded successfully. If xv runs into any problems, you'll hear about it. The load window will remain on the screen while the utility displays an error message.

The xv utility provides a couple of shortcuts for loading images. We already talked about pointing and double clicking the left mouse button. Here is an even faster method if the image was previously loaded. Each time an image is loaded, the name of the file that contains the image is added to the controls windows list. All you need to do is click on the name of the file in the controls windows to reload the image.

And if you don't like to pick file names from a list, you can always enter the file name directly into the Load file text box. Press ENTER and xv will try to load the file. If you typed a directory name, the utility will make it the current directory. You'll also find that you can use emacs-like editing keys to edit your entry in the Load file text box. Table 10-6 contains a sample of these key commands.

Cropping the Image

Any image that is displayed by xv can be cropped by using a few simple commands. The commands are contained on the xv controls windows that is displayed by typing ?, or by placing the cursor inside the image window, then pressing the right mouse button. From here on, the mouse button is about the only tool you'll need to use.

Before xv can crop an image, you must tell it what part of the image that you want cropped. You do this by placing a rectangle around the segment of the image. Is this hard to define? Not at all! Move the cursor to the upper-left corner of the piece of the image that you want to crop. Hold down the middle mouse button and drag the mouse until the rectangle is in position. It's that simple.

COMMAND	DESCRIPTION
CTRL-F	Moves the cursor forward one character
CTRL-B	Moves the cursor backward one character
CTRL-A	Moves the cursor to the beginning of the line
CTRL-E	Moves the cursor to the end of the line
CTRL-D	Deletes the character to the right of the cursor
CTRL-U	Clears the entire line
CTRL-K	Clears from the cursor position to the end of the line

TABLE 10-6. *Load File Text Box Edit Commands*

If you don't like the position of the rectangle, just press the middle mouse button again and draw another rectangle, or just press the middle mouse button without moving the mouse; the rectangle will go away.

Want to know more about the area of the image that you are cropping? The xv utility can answer nearly any question you can ask. Xv's control window contains an Info button. Clicking this button or typing the **i** command will bring up the Info window. In it you'll see a variety of information such as the size and position of the cropping rectangle. These are given in terms of the image coordinates.

Let see how this works. The following listing contains typical data that is displayed in the Info window. The first two numbers (114, 77) indicate the cropping rectangle's width and height in pixels. The next two numbers (119, 58) indicate the location the rectangle is from the edge of the entire image. In this example, the upper-left corner of the rectangle is located 199 pixels from the left edge of the image and 58 pixels from the top edge.

```
114x77 rectangle starting at 119,58
```

You can finish the cropping operation by using the mouse to click the Crop button on the control windows, or by simply typing **c**. You'll notice that the image window will now show you only the area of the image that was inside the rectangle. Whoops! Did you make a mistake? Don't worry, xv will fix it for you. All you need to do is click the mouse on the Uncrop button or press the **u** key. The uncropped image will return inside the window.

Printing the Image

The principle purpose of xv is to display and manipulate images on the screen. However, you can also use it to print the image in true PostScript style. From the control window you can choose Save, which opens another window. From this window you can set the paper size and the size and position of the image on the paper, and determine the file format. PostScript is one of the those options. You also determine whether the image is printed in landscape or portrait.

When everything is just right, press the Ok button or the ENTER key. The PostScript window is removed from the screen once the image is sent to a PostScript printer. If there are any problems, you'll receive an error message displayed on the screen.

Command-line Options

Most of the time, you'll be controlling xv using interactive commands. However, you can also pass commands as arguments to the command line when launching the utility. There are dozens of command-line options that are available to you. You'll have to read the utility's documentation for the complete list. However, we've included a sampling of the list in Table 10-7 to get you started.

OPTION	DESCRIPTION
-help	Prints instructions and lists command-line options
-fg	Sets the foreground color used by the windows
-bg	Sets the background color used by the windows
-hi	Sets the highlight color used for the top-left edges of the control buttons
-lo	Sets the lowlight color used for the bottom-right edges of the control buttons
-bw	Sets the width of the border on the windows
-geometry	Specifies the size and placement of the image window
-ncols	Sets the maximum number of colors that xv will use
-root	Displays images in the root window
-max	Automatically stretches the image to the full size of the screen

TABLE 10-7. *A Sampling of xv Command-line Options*

CHAPTER 11

Electronic Mail
Utilities

There isn't a lot new in electronic mail software these days. All the packages can pretty much handle the normal requirements of electronic mail. However, we uncovered three mail packages that are unique enough to include them in this chapter for your review.

The first package that we'll review is elm. This utility is an agent system, designed to be used with your current email utility, which allows you to read your mail in a very orderly way. Just read our review for the details.

One of the concerns heavy users of netnews have is the efficiency with which they receive their information. So we searched for a product that would meet their needs, and we found the cnews utility. No, this isn't a news reader, it's software that lets your system become a netnews node. Be sure to read this review if you're heavily into netnews.

The chapter ends with a software package that can handle the latest type of communications, namely, sending and receiving a fax. The Netfax utility is the perfect software for managing the transmission of a fax across telephone lines.

The elm Utility: Electronic Mail Software
The cnews Utility: Netnews Linking Software
The Netfax Utility: Fax Software

The elm Utility: Electronic Mail Software

Not another email! Please! Well, this is not just another email, but one that makes your life using email a little better. Dave Taylor, the author of elm, felt that the line-oriented email utilities that are currently available on UNIX are hard to use, especially with high volume mail. So instead of getting mad, Taylor did something about it. He created a new mailer called elm.

On UNIX systems, mail functions are divided into two parts: the part that you are most likely familiar with (the reading and writing part) and the delivery system. It is the reading and writing part that elm is concerned with. The elm utility will work with most delivery systems, such as sendmail, and is a full replacement for the mail and mailx utilities.

Inside elm, you'll find other software that will provide a list of your mail and that produces clean, paginated printouts of your email. Also, there is a systemwide daemon that can automatically answer your email when you're unavailable.

The striking difference between elm and other email systems is how Taylor centered elm's features around the screen. Let's say as a usenet user you receive an email from your friend who is on ARPANET. Beside sending you the letter, she also "cc'd" another friend on ARPA. Replying to the letter could be tricky. However, with elm, just press **G** for group reply on the utility menu and elm will correctly address your return email.

Taylor had several objectives in mind when he developed elm. He wanted to build a system that exploited the CRT, instead of assuming that the user is working with a teletype. He wanted a system that needed no documentation for the casual user but still had the power that the sophisticated mail expert expected. Taylor also set out to correct a few of the dumb things that are typical of some current mailers. Did he succeed? You bet, and it's all yours for the taking.

Restrictions

The elm utility contains very few restrictions. Taylor grants you permission to copy and distribute it and its source files without charge and without permission from the author. The key restriction is that you can't charge anyone for a copy of elm, even if you've included it in your own software that you offer for sale. Taylor explains how this works in the elm documentation.

Keep in mind that Taylor makes no guarantee about the utility—and you shouldn't either. Anyone using elm uses it at their own risk. Neither Taylor nor anyone else can be held liable for any damages. Be sure to include a similar statement if you distribute the utility.

Taylor doesn't mind if you add your creative ideas to elm; however, he requests that you send along a copy of your new version to elm@DSI.COM.

Known Problems

If you're already a fan of elm and have upgraded to version 2.3, you might be in for a surprise. In fact, this version of elm can be a little unpredictable.

TIP

After you install the upgrade, make sure that you run the newalias script. This will take care of a potential problem with aliases.

Here's a problem that some UNIX 5.3.2 users have experienced when trying to compile elm. It simply doesn't compile and you receive an error message that the compiler can't locate all the files that are necessary for the *curses.c* source file. This problem stems from the fact that only the runtime version of UNIX is installed on some systems. Missing are include files such as *ptem.h*, which contains the window sizing structure. What's the fix? Comment out the window sizing code in the *curses.c* file, or install the remaining includes files.

And for those of you who are running the utility on SCO Xenix, you might be receiving all your mail from anonymous. No, anonymous isn't your biggest fan. The problem is with the mail delivery agent. The mail delivery agent should be changed from */usr/bin/rmail* or */bin/rmail* to */usr/lib/mail/execmail*.

These aren't the only known problems. The documentation contains a listing of the more common bugs, along with suggested fixes. However, for the latest news about elm, connect to the elm usenet news group at *comp.mail.elm*. There you will find discussions about bugs, fixes and work-arounds. You'll also notice a monthly status report that lists archive sites that have the latest patches for bugs. These patches are posted to *comp.mail.elm* in addition to *comp.sources.unix*.

Installation

Installing the elm utility isn't difficult. The documentation that comes with the utility contains complete, step-by-step instructions for installation.

CAUTION
Don't attempt the installation before reading the instructions; otherwise, you'll be making this process more complicated than necessary.

Create a directory for the elm utility, then copy the utility's files from:

/.0/BSD/386bsd/386bsd-0.1/unofficial/from-ref/public on *gatekeeper.dec.com*

Once the files are in place, make the elm directory the current directory and type **sh configure**. The configure program will prompt you for information before it creates the makefile for you.

Next, create the binary files. The commands you'll need are shown here:

```
$ make documentation
$ make all > MAKELOG 2>&1 &
$ tail -f MAKELOG
```

Here's a hint! Substitute the following **make** command if you are running in the C shell:

```
make all >& MAKELOG &
```

If all goes well, your bin directory should contain the files that are shown in Table 11-1. The final step is to execute **make install**.

If you have problems compiling or running elm, don't panic. The first step is to reread the installation instructions that come with the documentation. Be sure that you haven't missed a step. Next, read the previous section about known problems and don't be afraid to post your problem on the elm news group *comp.mail.elm*. There are many elm users who have been down the same path before and they are usually more than willing to lend a hand. And if all else fails, you may want to drop a line to Taylor at:

taylor@hplabs.HP.COM.

answer	checkalias	filter	messages	printmail
arepdaemon	elm	frm	newalias	readmsg
autoreply	fastmail	listalias	newmail	

TABLE 11-1.   *Files in the Bin Directory*

Up and Running

Running elm is straightforward. After all, that was one of Taylor's objectives. For example, if you want to check your mail, type **elm -z**. If there isn't any mail, elm will display "no mail" on the screen; otherwise, the elm program will start up.

TIP

The elm utility comes with some test mail for you to play with. You'll find the test mail in *test/test.mail*. Just type **elm -f test/test.mail** at the prompt and elm will read eight messages and allow you to enter commands. Table 11-2 contains a sampling of the commands that are available in elm. The documentation contains a complete list of commands and instructions on how to use each command. Type **Q** to quit the elm utility and return to the prompt.

COMMAND	DESCRIPTION
?	Provides help on a specific key or summary of commands
a	Adds the return address of current message to alias database
d	Deletes a user alias from alias database
l	Lists all aliases in the database
m	Makes a new user alias and adds it to alias database when done
r,x	Returns from the alias menu
p	Searches for a person in the alias database
s	Searches for a system in the host routing/domain database

TABLE 11-2.   A *Sampling of elm Commands*

The cnews Utility: Netnews Linking Software

Tired of spending hours logged into a remote computer just so you can read netnews? Would you like to have your own news feed, and maybe even share it with others? Then maybe you should be running the same software the big boys (and girls) run. If you can find a site willing to give you a news feed (or sell you a feed for a reasonable price), cnews is the utility that will help make this happen.

The cnews utility software allows your computer to be a netnews node. It contains three utilities including a primitive newsreader: readnews, expire, and postnews. It includes all the utilities you need to manage and read news. However, you will probably want to get a copy of your favorite newsreader to supplement the readnews program supplied with cnews. One suggestion is the rn program, available from numerous servers on the net, such as *ftp.uu.net* in */networking/news/readers/*.

First, let's look at the heart of cnews: its ability to make receiving and sending netnews more efficient on your machine. Right now, you probably have to log onto an Internet host to run your favorite newsreader. This is the way most of us connect to netnews today. However, by running cnews, you don't have to log onto the Internet host to receive the netnews feed. This can save you hours of telephone time.

The cnews utility also provides you with a newsreader. Michael Rourke of the University of N.S.W. (*decvax!mulga!michaelr:elecvax*), designed the readnews and postnews utilities to work hand-in-hand with each other. Readnews goes out to your news spool directory, built by cnews, and finds all the postings from news groups to which you subscribe. It then lets you display those postings to the screen.

Wait! Who wants to have old articles taking up valuable space on a disk? That's a good point. Henry Spencer and Geoff Collyer from the University of Toronto developed the expire utility for that purpose. Just run expire and all those old articles are purged.

The last of the cnews utility set is postnews. This utility submits your news articles to news groups on netnews. Just write your article using your favorite editor, then pass both the name of the news group and the name of the file that contains the article as arguments to postnews. At nearly the speed of light, your thoughts are made available to the worldwide Internet community.

Installation

You'll find cnews at many places on the Internet. Here's just one location: */pub2/unix-c/usenet* on *rigel.acs.oakland.edu*. Copy the utility files to your system. The utility comes with a makefile; however, we suggest that you carefully inspect the configuration settings for this file. You may need to modify the configuration to suit your environment.

Once you're satisfied with the makefile, **make install**. Make will then do the rest of the work for you. Fortunately, there is only one file that needs to be compiled. This is the *batchmake.c* file. The rest of the utility is written as a Bourne shell script.

We also suggest that you take a close look at the *queuelen* and *roomfor* files. These files are system dependent and may require a little tweaking to get them working on your system. You can read more about the installation procedures in the utility's documentation.

If you have any problems running cnews, try posting your problem to *news.software.b*. The other users of the utility might be able to lend you a hand.

Restrictions

The cnews utility is copyrighted; however, you are given permission to use the software for any purpose. You can even modify the utility and redistribute it freely. The only restrictions are that you must give the authors credit in the documentation, and you must plainly mark any modified versions of the utility as not being the original software. You can read all about these restrictions in the utility's documentation.

Known Problems

We found reports of several known problems with cnews. For example, readnews may sometimes falsely report that you have news.

The expire utility also has a few little problems. The utility archives by copying files, not by linking them. This can cause the existence of several independent copies of cross-posted articles. Another problem that we've heard about with expire is with the **-p** command-line switch used to find subjects. The switch actually botches the "Subject:" lines on rare occasions.

We'll let you read the latest problems with cnews in the utility's documentation and on netnews.

Up and Running

The newsfeed is provided by an outside source. You can read the utility's documentation for more information about how to link to such a source. You'll notice that you must edit a set of configuration files. These settings determine how much of a newsfeed you will receive. A similar setting is also made in your newsfeed supplier's configuration file.

We suggest that you carefully review the amount of news that you want fed to your system daily. A daily feed of all the news is well over 10 Megabytes of information. And this is increasing at about 10% a month. So, be sure to have sent only those news groups that you are interested in reading. The volume can indeed be a problem if you have a slow modem (less than 9600 baud) or a small amount of disk space left on your system.

Once you have configured and run cnews, your feed will be loaded onto your computer's hard disk. You will run cnews periodically to get the latest articles, as well as delivering your postings to netnews.

We'll now turn to the utility's newsreader. The first place to start is with readnews. This is the segment of cnews that allows you to read all of the netnews articles for the news groups to which you subscribe. You execute the utility by typing **readnews** at the prompt. If you don't provide any command-line switches, readnews begins in the command mode. Table 11-3 contains a sampling of commands that you can use to control the readnews utility. You'll find a complete listing in the utility's documentation.

Another way that you can control the operation of readnews is by using command-line switches. For example, you can add a news group to your subscription list by using the **-s+** switch, followed by the name or names of the news groups. Each news group name must be separated by a comma. Table 11-4 contains a partial listing of these switches. You can learn how to use these and other switches by reading the utility's documentation.

COMMAND	DESCRIPTION
RETURN	Either prints the current article or goes to the next article and prints its header
.	Prints the current article
-	Goes back to the previous article
number	Goes to the article number in the current news group
s [file]	Saves the current article
N [newsgroup]	Goes to the next news group
q	Quits
DEL	Terminates current activity and returns to command mode

TABLE 11-3. *A Sampling of readnews Commands*

SWITCH	DESCRIPTION
-c	Checks if there is news, and if so, prints 'You have news.'
-C	Checks if there is news, and prints the groups and number of articles to be read
-l	Lists the titles of available news articles
-p	Prints all articles on standard output, and updates newsrc
-s	Prints the news group subscription list
-s+ group	Adds group to the subscription list
-s- group	Subtracts group from the subscription list

TABLE 11-4. *A Sampling of Command-line Switches for readnews*

The expire utility is used to remove old, expired news articles. (We suggest that you run expire daily.) The actions of expire are dictated by a control file that contains instructions for each news group that you subscribe to.

Each line in the control file is a record that is separated into fields by white space. The first field contains the names of one or more news groups. If more than one news group is given, each name must be separated by a comma. A word of caution! Don't use spaces to separate these names. This is a common mistake that you can avoid making.

TIP
You don't have to enter the full names of the news groups; you can enter just the news group's prefix, such as **comp**. All the news groups that have this prefix will be affected by the operation.

The next field contains a single letter that specifies the type of groups that will be removed from the file. These letters are "m" for moderated groups, "u" for unmoderated groups, or "x" for both moderated and unmoderated groups.

The third field specifies the period that the affected articles are to be removed from the file. The period is defined in number of days. The value of this field can be a little tricky to understand since three different values are entered, each one separated by a hyphen.

The first value indicates the retention period. It shows how much time passes before the article is a candidate for removal. The second value is the default date. It specifies the number of days that must pass before the article is removed. The last value is called the unconditional removal date. After this number of days have passed, the article is removed.

The fourth field on the line specifies the archival directory. You can use the at sign (@) in place of the name. In this case, expire will automatically use the default archival directory. You can read more about how to set up this file in the utility's documentation.

Another way to control the operation of expire is to use a command-line switch. There are only a few switches that are available to you. The **-a** switch, for example, specifies a default archival directory and is used in place of the directory that is specified in the control file. The **-p** switch causes the utility to print an index line for each archive article. This line contains the article's path name, message ID, the date the article was received, and the subject line of the article. The last switch is the **-o** option, which tells expire to use a format that is compatible with earlier versions of cnews.

The last utility in the cnews' set is postnews, which submits news articles to netnews. This utility is driven by command-line switches used to tell the utility the name of the news group, where to post the article, and the name of the file that contains the article.

Table 11-5 contains a sampling of command-line switches for postnews. You can read the utility's documentation for more information about how to use these switches to control the utility's operation.

The Netfax Utility: Fax Software

Imagine this scenario: You're set to demonstrate your new application, then at the last minute comes a call that most developers dread—can you provide the capability to send a fax using your application? A fax! Now isn't that a can of worms. Unless you're knowledgeable about communications, you'll have to hit the books and take a few communications experts to lunch before you can give the user a positive response.

SWITCH	DESCRIPTION
-s subject	Specifies the subject of the article
-n newsgroups	Specifies a list of news groups to which the article will be posted
-e expiredate	Specifies a date for the article to expire
-c control_command	Specifies special control commands

TABLE 11-5. *A Sampling of Command-line Switches for postnews*

Hold on! Keep those books on the shelf and don't invite your friend, the communications expert, to lunch. Here is a utility that will handle all your faxing software needs and it's free. Netfax provides Group 3 fax transmission and receiving services for networked UNIX systems.

Basically, all you'll need to run Netfax is a fax modem that conforms to the new EIA-529 Asynchronous Facsimile DCE Control Standard. Thanks to the work of Henry Minsky and David Siegel of the MIT AI Lab, you can easily incorporate their work into your application and meet any user demand, without having to create your own, sometimes complicated, fax routines.

Netfax actually consists of three subutilities. The main piece is the fax utility, the software that sends and receives a fax. The faxq and faxrm utilities are used to maintain the fax spooler. Faxq lists the fax spooler queue while faxrm is used to remove a job from the spooler.

We've found Netfax to be a worthwhile addition to anyone's UNIX toolbox. And for the price, you can't beat it!

Installation

You'll find Netfax on *athos.rutgers.edu.* in the */ietf* directory. This utility is also available elsewhere on the Internet. We suggest that you copy the distribution that is the closest to your location. The utility comes with a prepared makefile that is designed to be used with the GNU make utility.

Before you attempt to create the binaries for the utility, we suggest that you examine the *conf.h, conf.mk, and fax_prog.mk* files very carefully. These files contain settings that are unique for each system. Make sure that their configurations conform to the environment on your system.

TIP

The Ghostscript utility (see review in Chapter 8) is required for imaging of G3 fax data. However, you must compile Ghostscript using the fax driver. If you want to use Ghostscript with Netfax, you must recompile Ghostscript using the digifax dfaxhigh device driver. Just add the following line to the Ghostscript utility's makefile:

```
DEVICE_DEVS=x11.dev dfaxhigh.dev dfaxlow.dev.
```

Now back to the Netfax utility's installation. Type **make** at the prompt to create the binaries for the utility. You shouldn't expect any trouble building these files or running this utility. If you do, we suggest that you double check the installation procedures that you'll find in the utility's documentation, before asking for help.

Be sure to read any bug reports that appear in the documentation. Next, read netnews and see what the community of Netfax users has to say. We suggest that you read and post your questions to the *comp.dcom.fax* group.

Restrictions

Netfax is covered under the Free Software Foundation's license. This license simply states that you can freely use, modify, and distribute the utility without prior permission and without paying any fee or royalty.

The only major limitation is that you can't prevent anyone else from using and receiving the utility's source code. This is especially important for developers. You can include Netfax in your own application; however, you must freely distribute the source code to this utility if anyone asks you for it. You can still protect your own source code.

Netfax is distributed "as is" without any warranty that the utility will work on your system, or any system for that matter. You can read about this in the utility's documentation.

Known Problems

Yes, free utilities can have their problems. In fact, you can find bugs in nearly every utility, regardless of whether or not you pay for it. However, we found one reported problem with Netfax. That is, there isn't a way to cancel a fax in the process of being transmitted. Basically, if you don't remove the fax from the queue, the fax is as good as sent.

While we heard of only one problem with the utility, you might stumble across a few of your own. If you're sure that the problem might actually be a bug in the software, we suggest that you send the information in an email to *bug-fax@ai.mit.edu.*

Up and Running

Netfax is a network-oriented fax utility. At the center of the utility's operation is a fax spooler, commonly referred to as a *queue manager*, in the utility's documentation. The queue manager runs on the host that contains the fax modem. As it's running, the utility scans a queue directory for faxes sent from individuals on the network.

Each user can place a fax on the queue by using the fax utility, or by sending an email from the email utility using the fax queue's address. You'll have to read the utility's documentation for details on how to set up this feature on your system.

The fax itself must be in ASCII text, PostScript, or TeX DVI file format. These are automatically converted to PostScript and placed on the fax queue by the fax utility. The fax is then transmitted over the telephone line when the fax reaches the top of the queue.

Netfax also automatically answers incoming telephone calls to the fax modem. Once the utility determines that the incoming message is a fax, the fax is placed in the queue manager's incoming fax directory. The fax remains in this directory until a user in the network reviews the directory and retrieves the fax.

Type **fax** at the prompt to send a fax from any terminal on the network. All of the pertinent information about the fax is passed to the fax utility by using command-line options. Table 11-6 contains a sample of these options. A complete option list is available in the utility's documentation.

NOTE
Here's a useful hint. You can use the at sign (@) as the prefix to the recipient's telephone number. This won't affect dialing the telephone, but it will suppress the telephone number from appearing in the fax queue.

Let's say that you want to fax the file called *mary.txt*. The recipient's telephone number is 222-555-1212. You also want to be notified by email when the fax has been sent. Here's what you would type at the prompt: **fax -p 2225551212 -m mary.txt**. When you press ENTER, the *mary.txt* file is placed on the fax queue ready for transmission.

Are you sure the fax reached the queue? Good question! Type **faxq** at the prompt and this utility will display a list of waiting faxes on the screen. If the queue manager is running on a host other than the current one, you can use the **-h** switch on the command line, then specify the name of the host to display the queue. You'll see how this is done when you read the utility's documentation.

Now you decide that you don't want to send the *mary.txt* file. The faxq utility shows that the fax hasn't been sent. What next? Type **faxrm mary.txt**. When you press ENTER, the faxrm utility will remove the mary.txt file from the queue. You can also use the **-h** switch to specify a different host.

OPTION	DESCRIPTION
-p phone	Specifies a recipient phone number for the fax
-m	Mails you a notice when the fax has been delivered
-h host	Specifies the host for the fax spooler
-c	Creates a cover sheet
-r name	Specifies the recipient's name to appear on the cover sheet
-s name	Specifies the sender's name to appear on the cover sheet

TABLE 11-6. *A Sampling of Command-line Options for the fax Utility*

CHAPTER 12

Programming Languages

Although we've called this chapter "Programming Languages," we have more to offer than just a few programming *languages*. Actually, some of the packages that we review here can be classified as programming *tools*. The XFree86 leads off the chapter and is an X Windows server for 386 and 486 machines. We found this to be valuable because we couldn't find the server component for X Windows available for personal computers. At least not at our price—free!

Following the review of XFree86, you'll find a review of another programming tool called the f2c utility. This tool is designed to give Fortran programmers a leg up when they attempt to convert their Fortran applications to C. It handles most of the conversion for you.

We then move directly into programming languages and libraries, the first of which is gcc, a powerful C and C++ language compiler. Be sure to try this for your next application—that is, unless your next application involves artificial intelligence. If so, we recommend you consider either KCL, which is a LISP language, or SB-Prolog, which is the language of choice for many AI researchers.

We finish the chapter with two reviews of industrial strength libraries. The first is the NIH Class Library, which contains many classes that are required for typical applications. All you need to do is use these classes—there's no need to re-invent existing code. The Readline Library is another time saver. With this library, your applications will have a built-in editor, without the hassles of building the editor.

The XFree86: An X Windows Server
The f2c Utility: A Fortran to C Converter
The gcc Utility: A C And C++ Language Compiler
KCL: A LISP Language
The NIH Class Library: A C++ Library
Perl: A Programming Language
The Readline Library: A Line Editor Library
SB-Prolog: A Programming Language

The XFree86 Utility: An X Windows Server

An X Windows server on a personal computer and free for the taking? Yep! For years, there has been a need for a free X Windows server for 386- and 486-based systems. Now there's XFree86, a port of the X11R5 that supports several versions of Intel-based machines.

There are basically two components of X Windows: the X client and X server. The X client component is part of your program. The X server component is primarily machine-specific. Thomas Roell created a stir in the X world when he wrote the first free X server to run on the inexpensive Intel 386. Since then, his work has been incorporated into the standard X11R5 distribution. We feel that the combination of free, high-performance X servers coupled with the inexpensive 386/486 hardware is of significance because it makes X Windows so widely available. XFree86 is distinguished in that it is faster and has fewer bugs than the standard X11R5 server for the 386.

XFree86 is a perfect way to acquire your own copy of X server for today's personal computers. XFree86 has a long history as it was derived from X386 version 1.2, which was the X server distribution of the X11R5.

David Dawes, Glenn Lai, Jim Tsillas, and David Wexelblat are the original authors of XFree86; however, there have been many contributors to the latest version. You'll find names and email addresses in the documentation.

Now here is the best part. XFree86 is available in binary form for many of the common architectures. This means that you can log onto the Internet and download the binary version of XFree86, which will be ready to run on your system without having to build the executable files.

Installation

You'll find XFree86 at various sites on the Internet. Here's just one of them: *ftp.x.orgon* in */contrib/XFree86*. You'll also find a long list of locations in the documentation where you can find the binary versions for specific machines. We suggest that you take a look at this list before you build your own binary files. You might save yourself a lot of time.

TIP
Make sure that you are copying the latest version to your system. Each binary distribution contains a README file, which, among other things, tells you the version of the distribution. Remember, you're looking for XFree86 version 2.0 or later.

You can find all the installation instructions for XFree86 in the documentation. However, you should be aware that you must have sufficient disk space available for XFree86. You'll need about 80MB to build XFree86 and an additional 50MB of space to install the built binaries and other files that are required for the operating system. Table 12-1 contains a list of directories that you can remove to minimize disk usage. You can also remove the large font files *k14.bdf, hang*.bdf,* and *jiskan*.bdf.*

mit/doc	mit/hardcopy
mit/lib/CLX	mit/server/ddx/dec
mit/server/ddx/ibm	mit/server/ddx/macII
mit/server/ddx/mips	mit/server/ddx/omron
mit/server/ddx/snf	mit/server/ddx/sun
mit/server/ddx/tek	

TABLE 12-1.   *Directories that Can Be Removed to Save Disk Space*

With a little tweaking, you should be up and running with XFree86 in no time. Be sure to read Chapter 3, "The Hacker's Guide," for tips on tweaking your distribution. If you have any difficulty building or using XFree86, we suggest that you read *comp.windows.x.i386unix* on netnews. There you will find hot discussions about XFree86 and related topics. Be sure to read the frequently-asked questions about XFree86 on netnews. This will provide you with a fast start using the utility.

If you still have problems, send email to *xfree86@physics.su.oz.au.* The team responsible for maintaining XFree86 will then place your concerns on their list to investigate. Members of the team are listed with their personal email addresses in the documentation.

Known Problems

XFree86 is a rather new release and therefore it has a few problems. In fact, the authors mention in the documentation that this is a complicated release. Here are some of the typical problems that have been reported:

- There seems to be a memory allocation and de-allocation problem in the xset fp operations. The authors provide a work-around to this problem in the utility's documentation; however, there isn't any permanent fix on the horizon.

- There is a problem with dot-clock frequency limitations in the S3 and Mach32 servers. You'll have do some special programming if you want the S3 cards to run above 85MHz and for the Mach32 boards to run faster than 80MHz. Check the documentation for more details. This fix is expected to be in the next release.

- If you intend to use XFree86 on some Esix systems, beware that you might experience keyboard mapping problems. One of the console driver patches for the Esix 4.0.3A causes the XFree86 server's default keymap to be corrupted. Here are two solutions. The faster solution is to remove the console driver patch. Another remedy is to use the **xmodmap** command to reset the default mapping after you start up the server. Type the following to reset the mapping:

  xmodmap /usr/X386/lib/X11/etc/xmodmap.std.

Up and Running

After you have the XFree86 software on your system, type **startx**.

CAUTION
Your distribution of this software might use a different startup command. We suggest that you read the utility's documentation for the proper startup command if the one we suggest doesn't work with your distribution.

Once XFree86 is running, your screen will change from character-based to graphical image and you'll be able to open several different sessions at the same time. The utility's documentation contains a complete tutorial on how to use the utility.

The f2c Utility: A Fortran to C Converter

Stuck with a ton of Fortran code? Wish they were written in C so you could maintain them? Then look no further and wish no more: you've come to the right place.

Here is a way to make you productive and save your employer money. We're talking about the f2c utility, which reads your Fortran programs and translates them into C. Too good to be true? Maybe, but you now have your own copy of f2c to add to your UNIX toolbox.

Installation Is Fast
You'll find f2c in the *f2c/src* directory at *research.att.com.* Copy the files to an empty directory on your system. You'll receive all the necessary files, including a file of checksums and source files for the program to compute the checksums. The checksums program is used to verify that all of the source files have been received undamaged.

Since the files arrive compressed, you must use the uncompress utility to restore the files to their proper size. For example, type **uncompress *.Z**. Table 12-2 contains a list of these files. You can then compile the programs according to the instructions that are contained in the documentation files supplied with f2c.

Running Quickly
You've heard about f2c, but how do you get it to work for you? First, you'll need source code written in Fortran 77. Next, you'll need to type

   f2c <*name of Fortran source*>

FILE	DESCRIPTION
f2c.h	Includes file necessary for compiling output of the converter
f2c.1	Man page for f2c
f2c.1t	Source for f2c.1 (to be processed by troff -man or nroff -man)
libf77	Library of non I/O support routines the generated C may need
libi77	Library of Fortran I/O routines the generated C may need
f2c.ps	Postscript for a technical report on f2c
fixes	Complete change log, reporting bug fixes and other changes
fc	Shell script that imitates the behavior of commonly found f77 commands

TABLE 12-2. *The f2c Utility Files*

then press the ENTER key—f2c will crank away and, if all goes well, create a file using the same name as the Fortran source file, but place a .c extension on the new file.

For example, suppose the source file for your Fortran program is called *hello.f.* Type **f2c hello.f** at the prompt and press ENTER; f2c builds the C language file called *hello.c.* Once the file is created, you still can compile the new source code using the C compiler.

The source code that is generated by f2c may require a little tweaking if the code doesn't compile or work properly. There are several steps that you might want to follow if you experience such a problem. The first place to look for help is in the f2c options. Table 12-3 contains a few of the options that have a similar meaning as they do in Fortran 77. Table 12-4 contains some of the options that are unique to f2c. You'll find a complete listing of options in the utility's documentation files.

The next place to look for assistance is in A Portable Fortran 77 Compiler, UNIX Time Sharing System Programmer's Manual, available from Bell Laboratories.

Restrictions
f2c is copyrighted by AT&T Bell Laboratories and Bellcore. Generally speaking, you have permission to use, copy, modify, and distribute the utility and its documentation for any purpose and without fee. All you need to do is to display the copyright notice and the appropriate disclaimer in all copies. You can't use the names of AT&T Bell Laboratories or Bellcore or any of their entities in advertising

OPTION	DESCRIPTION
-C	Compiles code to check that subscripts are within declared array bounds
-I2	Renders INTEGER and LOGICAL as short, INTEGER*4 as long int
-onetrip	Compiles DO loops that are performed at least once if reached
-U	Honors the case of variable and external names
-u	Makes the default type variable 'undefined' rather than default Fortran rules
-w	Suppresses all warning messages

TABLE 12-3. *Some f2c Options*

or publicity pertaining to distribution of the utility without prior specific, written permission of AT&T Bell Laboratories or Bellcore.

As for the disclaimer, use the f2c utility at your own risk. AT&T and Bellcore disclaim all warranties with regard to this utility. This means there are no claims that it will work. You'll find all the legal notices in the f2c documentation.

OPTION	DESCRIPTION
-A	Produces ANSI C. Default is old-style C
-a	Makes local variables automatic rather than static
-C++	Outputs C++ code
-c	Includes original Fortran source as comments
-ec	Places uninitialized COMMON blocks in separate files
-f	Assumes free-format input
-72	Treats text appearing after column 72 as an error
-g	Includes original Fortran line numbers in #line lines
-P	Writes a file.P of ANSI (or C++) prototypes for definitions in each input file
-!bs	Does not recognize backslash escapes in character strings

TABLE 12-4. *Helpful Options that Are Unique to f2c*

Known Problems

f2c will provide you with self-explanatory diagnostics whenever you use it to translate Fortran source code. However, there are a few known problems. For example, floating-point constant expressions are simplified in the floating-point arithmetic. This means that floating-point arithmetic is accurate to at most 16 to 17 decimal places.

You'll find a complete list of bugs and their fixes in the files that are supplied with f2c. If you stumble across a new bug, send an example of the source code to *research!dmg* or *dmg@research.att.com*.

TIP
Before sending the example of your bug, turn off the optimization and see if the problem goes away.

The gcc Compiler: A C and C++ Language Compiler

Here comes another C compiler. Do you really need it? After all, a C compiler is probably part of the UNIX distribution that you have on your system, so you might be apprehensive about using a free compiler of any kind—if it's free then it probably isn't any good, you may think.

Don't think this way or you'll miss out on a powerful compiler that should be included in your arsenal of UNIX software. Here's what you get: a compiler that will work with standard C, C++, and Objective C. It can even convert your source code to standard ANSI C for portability.

And talk about portability, you're in for a treat if you develop applications that must run on various platforms: gcc can compile your source code to run on a machine that is different from your own system. All you need to do is tell the utility which machine will run your application, and it will create the proper binaries for you. The following are just a few of these systems:

M680x0	RT
VAX	MIPS
SPARC	i386
Convex	HPPA
AMD29K	Intel 960
M88K	DEC Alpha
RS/6000	System V

You'll find that gcc allows you to take control over as much of the building of your application as you need. For example, you can fine-tune the preprocessing operations, compiling, optimization, linking, and debugging. The utility's documentation shows you all that you need to know to take control.

Still not convinced? Well, here is a fact that will clear up any doubts: gcc is the compiler that is distributed with Data General Aviion and Next computers. What more can we say?

Installation

CAUTION

gcc uses GNU Bison (the free replacement for yacc). Please obtain a copy of Bison, which is usually available at the same FTP site as gcc. Bison is easy and quick to install.

You'll find gcc in the */pub/Z* directory on *moxie.oswego.edu.* Copy the gcc utility files into an empty directory on your system. The utility comes with a script that will configure the makefile for your system. Just type

configure —*target*

where *target* is the name of your system. For example,

```
configure —target=sparc-sun-sunos4.1.
```

Table 12-5 contains a list of some of the system names. See the utility's documentation for more names.

TIP

You can enter **CPU-SYSTEM** instead of the target name and the configure script will setup the makefile to create the proper binaries for you.

Don't be too concerned if you enter incorrect information. The configure script will either catch the error and display an appropriate error message or ignore the error and guess the missing data. Usually, the guess is sufficient to create the makefile. There are other command-line options that you may want to use when running the configure script. The document lists all of these and provides tips on when to use them.

You're almost ready to create the binaries. But before you do, make sure that the Bison parser generator is installed. Read the installation instructions in the utility's documentation for installation procedures. Build the gcc utility by typing **make LANGUAGES=c**. (Be sure you are in the compiler directory before executing the make utility.) Although only the C compiler is specified, the makefile normally builds compilers for C and C++.

alliant	altos	apollo	bull	cbm	convergent
convex	crds	dec	dg	dolphin	elxsi
encore	harris	hitachi	hp	ibm	intergraph
isi	mips	motorola	ncr	next	ns
omron	plexus	sequent	sgi	sony	sun
tti	unicom				

TABLE 12-5.   *A Sampling of Target Names for the Configure Script*

There are a few additional steps that you'll need to follow to complete the installation. These are all contained in detail in the utility's documentation. Follow these steps carefully and you'll end up with a successful installation.

Known Problems

If you run into problems, don't panic. The gcc utility's documentation lists a few known problems. However, if the problem that you're experiencing isn't listed in the gcc utility's documentation, you might have stumbled across a new problem. Don't keep it a secret!

Send all the specifics about your system and the problem to:

bug-gcc@prep.ai.mit.edu {ucbvax|mit-eddie|uunet}!prep.ai.mit.edu!bug-gcc

If the problem involves the C++ compiler, drop the email to:

bug-g++@prep.ai.mit.edu {ucbvax|mit-eddie|uunet}!prep.ai.mit.edu!bug-g++

And finally, if you suspect that the difficulty is caused by the class library rather than the compiler, email your suspicions to:

bug-lib-g++@prep.ai.mit.edu

For those who are unable to use email, you can report your problem via regular mail. Send your letter to:

GNU Compiler Bugs
Free Software Foundation
675 Mass Ave
Cambridge, MA 02139

TIP
Don't be too quick to report a bug! Do some research first. Read the
gnu.gcc.help, bug-gcc, and *bug-g++* news groups. The help news
group will let you determine if your problem is really a problem or
just your lack of experience.

There are other gcc news groups that will tell you if others have experienced a
similar problem. These group might also have reported a possible fix. Here are a
few of them:

- *gnu.gcc.announce*
- *gnu.gcc.bug*
- *gnu.gcc.help*
- *gnu.g++.announce*
- *gnu.g++.bug*
- *gnu.g++.help*
- *gnu.g++.lib.bug*

Up and Running
Compiling an application is straightforward. Type **gcc** *filename.c.* (Gcc uses the
UNIX standard for specifying libraries.) Press the ENTER key and gcc will begin
its four-stage process of building your application, unless you specify that you
want only specific ones done. (These are preprocessing, compilation, assembly,
and linking.)

The file suffix determines the type of compilation that is executed by gcc. Some
of these should be familiar to you since they are standard among other C
compilers. We've included a sample of other suffixes in Table 12-6.

gcc allows you to control which stage of compilation to perform. You'll find
this useful whenever you debug a large application. After you fix the problem in
one of the source code files, you need only execute those stages that are necessary
to link the code into the application.

You can specify the stage of compilation to perform by using the proper
command-line option. For example, type

gcc <option> <filename>.

Table 12-7 contains a sampling of the options and features that you can control.

SUFFIX	DESCRIPTION
.c	C source code that must be preprocessed
.i	C source code that should not be preprocessed
.ii	C++ source code that should not be preprocessed
.m	Objective-C source code
.h	C header file (not to be compiled or linked)
.cc	C++ source code that must be preprocessed
.cxx	C++ source code that must be preprocessed
.C	C++ source code that must be preprocessed
.s	Assembler code
.S	Assembler code that must be preprocessed

TABLE 12-6. *A Sampling of File Suffixes*

More Than ANSI C and C++

Is gcc truly an ANSI C and C++ compiler? Yes, and more! The authors of gcc built a compiler that contains all of the ANSI features you would expect. But they didn't stop there. They also included features that improve upon the current standard compilers. Table 12-8 contains a sampling of these new features.

OPTION	DESCRIPTION
-c	Compiles or assembles the source files, but does not link
-S	Stops after the stage of compilation proper and doesn't assemble
-E	Stops after the preprocessing stage and doesn't run the compiler
-o FILE	Places output in file FILE
-v	Prints the commands executed to run the stages of compilation
-pipe	Uses pipes rather than temporary files for communication between stages

TABLE 12-7. *A Sampling of Command-line Options*

FEATURE	DESCRIPTION
Statement Expressions	Puts statements and declarations inside expressions
Local Labels	Locals to a statement-expression
Labels as Values	Gets pointers to labels, and computed gotos
Nested Functions	As in Algol and Pascal, lexical scoping of functions
Constructing Calls	Dispatches a call to another function
Naming Types	Gives a name to the type of some expression
Typeof	Refers to the type of an expression
Conditionals	Omits the middle operand of a '?:' expression
Long Long	Double-word integers—'long long int'
Zero Length	Zero-length arrays
Variable Length	Arrays whose length is computed at run time
Macro Varargs	Macros with variable number of arguments
Subscripting	Subscripts any array, even if not an lvalue
Pointer Arithmetic	Arithmetic on 'void'-pointers and function pointers
Initializers	Non-constant initializers
Labeled Elements	Labels elements of initializers
Cast to Union	Casts to union type from any member of the union
Case Ranges	'case 1 ... 9' and such
Function Prototypes	Prototype declarations and old-style definitions
Dollar Signs	Allows dollar sign in identifiers
Character Escapes	\e' stands for the character ESC
Variable Attributes	Specifies attributes of variables
Alignment	Inquires about the alignment of a type or variable
Inline	Defines inline functions (as fast as macros)
Asm Labels	Specifies the assembler name to use for a C symbol
Explicit Register	Defines variables residing in specified registers
Alternate Keywords	'__const__', '__asm__', etc., for header files
Incomplete Enums	'enum foo;', with details to follow

TABLE 12-8. *A Sampling of New Features*

CAUTION
If you use any of these extended ANSI features in your application, you might run into portability problems with your source code. You could find yourself having to rewrite portions of your application that use these enhanced features of gcc.

Convert To ANSI C

gcc contains a easy way to add prototypes to your program, which, in effect, converts your program to ANSI C. All you need to do is run the utility's protoize program. Don't worry if you make a mistake. The utility also has an unprotoize program that reverses the action of the protoize program.

The protoize utility scans the source files that you specify on the command line and creates an information file. It is from this information file that the protoize program actually converts your program to ANSI C.

CAUTION
Although any file is eligible to be converted, the program converts only the source and header files that are found in the current directory. You must specify other directories using a command-line option.

The conversion consists of a rewrite of nearly all of the function definitions except for **varargs** functions. Through a command-line option, you can have the protoize program insert prototype declarations at the top of the source file. This makes a function's name known before its definition.

Converted files automatically replace the original source code file. But don't be too concerned! The program renames the original source code file with the *.save* extension. You can always recover your original source code.

Table 12-9 contains a sampling of command-line options that can be used with either protoize or unprotoize. Keep in mind that neither program will run unless the gcc utility is fully installed on your system.

KCL: A LISP Language

Want to try your hand at some Artificial Intelligence applications? Nearly every programmer has taken a crack at trying to give a computer the ability to behave like humans. You've probably tried using the C programming language or some other general purpose programming tool.

Don't be surprised if you were disappointed with the outcome of your work. General purpose programming languages by themselves just don't have the power that is required for the symbol and list manipulation that is required for an Artificial

OPTION	DESCRIPTION
-B DIRECTORY	Specifies the directory that contains the source code
-C	Renames files to end in '.C' instead of '.c'
-g	Adds explicit global declarations
-k	Keeps the '.X' files after conversion is finished
-l	Adds explicit local declarations
-n	Makes no real changes
-N	Makes no '.save' files
-q	Suppresses most warnings
-v	Prints the version number

TABLE 12-9. *A Sampling of Command-line Options for the protoize and unprotoize Utilities*

Intelligence project. You've heard the old expression, "Use the right tool for the job"—this holds true when you're developing an AI application.

There are a number of tools that are designed for Artificial Intelligence work. One of these was developed in the late 1950s by John McCarthy and is called LISP, which stands for List Processor. Now we're not recommending that you go out and purchase LISP software. We're suggesting instead that you connect to the Internet and download a very powerful version of LISP free of charge.

This free version is the Kyoto Common LISP, commonly known as KCL. KCL was developed in Japan by Taiichi Yuasa and Masami Hagiya for their work in Artificial Intelligence research. Fortunately, Yusas and Hagiya are willing to share their efforts with you.

KCL is special in that it can either interpret LISP (as most Lisp systems do) or compile it into C. Your local C compiler can then be used to produce a binary executable.

KCL isn't for everyone. It's designed for those who are serious about developing applications that employ AI techniques. If you're one of those developers, get prepared to receive one of the most powerful tools that you can acquire to build Artificial Intelligence software.

Installation

You'll find KCL on *rascal.ics.utexas.edu* on the Internet. The source files for KCL are stored in four directories: */h, /c, /lsp,* and */cmpnew.* The names of the */h* and */c* directories indicate the type of files that you can find there. The */lsp* directory contains the source files for LISP and the */cmpnew* directory contains the source files for the compiler.

The utility comes with complete instructions for installation on your system. In addition, you'll also receive several makefiles that are almost ready for building the binaries. Nearly all of the source files for the utility are system independent; however, a few files are system specific. The utility's documentation shows you how to wade through the switch settings that are necessary for your system.

Restrictions

KCL has a few restrictions that are different from those attached to other software reviewed in this book. The major restriction is that you are required to receive a license to use the utility on your system. Don't worry; there's no charge for this license.

The documentation contains a license agreement that the authors request you sign, copy, and return (original and one copy) to them. You are expected to do this before copying the utility to your system. You can read this agreement on the remote Internet host that contains KCL's source files.

Another restriction is that the license is only good for your own home or office. This means that you can't make any further distributions of the utility unless the recipient of your distribution also sends the author the license agreement. The authors' objective isn't to limit distribution of the utility but to preserve its quality and integrity.

Like nearly all of the software we review, KCL comes to you without any warranty. The authors won't be responsible to correct any bugs or deficiencies that you find in the utility.

If you find this all a little confusing, you may want to drop Yuasa and Hagiya an email at Kyoto University. They can be reached at:

siglisp@kurims.kurims.kyoto-u.junet

or

siglisp%kurims.kurims.kyoto-u.junet@utokyo-relay.csnet

Known Problems

Any utility has its problems and KCL is no exception. For example, when you attempt to compile a Lisp program, your C language compiler may display an error message stating that the code produced by KCL is too big. The compiler might state that it cannot compute the jump addresses. There is, however, a way to work around this problem.

The trick is to use the -J option with the assembler, if available. First, compile your LISP file by typing

```
>(compile-file "foo.lsp" :c-file t :h-file t :data-file t :o-file nil).
```

Be sure to replace *foo.lsp* with the name of your file. Next, compile the output of KCL using the -S option as illustrated here:

```
% cc -S foo.c.
```

Now for the trick. Assemble the output with the -J option as is shown here:

```
% as -J foo.s -o foo.o.
```

Just concatenate the data file at the end (*% cat foo.data >> foo.o*) and you've resolved the compiler error.

You can read more about potential bugs with KCL by reading the *comp.lang.lisp* news group on the Internet. If you discover a new bug, post it to the netnews group or send a bug report via email to the authors.

Up and Running

KCL is a compiler that translates a LISP program into a C language program that can be compiled with your existing C compiler. You never need to touch the C programs that the compiler generates. Simply write your LISP application and debug it using KCL's interpreter. When you are satisfied, you can then compile it using KCL.

You'll find that KCL uses most of the standard syntax and conventions of the LISP language. However, there are a few of these language features that aren't supported. You can read more about these in the utility's documentation.

There's really nothing much we can say about KCL without having to provide you with a LISP tutorial. We'll let you read the utility's documentation and other publications to help you construct a LISP application. The authors of KCL offer a manual that will help you with LISP and their utility. It's called *The KCL Report* and is comes with the KCL distribution.

The NIH Class Library:
A C++ Library

Why waste your time recreating classes that others have already built? Now you can directly benefit from your federal tax dollars and use classes that were built by the National Institute of Health, an agency of the federal government.

The C++ language is catching on like wildfire. Everyone is trying to capitalize on implementation of the C++ language in object-oriented designs. Well, did you know that the National Institute of Health had a head start? They started to develop an extensive C++ library years ago, before this concept caught on in industry. At that time their work was known as the OOPS Class library.

Fortunately, their work couldn't be kept behind locked doors. In fact, the NIH Class Library is available for everyone to use. And best of all, you can acquire the complete library at no cost. That's right. It's free!

The National Institute of Health designed their library to be used as a resource for software developers and to be portable to any system that uses System V or 4.2/4.3 BSD. These systems must support the AT&T C++ translator release 2.00,2.1, or other compatible C++ compilers. It is known to work trouble free on the Sun-3 or Sun-4 with SunOS 3.5 or 4.0.

Restrictions

There are no—well, almost no restrictions. Since the NIH Class Library was developed by the National Institute of Health (which is part of the United States government), it is freely available to the public. This is because the government cannot copyright its work.

This applies to nearly all the software that you'll find in the NIH Class Library. However, there are two files that were not produced by the government. These are *regex.h* and *regex.c*. The use of these files is restricted by the Free Software Foundation, Inc., license.

Don't be too concerned about the restrictions on these files. The Free Software Foundation, Inc., allows you to use these files any way that you desire without any fee or royalty payment. The only catch is that you can't prohibit anyone else from using these files. You can read about the latest restrictions for using the NIH Class Library in the library's documentation file.

Installation

You'll find the library in the */pub/NIHCL* library on *alw.nih.gov*. Installing the NIH Class Library is an involved process and beyond the scope of this book. However, you'll find all the details in the library's documentation. If you run into any problems, read the *comp.lang.c++* netnews group for tips on using the library. Remember, you can always post your own questions about the library. The NIH Class Library user community is broad-based, so someone can probably lend you a helping hand.

If all else fails, drop a line to Keith Gorlen at the National Institute of Health. His email address is *kgorlen@alw.nih.gov*. You can also reach him at:

National Institute of Health
Division of Computer Research and Technology
Computer Systems Laboratory
Building 12A, Room 2033
Bethesda, MD, 20892

Up and Running

The NIH Class Library can be used just like a typical C++ library. You can feel free to use these classes throughout your application—they'll work fine if you remember to link the NIH Class Library along with your code.

You'll find a wealth of classes in the library. In fact, there are so many useful tools that we would need half a book to tell you about them. So instead of writing another book, we'll provide a preview of what's in store for you in Table 12-10. You'll find a complete listing of classes, descriptions, and tips on how to use them in the library's documentation files.

When you use any of these classes in your program you can eliminate the need to have many global functions and variables. This is because all NIH classes inherit member functions and variables. And if you want to use a member function or variable outside the class, you can access them by using the C++ scope qualifier in your code. The following illustrates how this is done.

```
NIHCL::setError(ERROR_CODE, DEFAULT);
```

You can also incorporate multiple inheritance in your application by defining the MI preprocessor symbol before compiling the NIH Class Library with your code.

CAUTION
If you decide to use the MI switch, be sure that all classes linked together in the program have been compiled with the same MI option setting.

Perl: A Programming Language

Extracting information from a text file, then having to writing a fancy report with the data can be a time-consuming tasks—that is, unless you use a programming language that simplifies the task. Now we're not talking about C or another programming language that allows you to build elegant code. We're talking about Perl.

CLASS	DESCRIPTION
Bitset	Set of small integers (like Pascal's type SET)
Class	Class descriptor
Collection	Abstract class for collections
Arraychar	Byte array
ArrayOb	Array of object pointers
Bag	Unordered collection of objects
SeqCltn	Abstract class for ordered, indexed
Heap	Min-max heap of object pointers
LinkedList	Singly-linked list
OrderedCltn	Ordered collection of object
SortedCltn	Sorted collection
KeySortCltn	Keyed sorted collection
Stack	Stack of object pointers
Dictionary	Set of associations
IdentDict	Dictionary keyed by object
IdentSet	Set keyed by object address
Date	Gregorian calendar date
FDSet	Set of file descriptors for use with select(2)
Float	Floating point number
Fraction	Rational arithmetic
Integer	Integer number object
Iterator	Collection iterator
Link	Abstract class for linked lists
LinkOb	Link containing object pointer
Process	Co-routine process object
HeapProc	Process with stack in free store

TABLE 12-10. *A Sampling of Classes that Are Available in the NIH Class Library*

Perl is an interpreted language that is specifically designed to efficiently read text files and extract information that will be printed in a report. Don't expect to write sophisticated, large applications with Perl. However, you can expect to efficiently produce information for the more common system management tasks.

Larry Wall developed Perl by combining the best features of the C programming language and the sed and awk utilities along with a few of the familiar conventions of csh, Pascal, and BASIC-PLUS. This is a major advantage to Perl programmers in that they can quickly come up to speed developing a Perl application.

You'll notice that the syntax used to create expressions uses nearly the same format as the C programming language. However, there is one major difference. There is no arbitrary limit on the size of your data. As long as your system has sufficient memory, Perl can work with as large a text file as you can create.

Special care has been taken by Wall to assure that performance isn't degraded. For example, Perl uses hash tables that can grow as necessary, allowing the operation of your program to continue running smoothly. Then there is the sophisticated pattern matching technique that allows your Perl application to scan large amounts of data very quickly.

We said that Perl was specifically designed to work with text files. While that's true—Perl can also work with files that contain binary data and can make dbm files look like associative arrays. So there's no reason for not using Perl for your next application that must find and report on data in a text file.

What's that you say? You already have the sed and awk utilities. You don't need another tool for text files. But try working with a large text file and you may have second thoughts. The file might exceed sed and awk's capabilities and both utilities might run extremely slowly—too slow for your taste. You can overcome these hurdles by writing your application in Perl. And here's the best part, Perl comes with a translator that can automatically turn your sed and awk scripts into Perl scripts.

Installation

You won't find Perl difficult to install on your system. The initial step is to create a Perl directory, then copy the utility's files to your system. There are numerous places where you'll find Perl on the Internet. Here's just one of them: the */pub* directory on *flash.bellcore.com*.

Each system has its own environment settings. Therefore, some adjustment must be made to the installation software before you can build the utility's binaries. Fortunately, all you need to do is run the configure script that is supplied with the Perl utility. This script will create the *config.h*, *config.sh*, and *Makefile* files for you.

Although the configure script does a good job, we suggest that you review the settings in these files before proceeding. The next step is to type **make depend**. This will look for all the include files and the necessary modifications to the makefile so that all the dependencies are available to the makefile.

Next, you must execute the make utility. Type **make** and the make utility will build the binaries for Perl. Two additional steps must be performed before you are ready to run Perl: running make test and make install. The make test routine performs a regression test on the binaries that you just created. If the test is successful, you'll see the message "All tests successful" displayed on the screen. If you don't see this, see the *README* file in the *t* subdirectory. The make install routine places all Perl files in their proper directories.

And if your installation seems to be flawed, don't panic. Your support group is ready and waiting to help you. First, review the Perl news group *comp.lang.perl*. If you don't find any listed tips that get you back on track, post your problem. Within a day or so, you can expect to receive a response from other Perl users. Then, if all else fails, drop an email to Wall at *lwall@netlabs.com*.

Known Problems
Although you'll find that Perl is a worthwhile language to consider for your project, there are a few points that should be considered. For starters, Perl is dependent upon your system's definitions of various operations. These include type casting and the **atof()** and **sprintf()** functions. Therefore, if certain features of Perl act suspiciously, chances are that the problem lies with a system definition.

You'll notice that Wall has made every attempt not to impose arbitrary limits on built-in data types; however, there are some restrictions. For example, any identifier must not exceed 255 characters. In addition, a regular expression is limited to 32,767 bytes internally. You can read more about these limitations in the language's documentation.

Don't be misled by Perl language conventions and syntax. Perl uses constructs that are similar to other languages. However, you'll find that there are differences that can lead you astray. Be sure that you review the section titled "trap" in the language's documentation. This section points out all of these pitfalls. You should also read the netnews group *comp.lang.perl*.

Restrictions
The Perl utility is distributed under the Free Software Foundation, Inc.'s license. This means that you have the freedom to use, modify, and distribute Perl without prior permission from either the Free Software Foundation, Inc., or the authors of the utility. The only restriction is that you cannot prevent anyone else from using this utility.

If you decide to include Perl as part of your own software, you still must make the source code to Perl—not your application—available free of charge to anyone who asks for a copy. You can read all the fine print about this restriction in the utility's documentation.

Up and Running

Create your first Perl program by entering Perl code in a text file just as you do with any programming language. There are two common ways to run your Perl program: line by line, or as an entire program depending on the command-line option. Table 12-11 contains a sampling of command-line options. Notice that the -e option is used to execute the program a line at a time.

In most cases, you'll run your entire program. Just enter the **perl** command and the name of your program file as a command-line argument. Perl then reads your program, checks it for syntax errors, then compiles your program into a special internal form before the program is run.

Inside Perl Data Types and Characters

Unlike many programming languages, Perl has only three data types: scalars, arrays of scalars, and associative arrays of scalars. A *scalar* is a value such as a single integer or a string (4, "abc") and is used for holding a single value. In comparison, an *array of scalars* is used for holding a series of values, such as a list of names such as "Moe," "Larry," "Curly." An *associative array of scalars* differs from an array of scalars in that the subscript can be any datatype, for example: $days {"Jan"}.

OPTION	DESCRIPTION
-0	Specifies the record separator ($/) as an octal number
-a	Turns on autosplit mode when used with a -n or -p
-c	Causes Perl to check the syntax of the script and then exit without executing it
-d	Runs the script under the Perl Debugger
-D	Sets debugging flags
-e	Enters one line of script
-I	Tells the C preprocessor where to look for include files
-P	Causes your script to be run through the C preprocessor before compilation
-S	Makes Perl use the PATH environment variable to search for the script

TABLE 12-11. *A Sampling of Command-line Options for Perl*

The execution of a Perl operation depends on the context of the operation or the value used for the operation. Perl recognizes three major contexts: a string, a numeric, and an array. Perl operations return either an array or a scalar value. What's interesting is that an operation that returns scalars isn't concerned if the context is seeking a string or numeric. The Perl's documentation is filled with information about how data types are to be used within your application.

Another interesting twist of the Perl language is the way in which Perl handles null strings. Perl recognizes two kinds of null strings: defined and undefined. A defined string is treated similarly to the way the C programming language handles defined null strings.

An undefined null string is returned when there isn't a real value for something. This occurs when an error is detected, when the end of file is reached, and when an application refers to an uninitialized variable or array element.

Once your application accesses the undefined null string, the string becomes defined.

TIP

You can always use Perl's **defined()** operator to determine whether a value or array element is defined or not. Once a variable or array element is defined, it can be used similarly to the way a defined null string is used in the C programming language.

If your application requires multi-dimensional arrays, you're almost out of luck. Perl doesn't directly support multi-dimensional arrays. However, don't give up all hope. The Perl documentation shows you how to emulate a multi-dimensional array by using subscripts with an associative array.

Here's another interesting feature of Perl. Each Perl data type has its own name space. This means that you can use the same name for a scalar variable, an array, an associative array, a file handle, a subroutine, and a label, without fear of conflict.

As you begin to use Perl to develop your application, you'll notice a wealth of special characters that you can use to help you fine-tune your code. Table 12-12 contains a sampling of these characters. You'll find a complete listing, as well as tips on how to use them in the Perl documentation.

Expressions and Flow Control Statements

You'll notice that Perl incorporates many of the same conventions as other programming languages. Perl is a free-form language, very similar to the C programming language. You can write expressions and flow control statements without regard to position (except for the logical flow of your code). Perl ignores white space.

We won't talk too much about the Perl syntax—you can read all about it in the Perl documentation. However, we will take a glimpse inside to give you a flavor for programming in Perl. For example, you can create an expression that Perl will

CHARACTER	DESCRIPTION
\t	tab
\n	newline
\r	return
\f	form feed
\b	backspace
\a	alarm (bell)
\e	escape
\033	octal char
\xlb	hex char
\c[	control char
\l	lowercase next char
\u	uppercase next char
\L	lowercase till \E
\U	uppercase till \E
\E	end case modification

TABLE 12-12. *A Sampling of Special Characters*

evaluate and test, and then use the proper flow control routine to execute the desired code.

You'll find a host of flow control statements that will give you flexibility in designing efficient code. Here are a few: *if EXPR, unless EXPR, while EXPR,* and *until EXPR. EXPR* represents the expression that must be evaluated by Perl before the appropriate block of code is executed.

Expression operators shouldn't be unfamiliar to you since they are almost exactly the same as the operators that you use to build expressions in the C programming language. However, there are some differences. Table 12-13 gives you a sampling of operators that Perl makes available to you that differ from those found in C. Table 12-14 shows you a sampling of C language operators that are missing from Perl. You'll find a complete listing and a detailed discussion about how to construct expressions in the Perl documentation.

It shouldn't take you too long to be able to develop an application in Perl. However, there are a few twists in the language that you should note. Let's say that you need to create a **for** loop. The following listings show you the traditional C language **for** loop and how you achieve the same functionality in Perl.

OPERATOR	DESCRIPTION
**	The exponentiation operator
**=	The exponentiation assignment operator
()	The null list, used to initialize an array to null
.	Concatenation of two strings
.=	The concatenation assignment operator
eq	String equality (== is numeric equality)
ne	String inequality (!= is numeric inequality)
lt	String less than
gt	String greater than
le	String less than or equal
ge	String greater than or equal
cmp	String comparison, returning –1, 0, or 1

TABLE 12-13. *A Sampling of Operators Found in Perl but Missing in C*

In C:

```
for ($i = 1; $i < 10; $i++) {
      ...
 }
```

OPERATOR	DESCRIPTION
unary &	Address-of operator
unary *	Deference-address operator
(TYPE)	Type casting operator

TABLE 12-14. *A Sampling of Operators Found in C but Missing in Perl*

In Perl:

```
$i = 1;
while ($i < 10) {
        ...
} continue {
   $i++;
}
```

Perl also allows you to create subroutines to isolate blocks of code within your application. You can declare a subroutine by using the **sub** command, followed by the name of the subroutine and the block of code that is to be executed when the subroutine is called. The listing below illustrates how to create the subroutine called **MAX**. Once the subroutine is defined, you can call the subroutine from anywhere in your application by using the **do** command.

```
sub MAX {
      local($max) = pop(@_);
       foreach $foo (@_) {
              $max = $foo if $max < $foo;
          }
       $max;
  }
```

For example, to call the **MAX** subroutine you'd enter the command **do MAX**.
You'll find the Perl documentation loaded with tips and techniques for using subroutines and how to pass data to a subroutine. Perl supports call by reference and call by value.

A Look at Perl Formats

The Perl programming language is designed to display information in reports. Perl is rich in format commands. Practically any report that you can conceive can be created using Perl. At the heart of this formatting capability is the Perl **format** command, which is used to define the format of an output record when the record is printed using the Perl **write** operator.

The format itself is defined in the formlist that appears below the **format** command. This is illustrated here:

```
# a report on the /etc/passwd file
format STDOUT_TOP =
                        Passwd File
Name                    Login   Office   Uid    Gid Home
---------------------------------------------------------------
.
format STDOUT =
@<<<<<<<<<<<<<<<<<< @|||||||| @<<<<<<@>>>> @>>>> @<<<<<<<<<<<<<<<<<<
$name,              $login,   $office,$uid,$gid, $home
```

You'll notice that there are two formlists used in this example. The first called STDOUT_TOP defines the form for the top of each page of the report. This is entered free-form in your source code.

Beneath the STDOUT_TOP form is STDOUT. This defines the columns of the report using the at (@) sign and identifies the Perl variables that contain the data that will appear in the report. Notice that a dollar ($) sign precedes each variable name and each variable is separated by a comma.

CAUTION
Notice that each formlist is terminated by a period displayed on the last line of the formlist.

There is a host of other formatting operators that you can use to create any fancy report that you require. You'll find all the information about how to use these operators in the Perl documentation.

Debugging Your Perl Programming

Wall didn't leave you hanging. He built a very useful debugger to help you locate trouble spots in your application. The debugger isn't a separate program but is invoked using the a -d switch when you begin Perl (**perl a -d**). Once you've set this switch, Perl will run your program using the debugging monitor.

The Perl Debugger is similar to other debuggers that you use with your favorite compiler. After you launch Perl in the debug mode, Perl stops at the first executable statement and prompts you to enter a debugging command. Table 12-15 contains a sampling of the Perl debugging commands. You can read more about how to debug your Perl program in the Perl documentation.

COMMAND	DESCRIPTION
h	Prints out a help message
T	Stack trace
s	Single step
n	Next
f	Finishes
c	Continues
<CR>	Repeats last n or s
l	Lists next window
–	Lists previous window

TABLE 12-15. *A Sampling of Debugging Commands*

The Readline Library: A Line Editor Library

If you like the command-line editing facilities of the Korn Shell or of bash, then you probably would like to give similar editing capabilities to your text-based programs. All you have to do is write your own text editor. Just kidding! Now thanks to Richard Stallman, you don't have to write your own.

Stallman has created the Readline Library, which enables you to incorporate the features of an editor in your application without the hassle of programming. And as a extra bonus, the Readline Library recognizes the same commands as emacs. This means your program can conform to a standard set of line editing conventions.

Will the Readline Library revolutionize your applications? Probably not, but it will enable you to create professional quality applications—applications that incorporate those "simple" features that the user community has learned to expect but are time-consuming for you to write.

Installation

Just like most of the libraries that are distributed by the Free Software Foundation, Inc., the Readline Library comes with a ready-made makefile. First, create an empty directory on your system, then copy the library's files from the */.0/BSD/net2/usr.bin/gdb* directory on *gatekeeper.dec.com*.

Before compiling the binaries, read the utility's installation documentation file for the latest tips on building your copy of the Readline Library. You might need to tweak the makefile to assure that paths correspond to your system.

Finally, move to the library's src directory and execute make. Within a few minutes, your copy of the Readline Library will be ready to be incorporated into your next program.

Restrictions

The Readline Library is distributed by the Free Software Foundation, Inc. As with all of their distributions, you have permission to distribute this library as is or in a modified form without paying royalties to either the Free Software Foundation, Inc., or the author of the library.

The only catch is that you can't charge anyone for use of this library or for your modification of the library. This may sound confusing at first since we're talking about a library that is expected to be included in a software product available to the public. However, the Readline Library is covered under the GNU library agreement rather than the General Public License.

You'll find a complete explanation of these restrictions in the Readline Library's documentation. If these permissions don't cover your intended use of the utility, you'll require written permission from the Free Software Foundation, Inc., before you distribute your application.

Up and Running

The Readline Library can be used as your customized editor within your application. The library's info file has a section called "Programming with GNU Readline" that provides you with all the details of how to make the library part of your program.

The user of your application will probably be familiar with how to use the Readline Library since it reacts to the same keystrokes as the emacs utility. In fact, the Readline Library also has a vi mode. This allows the user to use the simple vi line-editing commands. Underline the word *simple*; the library doesn't have the full set of vi editing functions.

When the Readline Library is executed, the user of your application can enter characters at the keyboard; the utility displays them at the current cursor position. The cursor is then automatically moved one space to the right. Make a mistake? Don't worry! Your user can press the DEL key to move the cursor back to delete a character. However, unlike other simple editors, the Readline Library also allows the user to quickly undo the previous change by using the CTRL-_ command.

We've only scratched the surface of the commands that are available with the Readline Library. There are commands that allow the user to move the cursor quickly anywhere on the line, to remove text from the line, and to change text. There are even commands that will change the case of a letter or series of letters.

Enough for the simple tasks. Here's something that most editors don't have—a history feature. Each command that is entered into the Readline Library is added to the library's history list. This means your user can simply scroll through the history list to find a previous command to re-execute. Table 12-16 contains a list of some of the history commands.

Although the author of the Readline Library has built-in all the standard functionality that you come to expect from an editor, you can add your own features. That's right! The Readline Library is capable of executing your own C language functions. Once you've created the function, assign the function to a key. Whenever the user presses the key, the Readline Library automatically runs your function. Look for the "Key Bindings" section of the library's info file for all the specifics on how to connect your function to a command key.

NOTE
You can type the ESC key instead of the META key for commands in Table 12-16.

SB-Prolog:
A Programming Language

Developing applications that test the world of artificial intelligence is a challenge to any programmer. Sure, you can build AI applications using the C programming

COMMAND	DESCRIPTION
CTRL p	Moves one command up the history list
CTRL n	Moves one command down the history list
<Meta> <	Moves to the beginning of the history list
<Meta> >	Moves to the end of the history list

TABLE 12-16. *A Sampling of History Commands*

language. But if you're a serious AI developer, you'll need a language that is designed for AI applications. We're talking about prolog.

Prolog isn't new—it's been available for years. But now it's yours and it's free! A team of developers from the State University of New York (SUNY) at Stony Brook created a version of prolog called SB-Prolog, and made it available to the public.

In the center of SB-Prolog is an emulator of a prolog virtual machine, which is an extension of the Warren Abstract Machine. Most of prolog is written in the C language to assure portability among systems. The rest of the language is written in prolog itself.

SB-Prolog isn't exactly like other prolog systems that you might have used in the past. You'll notice that SB-Prolog offers features that are not found on most prolog systems. For example, SB-Prolog has dynamic loading of predicates and makes provision for generating executables on the global stack. This stack space can be later reclaimed. You'll also find full integration between compiled and interpreted code. You can read about these and other features that make SB-Prolog outstanding in the SB-Prolog's documentation.

Let's be up-front. There are some typical features of a prolog system that you won't find in SB-Prolog. These include a garbage collector for the global stack and the *record/recorded/erase* feature of C-Prolog. These shortcomings are also talked about in the documentation.

Installation
You'll find SB-Prolog in the */pub* directory on *ftp.cis.ohio-state.edu*. Create an empty directory for SB-Prolog on your system, then copy the files from the remote host. You'll notice that the authors of SB-Prolog have made building the binary files very simple. They provide a script called INSTALL. All you need to do is run this script; everything else will be done for you.

Restrictions
Like so many utilities mentioned in this book, SB-Prolog can be copied and distributed without prior permission from State University of New York (SUNY) at Stony Brook, which holds the copyright to the software.

You can freely modify the SB-Prolog source code and include SB-Prolog in your own application. The only catch is that you can't restrict anyone else from doing the same. This means that if you include SB-Prolog in your application, the user of your application must have access to the SB-Prolog source code. Your code can remain confidential.

Above all, remember that the SB-Prolog comes without any warranties. This means the software may not work on your system. Be sure to provide the same warranty if you include SB-Prolog in your application.

You'll find more information about these restrictions in the SB-Prolog documentation. If you are confused about these restrictions, Saumya K. Debray, at the University of Arizona (602-621-4527), might be able to answer your questions.

Known Problems

Don't expect SB-Prolog to work bug free. There are a few areas that could cause problems, such as when attempts are made to set trace points using *trace/1* on system and library predicates. This can cause bizarre behavior.

You'll find some of the other problems with SB-Prolog listed in the documentation. However, for a more comprehensive and up-to-date list, we suggest that you read the *comp.lang.prolog* netnews group. There you can find tips and problems that other SB-Prolog users will share with you. You can even post your own questions about SB-Prolog and have other users suggest answers.

Up and Running

We can't provide you with a full lesson on how to develop a prolog application in this book. You will find all you need to know about how to use SB-Prolog in the SB-Prolog documentation. We'll just highlight a few points that illustrate some of the versatility that you'll find when you start using SB-Prolog.

SB-Prolog is design for efficient use of memory. For example, SB-Prolog uses a technique that makes it unnecessary for you to explicitly link in all the predicates for your SB-Prolog program. Here's how it works. During execution, if an undefined predicate is required, SB-Prolog hunts down the predicate, then dynamically loads and links the file that contains the predicate, before continuing with the execution of the program.

At the heart of this technique is the SIMPATH environment variable. This variable contains the search path the SB-Prolog follows to locate the predicate file. All you need to do is properly set up the value of the SIMPATH variable. The following illustrates how this is done in the C shell.

```
setenv SIMPATH path
```

Replace the word "path" with the directories that are to be searched. Be sure to separate each directory name with a colon (*src1: src2 : src3*).

An SB-Prolog program can be executed in one of two ways. The first is the more traditional approach—enter your code into a text file, then use the SB-Prolog compiler to convert the file into a byte-code file. The byte-code file can be dynamically linked into an executing SB-Prolog program. The compiled program can also be directly executed.

Another way to execute your SB-Prolog program is interactively from an SB-Prolog prompt. SB-Prolog uses the **consult** command to read text in from a file.

This is a perfect way to test out a few lines of code before including them into your SB-Prolog application.

Compiling your SB-Prolog application isn't difficult at all. Just type

compile (InFile, OutFile, OptionsList, PredList)

at the command line. Replace *InFile* with the name of your source code file. *Outfile* is the name of the executable file. *OptionsList* must be replaced with any compiler options, and the *PredList* contains the list of predicates that are used in your application.

SB-Prolog then starts the four-phase compilation process. First, your source code is read and passed through a preprocessor that essentially creates another prolog source program. The next phase requires that the output of the preprocessor is transformed into an annotated abstract syntax tree. This information is then turned into WAM assemble code, which is then processed by the assembler to generate the byte code.

There's a lot more to developing an SB-Prolog application than we've presented here. We haven't even scratched the surface when it comes to the full power of SB-Prolog. For that, you'll have copy SB-Prolog onto your system and experiment yourself. Who knows, maybe with your own copy of SB-Prolog, you might come up with a trend setting AI software package.

Index

More Programming Tools on CDROM!
◆ see next page for detailed product information.

1️⃣ Please Fill Out Completely 2️⃣ Payment Method

Shipping Address

Company

Name

Address/Mail Stop

City

State/Zip/Country

Telephone -- with an Area and Country code.
(in case there is a question about your order)

If you are ever unsatisfied with one of our products, simply
return the item with your invoice number and a short note
saying what is wrong.

◆   Check enclosed. (Drawn on a United States Bank.)

◆   Please charge to my:
❑ Visa   ❑ MC   ❑ Discover   ❑ American Express

Name on Card

Cardholder Signature

Account #

Expiration Date

3️⃣ I'd Like to Order:

Qty	Product	Description	Price	Total
____ x	Hobbes	600 MB current Shareware for OS/2	$ 29.95*	Total $_____
____ x		Subscription: new every 3 months	$ 19.95*/issue	Total $_____
____ x	CICA	4000 new Windows™ programs	$ 29.95*	Total $_____
____ x		Subscription: you get yours first	$19.95*/issue	Total $_____
____ x	Simtel	Classic: 650 MB Shareware for MSDOS	$ 29.95*	Total $_____
____ x		Subscription: quarterly updates!	$19.95*/issue	Total $_____
____ x	Space&Astronomy	Thousands of NASA images and data files	$39.95*	Total $_____
____ x	Giga Games	3000 hot Games for MSDOS & Windows™	$39.95*	Total $_____
____ x	CoC	CDROM of CDROMs -- 4067 descriptions.	$ 39.95	Total $_____
____ x	Libris Britannia	DOS Scientific & Engineering with doc	$ 59.95*	Total $_____
____ x	La colección	MSDOS/OS/2/Windows™. Spanish indexes	$ 39.95*	Total $_____
____ x	QRZ!	Ham Radio call sign database + files	$ 29.95*	Total $_____
____ x		Subscription: auto. new every 3 months	$ 19.95*/issue	Total $_____
____ x	Tax Info '93	335 IRS Tax forms & instructions	$ 39.95	Total $_____
____ x	ClipArt	ClipArt Cornucopia -- 5050 images	$ 39.95	Total $_____
____ x	Fractal Frenzy	2000 beautiful high resolution fractals	$ 39.95	Total $_____
____ x	Travel	202 Hi-Res US, Europe travel images	$ 39.95	Total $_____
____ x	GIFs Galore	5000 GIF images - all categories - no adult	$ 39.95*	Total $_____
____ x	Gutenberg	Project Gutenberg: classic literature, docs	$ 39.95	Total $_____
____ x		Subscription: about every 6 months	$ 24.95/issue	Total $_____
____ x	Internet Info	15,000 computer and Internet documents	$39.95	Total $_____
____ x	SysV r4	610 MB ready-to-run Unix Sys V utilities	$ 59.95*	Total $_____
____ x	Nova	600 MB Black Next app's, src., docs, etc.	$ 59.95*	Total $_____
____ x	Nebula	600 MB NeXTSTEP Intel app's, docs, etc.	$ 59.95*	Total $_____
____ x	Aminet	650 MB new files for the Amiga	$ 29.95*	Total $_____
____ x		Subscription: you get yours first	$ 19.95*/issue	Total $_____
____ x	GEMini	616 MB 3000 programs for Atari	$ 39.95*	Total $_____
____ x	Info-Mac	10,000 Mac files from Sumac archive	$ 49.95*	Total $_____
____ x	X11R5 /GNU	X Windows and GNU software for SPARC	$ 39.95	Total $_____
____ x	Source	600 MB Unix & MSDOS source code	$ 39.95*	Total $_____
____ x	CUG	C User Group C source code	$ 49.95*	Total $_____
____ x	Ada	Programming tools, source code and docs	$ 39.95*	Total $_____
____ x	Sprite	Berkeley distributed OS for SUN	$ 29.95	Total $_____
____ x	Linux	Yggdrasil Linux O/S. GNU & X11 src.	$ 49.95	Total $_____
____ x	Toolkit	For Linux - 600 MB util. + Slackware	$ 39.95*	Total $_____
____ x	FreeBSD	Berkeley BSD for PC, w/GNU & X11 src.	$ 39.95	Total $_____
____ x		Subscription: new about every 4 months	$ 24.95/issue	Total $_____
____ x	FAQ	alt.cd-rom Frequently Asked Questions	$ 1.00	Total $_____
____ x	Jewelbox	Clear plastic CD boxes (pack of 10)	$ 5.00	Total $_____
____ x	Caddy	Quality standard caddies — Best Price!	$ 4.95	Total $_____

Shareware requires payment to author if found useful

Sub-Total $_____
Tax 8.25%, (California residents only) $_____
Shipping & Handling ($5 US/Canada, $10 Air Overseas per order) $_____
                                                     Grand Total $_____

Walnut Creek CDROM
4041 Pike Lane, Suite D-854   Phone: 510 674-0783
Concord CA 94520   Fax: 510 674-0821
USA   Email: orders@cdrom.com

Call 1 800 786-9907

More Programming Tools on CDROM!

FreeBSD CDROM

 $ 39.95

FreeBSD is a complete 4.3 BSD compatible, 32 bit operating system for 386/486/Pentium. It comes with XFree86 (X11R5), TCP/IP networking, SLIP, PPP, telnet, ftp, gopher, archie, and NFS. There is a complete ANSI/POSIX-1003.1 compliant development environment - including kernel source, Gnu C and C++ compilers, GDB, lex and yacc, source level debuggers, profilers, Gnu emacs, perl, etc. You get TeX, ghostscript, FlexFax fax software, ksh, tcsh, and bash shells, sc spreadsheet, etc. Also audio support for many boards. EVERYTHING comes with source code. With FreeBSD you get a tightly integrated build system, you can make the whole source tree with one command. The disc is in Rock Ridge format. Call today, and put a great system on your computer.

Internet Info CDROM

 $ 39.95

This disc is a collection of the wealth of information that is available on the Internet. There are over 12,000 documents about computers and networks: answers to Frequently Asked Questions (FAQs) about almost every subject imaginable. Internet RFCs and IENs. Documents on computer security. Internet Network maps. Archives of technical discussions from USENET. Lists of ftp-sites, and descriptions of the archives they hold. You get extensive bibliographies and technical book reviews, and hundreds of documents on computers and information standards. If computers and networking interest you, this CDROM is indispensable.

Other CDROMs produced by Walnut Creek CDROM include:

Cica MS Windows CDROM	Thousands of programs for MS Windows
Giga Games CDROM	Games for MSDOS and MS Windows
Space and Astronomy CDROM	Thousands of NASA images and data files
C Users Group Library CDROM	A collection of user supported C source code
Simtel MSDOS CDROM	Shareware/Freeware for MSDOS
Clipart Cornucopia CDROM	Clipart for Desktop Publishing
QRZ Ham Radio CDROM	FCC Callsign Database plus shareware
Gifs Galore CDROM	Over 6000 GIF Images
Project Gutenberg CDROM	Classic Literature and historical documents
Hobbes OS/2 CDROM	Shareware/Freeware for OS/2
Source Code CDROM	650 Megabytes of source code for programmers
Internet Info CDROM	Thousands of computer and network documents
X11/Gnu CDROM	X Windows, and Gnu software for Unix and SPARC
Aminet Amiga CDROM	Shareware/Freeware for Amiga
Ada Programming CDROM	Programming tools, Ada source code and docs
Nova for NeXT CDROM	Programs for black NeXT
Nebula for NeXTSTEP Intel CDROM	Programs for NeXTSTEP Intel
Garbo MSDOS/Mac CDROM	MSDOS and Macintosh Shareware/Freeware
Fractal Frenzy CDROM	High resolution images of fractals
FreeBSD CDROM	Complete FreeBSD Operating system, X11R5/GNU
Toolkit for Linux CDROM	Programs and Documentation for Linux OS
GEMini Atari CDROM	Programs for the Atari ST

SEE REVERSE PAGE FOR ORDER INFORMATION

OR CALL TOLL-FREE

1 800 786-9907

Walnut Creek CDROM

4041 Pike Lane, Suite D-854
Concord CA 94520
Phone   510 674-0783
Fax   510 674-0821
Email   orders@cdrom.com